ART AND ARTIFACT

Murals from the Minneapolis Uprising

Published by the Katherine E. Nash Gallery
in association with Memorialize the Movement

ART AND ARTIFACT

Murals from the Minneapolis Uprising

TEXTS BY

Leslie Guy
Leesa Kelly
Amira McLendon
Howard Oransky
Seph Rodney

Curated by Amira McLendon

CONTENTS

Howard Oransky

FROM RED OCHRE TO EGYPTIAN BLUE

Preface

"Let the facts speak for themselves, with you as a medium."

— Ida B. Wells

There is a book in the Wilson Library at the University of Minnesota titled *Without Sanctuary: Lynching Photography in America.*[1] The book includes photographs and postcards from nearly one hundred lynchings—a very small sample from the thousands of public murders committed against Black people in this country. One of the postcards shows the murdered bodies of Elias Clayton, Elmer Jackson, and Isaac McGhie, surrounded by a crowd of white men clearly proud of their work. One, fashionably dressed in a bow tie, smiles broadly for the camera. Automobile headlights were used to illuminate the nighttime scene for the photographer. The postcards were sold as souvenirs.[2]

Elias Clayton, Elmer Jackson, and Isaac McGhie were lynched in Duluth, Minnesota, on June 15, 1920. They were employed by the John Robinson Circus and arrived in town for a parade and performances on June 14. Along with three other Black men from the circus they were accused of raping a white woman and held in the Duluth city jail. A crowd of white men estimated to be in the thousands converged on the jail, Duluth Commissioner of Public Safety William F. Murnian ordered the twelve officers inside to holster their guns, the mob forced their way inside, dragged the men out of the jail, and hanged them from a lamppost.[3] When they died, Elias Clayton was nineteen, Elmer Jackson was nineteen, and Isaac McGhie was twenty years old. In 2000 the Clayton Jackson McGhie Memorial Inc. was formed. It operates the Clayton Jackson McGhie

Memorial Plaza at the corner of 1st Street and 2nd Avenue East in downtown Duluth.[4]

On May 25, 2020—one hundred years after Elias Clayton, Elmer Jackson, and Isaac McGhie were lynched in Duluth—George Floyd, accused of passing a counterfeit $20 bill, was lynched by Minneapolis police on the street outside the Cup Foods convenience store at the intersection of 38th Street E. and Chicago Ave. A seventeen-year-old girl, Darnella Frazier, recorded the killing with her cell phone and posted it on the internet. She spent nights afterward apologizing to Mr. Floyd for "not doing more" and later described the scene as that of "a man, terrified, scared, begging for his life."[5]

Days of protests and unrest followed. In response to broken windows, business owners across the Twin Cities began to cover their storefronts with sheets of plywood. Soon thereafter many of these boards were covered with painted messages and murals. The Cities were in turmoil and the urban landscape was transformed into a living visual chronicle of the moment. People turned to painting because, like storytelling, it fulfills a basic human need. Painting can be found in human cultures around the world, and it can be traced back to our common ancestors in Africa. In 1991 ancient paintings were unearthed inside the Blombos Cave, near present-day Cape Town. The cross-hatched patterns were created 73,000 years ago by brilliant artists working with red ochre, silcrete, and bone.[6] Separated by thousands of years and thousands of miles, the artistic legacy bequeathed by the artists in South Africa was employed on the streets of North America and in cities around the world as the protests spread. Some of the murals included portraits of George Floyd that were made using a stencil created by Seitu Jones, a St. Paul–based artist. After he posted it on his website as a free download, the *Blues for George* image quickly appeared in public locations across the Twin Cities. The portrait uses a shade of Egyptian Blue that was created and patented by George Washington Carver, making the image a tribute to two Georges.[7]

At the time, I thought it would be amazing to one day have an exhibition of the murals in the Katherine E. Nash Gallery. That idea faded as businesses reopened, the boards were removed, and the murals began to disappear. Fortunately, Leesa Kelly had the inspiration and the presence of mind to save and collect the murals. As the collection grew, she established Memorialize the Movement, dedicated to the collection, preservation, and documentation of the murals. This activity was repeated in other cities as part of an effort to collect and preserve the evidence of the protests that began in the Twin Cities and were happening nationwide. In Washington, DC, curators from the Smithsonian Institution toured the areas outside the White House and collected art, signs, photographs, and other artifacts that remained from the protests. "It is critical that we collect so that this moment does not get lost," said Aaron Bryant, a curator at the National Museum of African American History and Culture. "We talk to people so we don't forget their stories. History is happening right before us."[8]

The message contained in the murals rang out loud and clear across the Twin Cities, Minnesota, the United States, and the world. Unfortunately, the message was not received by all those people who need to hear and understand it. Less than one year after the police killed George Floyd, a young Black man, Daunte Wright, was killed by the police during a traffic stop in Brooklyn Park, Minnesota. He was twenty years old when he died on April 11, 2021. The officer who killed him less than fifteen miles from the intersection of 38th and Chicago in Minneapolis, a twenty-six-year veteran of the police force, claimed that in a moment of confusion she mistakenly pointed her firearm at Daunte Wright, instead of her Taser gun.[9]

In the summer of 2023 I hired Amira McLendon, a senior undergraduate student in the Department of Art, for the position of Undergraduate Gallery Preparator, an annual internship we offer in the Katherine E. Nash Gallery. I saw on Amira's résumé that she had worked as an intern with Leesa Kelly at Memorialize the Movement, and I asked her to introduce us. The three of us met and agreed to present an exhibition of the murals, curated by Amira, at the University of Minnesota. This collaboration builds on a foundation of previous engagement between Memorialize the Movement and the University of Minnesota. Amira's internship at MTM was made possible through Minnesota Transform, an initiative funded by the Mellon Foundation at the University of Minnesota. Memorialize the Movement has been in residence during the 2023–24 academic year at the College of Liberal Arts' Engagement Hub, offering our students pathways through the University of Minnesota and the surrounding community via its Community Creates program.

Art and Artifact: Murals from the Minneapolis Uprising is presented by the Katherine E. Nash Gallery in association with Memorialize the Movement, September 10–December 7, 2024. The exhibition and this catalogue were made possible by the generous support provided by the Associate Dean for Art and Humanities, College of Liberal Arts; College of Liberal Arts Public Engagement; the Office of Diversity, Equity, and Inclusion, College of Liberal Arts; the Department of American Studies; the Department of History; The Imagine Fund Special Events Award; the Institute for Advanced Study; Minnesota Transform: A Mellon Foundation Just Futures Project at the University of Minnesota; The Givens Foundation for African American Literature; Harlan Boss Foundation for the Arts; Stuart and Kate Nielsen; Rosalie O'Brien; and an anonymous donor.

The Katherine E. Nash Gallery is operated by the Department of Art and supported by the faculty and the administrative and technical staff in the Department of Art, the College of

Liberal Arts, and the University of Minnesota. My thanks to Nicholas J. Allyn, Christine Baeumler, Kay Briese, Mindy Breva, Alexandra Brown, Greg Brown, Louis Clark, Almena Dees-Sims, Tracey Deutsch, Colleen Donahue, Brad Engelmann, Carrie Ryan Galia, Jim Gubernick, Karen Haselmann, Regina Hopingardner, Kathy Kipp-Huspeni, Shannon Birge Laudon, Josephine Lee, Elizabeth Lim, Paul Linden, Kevin McKoskey, Logan Morrow, Rana Murphy, Logan Nelson, Michael Oakes, Michelle Orr, Lynda Pavek, Sonja Peterson, Kimberlee Roth, Robin Schwartzman, Clayton Smith, Caroline Houdek Solomon, Patricia Straub, Victoria Troxler, Ann Waltner, Russ White, Amelious Whyte, and Pamela Windingstad. Teréz Iacovino, Assistant Curator of the Katherine E. Nash Gallery, has enthusiastically supported this project on both the administrative and technical sides. Our current and past Undergraduate Interns Kathryn Blommel, Jordan Bongaarts, Amira McLendon, and Corrie Steckelberg, and Graduate Teaching Assistants Mikayla Ennevor, Kayla Fryer, and Alter Hajek have helped this project move forward. Kathryn Blommel, Rob McLain, Corrie Steckelberg, and Eleanore McKenzie Stevenson skillfully helped install the exhibition in the gallery.

I am grateful to our authors for their beautifully written essays included in this publication: Leslie Guy, Leesa Kelly, Amira McLendon, and Seph Rodney. I appreciate the excellent work by our designer Emily Swanberg, copy editor Miles Champion, and photographer Easton M. Green. My thanks to Seitu Jones and Springboard for the Arts for allowing us to reproduce the *Blues for George* mural on the cover of this book. Seitu was one of the first artists I met when I moved to Minnesota thirty years ago, as we were both on staff at Walker Art Center. Throughout his career Seitu has shared a spirit of love, pride, and hope in his work with the people of Minnesota and beyond. This publication is distributed by the University of Minnesota Press: my thanks to Pieter Martin, Senior Acquisitions Editor, and Laura Westlund, Managing Editor, for welcoming this project and for bringing it to the Press; Heather Skinner, Publicity Director and Assistant Marketing Manager, and Shelby Connelly, Marketing Associate, for their help with promotion; and Rachel Moeller, Assistant Production Manager and Art Director for help with production.

Art and Artifact: Murals from the Minneapolis Uprising would never have happened without the dedication and hard work of Leesa Kelly, founder and executive director of Memorialize the Movement. Thank you, Leesa. My thanks to our project curator, Amira McClendon, for compiling this powerful exhibition. And my thanks and appreciation to my wonderful life partner, Annette Igra, whose love and support have been my north star for this project and all the exhibitions I have presented in the Katherine E. Nash Gallery during my time as director.

Amira McLendon

ART IN ACTION

I had only just begun my studies as a higher education student when the world was turned upside down in 2020. What started as an extra week of break turned into months of isolation. When news broke in May of George Floyd's murder, I felt called to action, along with many in my community. I watched as our protests and rallies touched every corner of the world and felt proud to be a part of the community leading the fight against injustice. Now, in 2024, we're four years removed from the Minneapolis Uprising in 2020.

When I decided to major in art at the University of Minnesota, I did so with no plan for my future. I knew I enjoyed art, but I found myself feeling profoundly insecure when surrounded by my seemingly more talented peers. I felt disconnected from my practice as an artist and found it difficult to figure out why I was so drawn to this particular realm despite having no sense of direction. That was until I joined Memorialize the Movement as an intern in 2022. It wasn't until I began my internship that all the possibilities for my future became apparent. I felt as though I had finally found my place within the arts and my drive to seek out opportunities for my communities was ignited. Through my experiences with Memorialize the Movement I was able to experiment with the practice of curation as cocurator of *Justice for George: Our Strength, Our Story* and other smaller exhibitions. I also developed an interest in archiving. This experience led me to working for the Katherine E. Nash Gallery and developing skills and perspectives in a more traditional gallery setting, which led me to curate this exhibition in collaboration with both Memorialize the Movement and the Katherine E. Nash Gallery. Memorialize the Movement has changed my trajectory in art and started me down a path of seeking justice and liberation through the arts.

Art is always at the forefront of movements and calls for justice. When people in the community began making art in the wake of George Floyd's murder, it was a form of self-expression and a means of communication. Art weaves a narrative of the people and bares their truths for all to see. In an age when, without context, things can be easily misconstrued, the artwork created during the Uprising contextualized the actions and feelings of the people. Feelings of grief and anger were expressed through paint. Now, as we look through the collection of over one thousand plywood panels in our stewardship and remember that time, these artworks have also become artifacts. They exist now as the cultural and historical records of our community. They are reminders of our collective past and hold history in every stroke of paint.

When pondering the title for this catalogue and exhibition, I spent a lot of time thinking about what these murals represented. Protest art and art made in the wake of civil unrest stands at an interesting intersection between artwork and historical objects. This observation helped me to arrive at the title *Art and Artifact* to reflect the intersection in which the murals reside. These murals paint a picture of what the local community was feeling during the Uprising in 2020. Now, looking back, I wonder what I would be able to remember about 2020 without these murals. There are articles and photographs online but viewing them through a screen feels distinctly distant. Although a photograph provides a snapshot of time, there is a separation that a photograph elicits. Looking at a photograph, it can feel like the object is in the past, and I am removed from it. Whereas with the murals, I can touch, breathe, and smell the past. It's important for us to emphasize that while these murals are works of art, they're also invaluable relics of the historical Uprising of 2020. The people of the community should be the stewards of their own histories and feel empowered to step into these roles.

As we move forward, let's continue to hold museum institutions accountable. In a country where the practice of erasure is commonplace, we need to demand space from the institutions that have contributed to this practice. It is our right to have the space to create what is necessary for our own empowerment, whether that be through the allocation of physical space to community causes or the funding and support of them. Black and Brown people can preserve and tell their own stories and champion the people of our communities to be creatives, leaders, and innovators that give future generations expectations to aspire to. To do this, we must also recognize what our roles are.

To the communities of Minneapolis and Minnesota, as the people who bore witness to the atrocious acts of the Minneapolis Police

Department in 2020, it's our job to be the spearheads of continuous conversations of action. If we forget, so will everyone else across the country and the world. Even in moments of seeming helplessness, there is strength and power in our community, in our neighbors.

To the communities outside of Minneapolis and beyond Minnesota, keep listening and keep acting. What happened to George Floyd happened to countless other Black people throughout the United States. The violence against Black people in this country does not disappear when we cross state lines. Although Mr. Floyd was a catalyst, let the injustice in your own communities drive you to action as well. He was just one of many Black people killed since 2020. Do not let the names of these people be forgotten. Say their names in your own cities and let the memories of their murders drive you to action.

As you view this catalogue or visit our exhibition, ask yourself, what am I doing to empower my community and take a stand against injustice? Everything is political, every action you take to intentionally disrupt or turn a blind eye holds weight. One day, we'll reach a future where injustice isn't tolerated, but right now we are in the fight to get there. It may be discouraging at times and feel like nothing we do means anything in the grand scheme of things, but your actions hold meaning. Every conversation, every protest, every antiracist action you take helps to create a brighter future that embraces everyone.

My hope is that you feel inspired by the strength and power of our community and feel driven to engage in dialogue and action. Pursuing justice is a collective effort that requires creative action. As you immerse yourself in the stories and expressions of resilience showcased in the catalogue and the exhibition, let them serve as a catalyst for your own commitment to justice. Whether through artistic expression, community organizing, or actively challenging discrimination in your own circles, your contribution matters. Continue to push boundaries and demand change.

Leesa Kelly

MEMORIALIZING A MOVEMENT

I write this essay from intersecting identities that inform my experience in Minneapolis—a predominately white city in the Midwest region of the United States. I am a Black queer woman who founded an organization rooted in protest and fostering representation through art conservation for Black communities. This context informs my daily lived experience and how I am forced to navigate predominantly white spaces that are, at their foundation, anti-Black, anti-woman, and anti-queer.

The lynching of George Floyd by Minneapolis police officers on May 25, 2020, sparked the largest worldwide uprising many of us have ever witnessed. From Minneapolis to Munich, people across the world protested the police brutality experienced by Black bodies. Police precincts were burned, statues of colonizers and oppressors were destroyed, and calls for justice rang out. But this movement did not begin with George Floyd. While the murder of Mr. Floyd in Minneapolis was the igniting flame for the eruption of protests and uprising, pressure had been building long before his murder occurred.

On November 15, 2015, twenty-four-year-old Jamar Clark was fatally shot by two Minneapolis police officers. Protests ensued outside of the 4th Precinct for eighteen days. In the end, his murderers did not face criminal charges, and, after paid administrative leave, they returned to work on January 6.[1] In July 2016, thirty-two-year-old Philando Castile was shot five times in his car in Falcon Heights, a suburb of St. Paul, with his girlfriend and her four-year-old child sitting in the passenger and rear seats. Protesters blocked off major

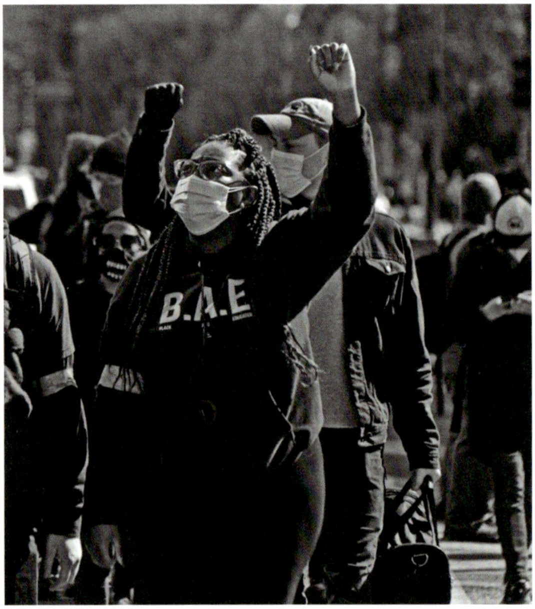

Fig. 1 - Protest in Minneapolis, January 2021.
Photo by Micki Benson

highways, stopping traffic to demand justice for his murder, but the officer was found "not guilty" and acquitted of all charges.[2] Between 2017 and 2020 we experienced the murders of countless other Black men and women across the United States—Stephon Clark, Botham Jean, Elijah McClain, Tony McDade, Breonna Taylor—for sleeping, holding phones, eating, sitting, standing, and existing. Each one led to powerful protests, yet many of the outcomes were the same.

Tension began building in 2020 when COVID-19 brought the world to a halt. While many people around the world lost their lives to the virus, in the United States Black communities experienced loss on a staggering scale.[3] Then, in March of 2020, we learned about the tragic murder of Breonna Taylor in her own home by police. Because of the pandemic, Black communities knew we could not protest, so we channeled our energy into the upcoming election. That experience led to more frustration and fear as former president Trump made a mockery of this country and threatened civil war should he lose the election.

By May, the tension was overwhelming in Minneapolis. Those three months, between March and May, when our communities felt most vulnerable, came to a head on May 25, 2020. On that day, we watched, helplessly, the video of George Floyd's final moments as Derek Chauvin held his knee on Mr. Floyd's neck in an unauthorized restraint over an alleged counterfeit twenty-dollar bill.

The response was immediate (fig. 1). After watching Breonna Taylor's murder go unprotested, with no justice in sight, our community knew we could not allow the same thing to happen to George. After witnessing his public execution, we were prepared to fight for justice. Residents of Minneapolis and St. Paul rallied, leading protests day and night at the Capitol building in St. Paul, the 3rd Precinct in South Minneapolis, the governor's mansion, the mayor's apartment building, Derek Chauvin's home, the steps of the courthouse, and, most significantly, the site where George Floyd took his last breath. I watched protesters burn down the 3rd Precinct at the corner of Minnehaha and Lake St., the fire a manifestation of our collective pain and anger.

In an effort to protect their businesses from looters or from burning, business owners boarded up their storefronts with large sheets of plywood. The material was in such high demand that hardware stores inflated the prices, and it became almost like a currency for business owners, trading goods and services for plywood to protect their assets. For our community, the plywood had a different value. To us, it was a blank canvas on which to express all that we were collectively feeling. Our community had so much to say, and instead of listening, the state and business owners alike boarded up the city and shut us out.

It seemed to happen overnight. I spent the evenings fundraising for supplies for families, then each morning I would wake up and check mutual aid accounts online to find out what supplies were needed and go pick them up. There were drop-off points in different parts of North and South Minneapolis and St. Paul, so I rotated, going to a different location each day. As I drove to a drop-off point in South Minneapolis, I noticed how colorful the streets had become. Murals now covered every inch of the boarded-up buildings, stories spanning for miles at a time. Over the next few days artists, protesters, community members, and children all joined in. Before long the entire city was covered in art. It was a beacon of light in the darkest of times.

The murals ranged from massive, multi-paneled elaborate pieces to single-paneled pieces with a simple message. They were both colorful and professionally painted, as well as rugged, dark, and pointed. There were quotes from famous activists, paintings of Mr. Floyd's likeness, impressive graffiti writing demanding that we "Say His Name," and community pieces, where people wrote messages of love and solidarity. These murals were our private journals made public—where our heaviest emotions went to live because we couldn't carry them home with us. So, we poured our hearts and souls into the murals we painted. There were messages of mourning and anger, and calls to action. There were demands for justice, demands for the officers involved to be prosecuted and sentenced, demands for our city to rise to the occasion and enact policy changes. There were also messages of hope, community, and tenderness. The murals became a method of communication between neighborhoods during the uprising, reminding one another that we were all in this fight together. That helped us keep going.

About mid-June, the looting and burning eventually subsided. The governor had activated the National Guard and there was a nightly curfew. Business owners felt safe enough to slowly begin reopening their storefronts, which meant that murals would disappear overnight. For me, this posed a new set of concerns. Where did the murals go? Where should they go? Who or what entity should be allowed to collect and preserve them? Should they even be preserved? I listened intently, following each conversation and news article that speculated on the future of the murals. With each passing day, more murals were seemingly disappearing from history. There were rumors that murals were being auctioned off by businesses and sold to wealthy art collectors. There were interviews where local museums tossed around the idea of collecting the murals themselves, a thought that enraged me. At the time, I couldn't understand why it upset me; it just felt wrong to allow a museum—rooted in colonialism and imperialism—to collect this art. It wasn't created for a museum. It was born in protest and should be honored as such.

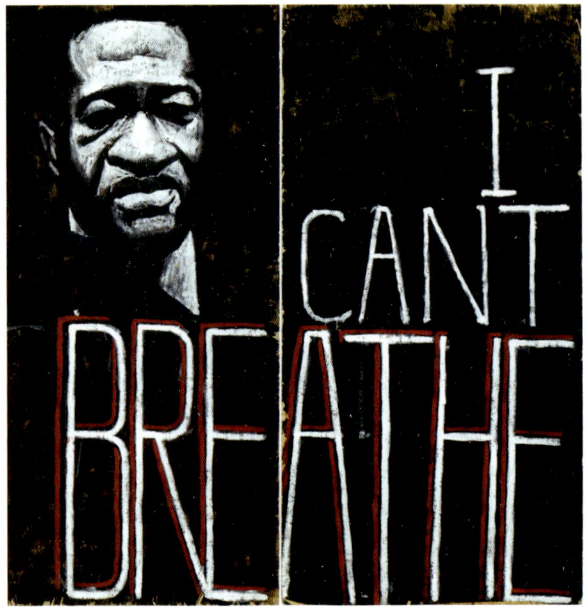

Fig. 2 - Portrait of George Floyd and text that reads "I CANT BREATHE," once located at Burch Steak, 1933 Colfax Ave. S., Minneapolis

It became clear to me that none of the Black art organizations in the city had a plan to collect the murals. Most of them were small, underfunded institutions without a means of collecting such large works. It also became clear to me that the entity who collects the murals would need to possess an active imagination in order to attempt to preserve these large-scale plywood murals. Many of the speculators were caught up in the logistics, the how and the where, but few people talked about the why. The why was clear to me from the beginning. When I walked the streets of the city I saw a story. If you went neighborhood to neighborhood, what you found was a complete written and visual history of the uprising. There were murals that recorded the date, time, and the minutes it took for Mr. Floyd to take his last breath. There were murals that depicted images of the city burning. There were murals that depicted people joining hands in protest. There were even messages that communicated which stores were Black-owned businesses, that children lived there, or instructions for how to access a business even though it was boarded up. What I saw when I looked at the murals was the full picture. Each mural working alongside the others to tell a story of a people who refused to accept that another Black man had been murdered by police. If these murals should be preserved, then who better to preserve them than us—the community most impacted by Mr. Floyd's murder? The people who were out in the streets protesting and providing mutual aid. Black people.

As I watched and waited, nobody acted. Each day, our murals disappeared, and I realized that this moment was fleeting and that waiting was not an option. I created a flyer and called the project Memorialize the Movement (MTM). I then went door-to-door to businesses with murals, handing out the flyers and talking to the owners about their plans for when they took their murals down. Many of the owners had no idea what to do with the art and were happy someone had come along with a solution.

In early June I was at Spectacle Shop in Uptown on Hennepin Ave. getting my annual eye exam. I gathered my nerve and asked them about the mural on their business and they agreed to let me collect it. A week later, as I was driving to Spectacle Shop, I stopped at the intersection of Hennepin Ave. and Franklin Ave. I looked to my right and saw a group of men removing murals from the now-closed Burch Steak. When the light changed, I pulled over and asked the men what their plans were for these murals. They explained to me that they were contractors hired to remove the murals from the building and place them against the trash to be thrown away. I asked them to show me where they were discarding the murals and they led me to the back of the building. When we reached the trash area, what I saw made my heart stop. Leaning against the trash can was a black-and-white mural with a portrait of George Floyd painted on one side, and the words "I CANT BREATHE" [*sic*] written below and on the other side in red and white letters. The portrait of George looked sad to me, like he was disappointed to be leaning up against that dirty trash can—like he knew he deserved better than this (fig.2).

I don't consider myself to be religious, but at that moment a divine message was clear. My heart hurt thinking that this mural would have been discarded, erased from history, if I hadn't pulled over when I did. I knew what I needed to do. I instructed the contractors to place all the murals they took down in my car. At the time I was in my partner's Jeep, and we had planned to let down the back seats and place the murals in the trunk. As the workers followed my instructions, the head contractor came back from lunch to find his workers under new management. He came up to me and asked what was going on, to which I responded with stubborn indignation, "These murals are coming home with me." He then asked, "And how do you plan to get these murals home?" After I explained about the back seat, he shook his head at me and walked away. A few moments later he came back with an armful of ratchet straps. He told me that the murals would never fit in the Jeep, and he showed me how to lay the murals on top of the Jeep and strap them down using the ratchet straps. I was in shock as I listened and worked the straps according to his instructions. When we were done, I asked him if he wanted money for the straps, and he looked me in the eyes and said, "If you're going to do this, then you better do it right." Then he and his workers left me standing there, with the weight of his words hanging in the air.

Over the next six months I devoted every waking moment to the collection of the murals. When my garage became too full, I started a GoFundMe campaign to raise money for a place to store the murals. By October of 2020 I had collected over three hundred pieces and rented a storage room at the Northrup King Building in North-

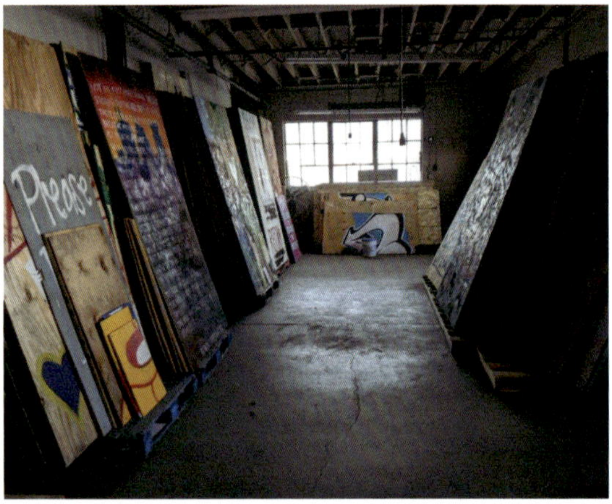

Fig. 3 - Memorialize the Movement's first storage space, October 2020. Courtesy of Memorialize the Movement

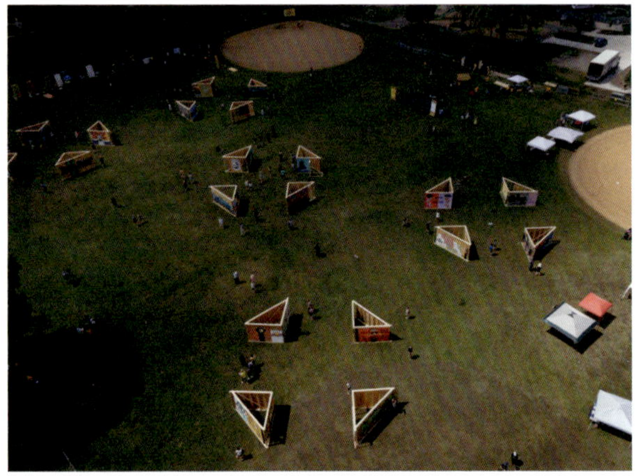

Fig. 4 - Justice for George, Phelps Field Park, Minneapolis, May 22, 2021. Photo by Christian Monterrosa

east Minneapolis (fig. 3). By the time the move was complete, the collection had doubled. I stood in our storage room alone, surrounded by all the murals, and new questions swam in my mind. "How do I give these murals life?" It wasn't enough to collect them and store them in a dark room; that's what the museums would have done. I'm supposed to do things differently. "How do I honor their original purpose and empower them to still make an impact on people?"

In December of 2020 I decided to curate a selection of the murals in an event I would call *Justice for George: Messages from the People. Justice for George* was an exhibition, a celebration of life, and an acknowledgment of everything my community had been through in 2020. I wanted to create a safe space where people could heal from the trauma caused by the pandemic and uprising, celebrate our power and resilience, and express themselves creatively through art, music, and dance. Over the next five months I would learn to become an event coordinator, a curator, a conservator, and, ultimately, an executive director. On May 22, 2021, we hosted the first of what would become an annual event. We saw over three hundred attendees at Phelps Field Park that day, a larger turnout than we could ever have expected (fig. 4). It was life-changing, seeing people interact with the murals and watching as the art and the music reignited the flames in their hearts that had been burnt out by exhaustion. After the media attention we received at the event, many artists and businesses reached out to donate their murals, and by the time 2022 came around we had collected over one thousand pieces.

Change is an iterative process. It involves questions and repetition to get it right. Throughout this process I have been posing questions to the universe, then allowing the answers I received to guide my next move. I wondered if I should be the one to collect these pieces, then I saw the mural of George next to the trash. I asked how to bring life to the murals, then *Justice for George* was born. In January of 2022 I asked, “How do I connect this work to my community?” Then, the very next month, the Paint to Express (PTE) workshops were born. The PTEs are free workshops that we host in a different location in predominantly Black communities each month, where we provide free art supplies, miniature plywood panels to paint on, free food, and music. We wanted to curate an experience where our community could feel comfortable expressing themselves creatively as part of the healing process.

As I reflect on the success that MTM has had in preserving these murals and the stories they hold, I'm reminded of my anger back in 2020 when museums entertained the idea of collecting these artifacts. At the time, I didn't understand why the thought upset me, but now, four years later, I realize that it's because there is little representation in the museum and conservation industries. Since 2020, I have learned that 5 percent of all conservators, less than 7 percent of all historians, and 4 percent of all curators in the United States are Black.[4] That means that if a museum had collected this art, there would likely only be one Black person, if that, in the whole institution who could tell this story, if they were even given the opportunity to do so.

As I continue this work, I now understand that there is so much more to this than just collecting and preserving the murals. Yes, the murals are powerful records of one of the greatest social movements of my generation, but only in the right hands. My mission is to be a steward, not only for the murals but for the story as well—a messenger, to pass on everything I'm learning in this process to the next generation. I hope to inspire and foster future historians, preservationists, and curators. While I know that there is still a long way to go, and I am just one of many people leading this work, I am proud to say that I can already see the buds of change peeking through the cracks.

This catalogue and exhibition are a testament to the progress that is already being made to improve representation, because neither would exist without the ambition of my good friend Amira (fig. 5). A former MTM intern, Amira McLendon worked with us for two years, during which time she gained an interest in curation and preservation. Now, just a year after the internship ended, she is curating the largest indoor Memorialize the Movement exhibition to date. Progress is slow, and change takes time. But I sleep peacefully at night knowing that this work makes a difference. This catalogue is tangible proof of that.

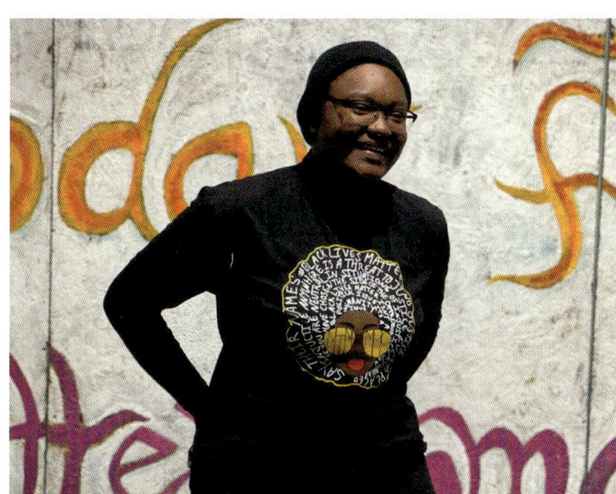

Fig. 5 - Amira McLendon. Courtesy of Memorialize the Movement

Leslie Guy

WHAT ARE WE DOING TO SAFEGUARD OUR HISTORY?

Memorialize the Movement (MTM) was a grassroots effort born out of a sense of urgency to prevent the erasure of history. Protest art decrying George Floyd's death had appeared on boarded-up storefront windows. These works around the Twin Cities were a window reflecting the range of our feelings at that time—anguish, shock, and fervent hopes for a brighter future.

In a surprisingly short amount of time, efforts to return to normalcy were underway. Reopening of businesses came with removal of the boards. MTM stepped in to reclaim the work from dumpsters, preventing these tangible connections to history from ending up in landfills or being recycled into mulch for landscaping or pulp for paper production. So it was that MTM set upon the task of creating "a living archive dedicated to collecting, preserving, and activating the plywood protest murals that were created during the Minneapolis Uprising of 2020 and beyond."[1]

Just a year into MTM's work, they were contacted about a large mural in peril that was soon to be removed from a salon's corner windows. The title of this work, *The Revolution Will Not Be Televised*, was taken from a seminal 1971 Gil Scott-Heron song. The mural's playful design references the song's lyrics while serving as an effective counterpoint to its powerful message. The compelling piece was actively degrading, its very substrate attacked by a fungal network. Areas with active delamination exposed white root-like mycelium with associated large fruiting bodies reminiscent of squashed cauliflower.

By expanding and then erupting to the surface, these fruiting bodies were further compromising the structure of the board. Mildew with the appearance of an oily black ooze was seeping from the cut edges of the pressboard. Taking advantage of this nutrient-rich environment, a broad cross section of insects had sought shelter in the welcoming space. The work was in a state of active biodeterioration. Without intervention, this mural would be reduced to a pile of gardening mulch interspersed with flecks of colorful paint. Fortunately for us, MTM intervened. A process of dehumidification, freezing, and surface cleaning saved the work. *The Revolution Will Not Be Televised* has been saved and is one of the most striking works in the collection (see insert at the back of this book).

The speed with which nature was reclaiming the mural was eclipsed by the efforts in Florida to censor the past. In 2021 Governor DeSantis introduced the legislative proposal Stop W.O.K.E. Activism and Critical Race Theory in Schools and Corporations.[2] Opponents of the bill raised the alarm, warning that, if passed, this legislation would "censor honest conversations about Black history, LGBTQ history, and the root causes of injustice and discrimination in schools and workplaces." In their words it was "censorship disguised as nondiscrimination."[3] Florida's Department of Education subsequently prohibited schools from mentioning the Black Lives Matter movement and the killing of George Floyd in their textbooks.[4] In 2024 the Florida legislature passed HB1291, a bill prohibiting teachers from introducing curricula or instruction based on theories that systemic racism, sexism, oppression, and privilege are inherent in the institutions of the United States and were created to maintain social, political, and economic inequities.[5]

While at the forefront of the effort to suppress the past, Florida is not alone. The American Library Association's Office for Intellectual Freedom (OIF) has released new data documenting attempts to censor books around the county. A record 4,240 unique book titles were targeted for censorship in 2023, a 65 percent increase over 2022 and a 128 percent increase over 2021. Books representing LGBTQIA+ or BIPOC individuals made up 47 percent of those targeted in censorship attempts.[6] Our national climate is becoming increasingly hostile toward the narratives MTM seeks to preserve.

The story of the *Celebration of Life* mural (1995–2001) is a cautionary tale of how easily the histories and concerns of underrepresented communities are disregarded and discarded. The world-renowned artist John Biggers (1924–2001) was commissioned by the Black community of North Minneapolis to create a monument to Juneteenth. This epic work once stood on the corners of Lyndale Avenue N. and Olson Memorial Parkway, a welcoming sentinel to the neighborhood.

"There is nothing left to do but cry."[7] These words were uttered in sorrowful resignation

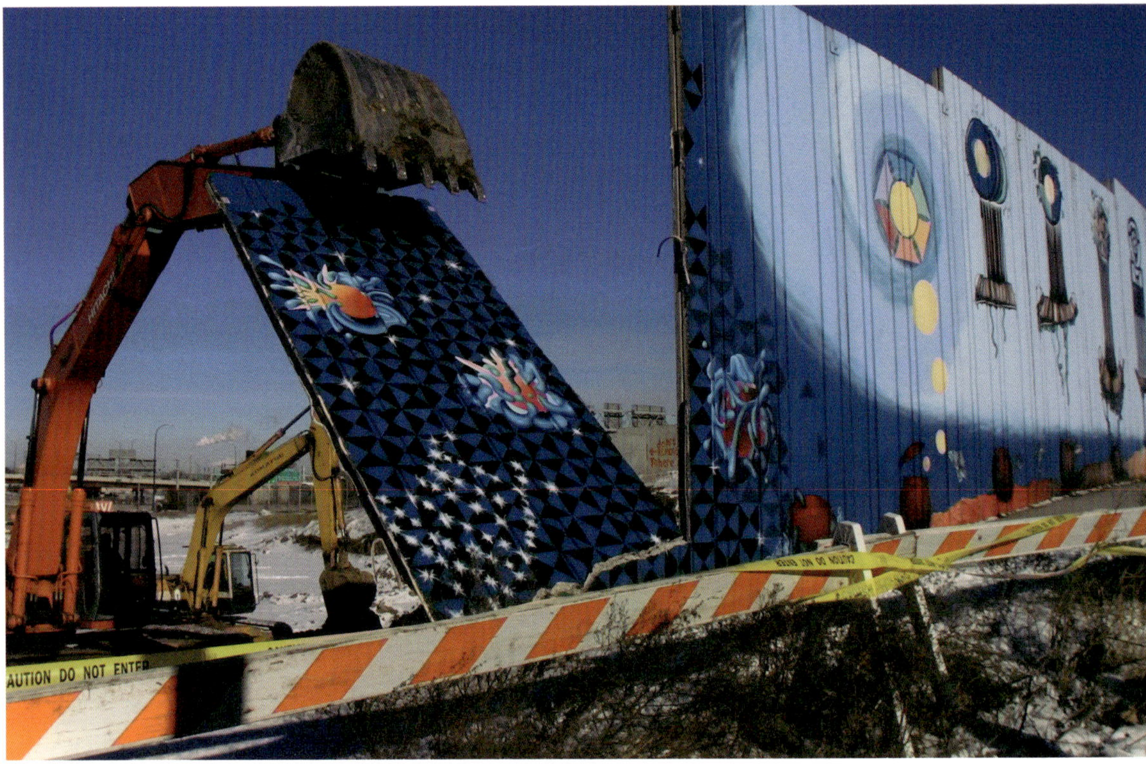

Fig. 1 - Destruction of the *Celebration of Life* mural, December 31, 2001. Photo by Bruce Bisping/*Star Tribune* via Getty Images

by a member of the Citizens Action Committee to Preserve the Celebration of Life Mural after losing a two-year fight to save the mural. December 31, 2001, was the last day for this mural, paid for and commissioned by the community of North Minneapolis in celebration of slavery's end. Like so many Black communities around the nation, North Minneapolis celebrated this day decades before it was nationally recognized. On this bleak December day a human chain was formed, with bodies encircling the massive concrete structure. It was the community's last resort to keep the cranes away (fig. 1). All their other efforts had failed. Protesters at the site decried the "terrorism of our art," asserting the city's indifference to African American art and history: "If this was one of [Charles] Schulz's pieces, it would have been relocated."[8]

Hearing these words, one is compelled to recall the history of this place. Less than ten miles away, Dred and Harriet Scott had been enslaved at Fort Snelling. Their illegal bondage at that location was reaffirmed in the now infamous 1857 ruling by the U.S. Supreme Court, which read that "[the negro] had no rights which the white man was bound to respect; and that the negro might justly and lawfully be reduced to slavery for his benefit."[9]

The Celebration of Life project began in 1994 as a dream. Organizers of the mural hoped that it would bring people together in cele-

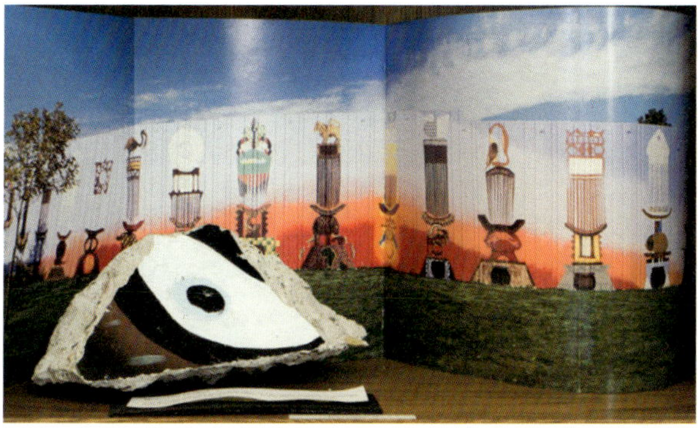

Fig. 2 - *Celebration of Life* by John Biggers et al., 1996, relic. Sumner Library display case. Courtesy of Hennepin County Library

bration of the history, humanity, and strength of African people. It was envisioned that the mural would provide inspiration to help others in a joint effort to transform the world. The project team gallerist, Patricia Phillips, along with lead artists Ta-Coumba T. Aiken and Seitu Jones, reached out to Biggers with a novel proposal. Their plan was to have Biggers design a mural that would be executed by the two lead artists with the assistance of apprentices. This project came toward the end of Biggers's long and storied career. As founder of the art department at Texas Southern University, John Biggers was a teacher at heart as well as a prolific artist. His murals can be found around the country and his work is in over forty museum collections. At the time, Biggers was in ill health and intent upon staying closer to his home in Houston. Fortuitously, it had been his lifelong aspiration to work collaboratively with a group of artists in a working style similar to Diego Rivera, so Biggers enthusiastically accepted.[10]

The Celebration of Life Project brought Biggers full circle in his career, connecting him to his experiences as a student at Hampton University. His use of African and Native American imagery can be traced back to his engagement with the extensive collections first established at the Hampton University Museum in the 1870s. A year before the Minneapolis commission, Biggers completed the *Tree House and House of the Turtle* in honor of the school's African, Native American, and Christian heritages.

Little remains of *Celebration of Life*, a 160-foot-long community-comissioned monument in commemoration of Juneteenth, save a few fragments no larger than the average end table. Though the original *Celebration of Life* mural is lost forever, a relic remains at Sumner Library—a piece of concrete from the mural wall, set in front of an image of the beloved work (fig. 2).[11] Public officials attribute the pulverization of this mural to the impossibility of removing the art without significant destruction. The *Star Tribune* reported that "the mural needed to be torn down to improve access and visibility for a new housing development called Heritage Park."[12]

Yet, in museums throughout Europe and the United States, there are countless examples of monumental antiquities that were moved safely across contents via nineteenth-century technology. Moreover, by 2001, the Science Museum of Minnesota successfully completed a $99.6 million museum building campaign that involved the relocation of 1.75 million artifacts. Dino Day—March 27, 1999—marked the kickoff of moving the large skeleton collection. The ceremony was attended by then Governor Jesse Ventura and featured the relocation of the famed triceratops (fig. 3). This massive endeavor gained national recognition with the pioneering publication *Moving the Mountain: Science Museum of Minnesota Guide to Moving Collections*.

The Celebration of Life project's organizers used the mural as a catalyst for a comprehensive educational and community outreach program. For the general audience there were community workshops on Black art conducted at the Walker Art Center; a mural arts curriculum was developed for school-age children in Minneapolis and St. Paul; and handouts with the mural's image were made for distribution. There was a Mural Unveiling Weekend where Maya Angelou, Alvia J. Wardlaw, and John Biggers signed books to raise funds for the mural. Under the tutelage of the project's lead artist, several young artists worked on the mural (fig. 4). Decades later, many of the participants are now established in the field. Many of the mural's original artists are part of the John Biggers Seed Project, "the legacy project of the John Biggers *Celebration of*

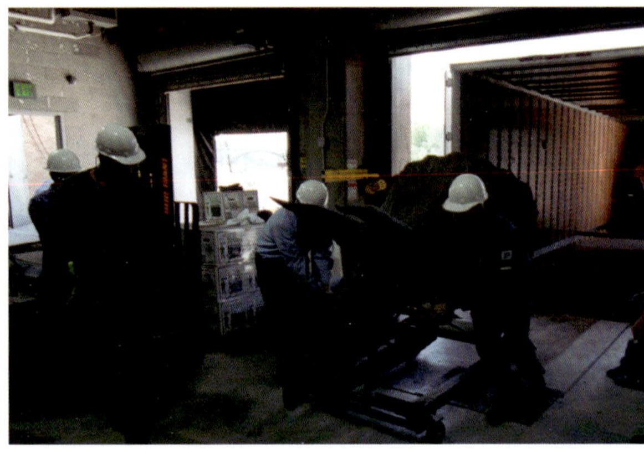

Fig. 3 - Relocation of the famed triceratops, Science Museum of Minnesota. Photo by Duane Braley, Star Tribune via Getty Images

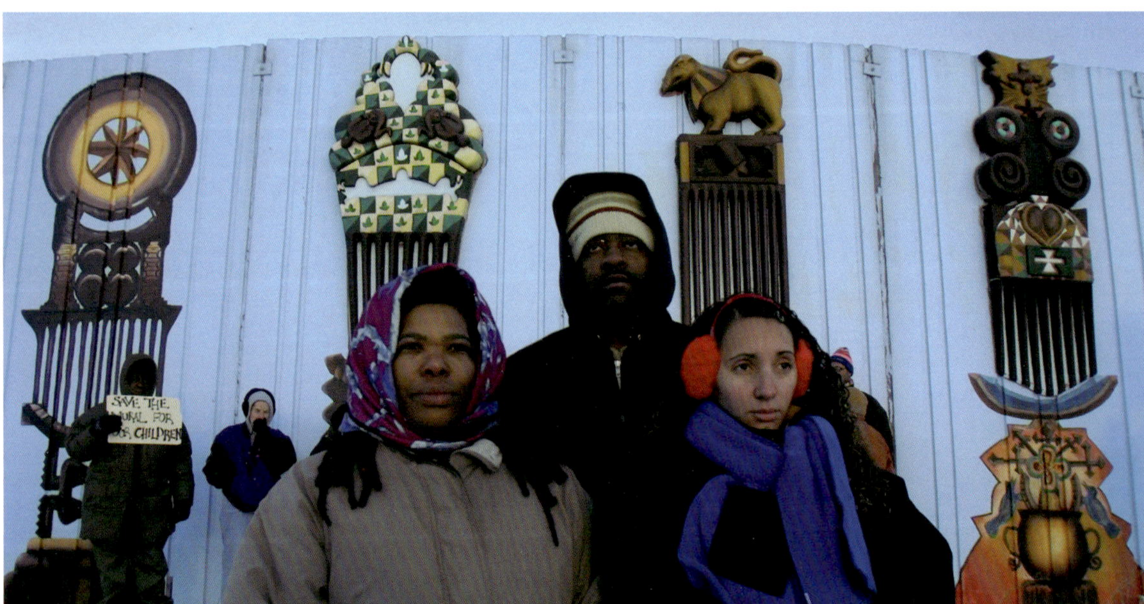

Fig. 4 - Left to right: Vanessa Sayers, Patrick Cunningham, and Loretta Day, three of the artists who worked on the *Celebration of Life* mural, December 31, 2001. Photo by Bruce Bisping, *Star Tribune* via Getty Images

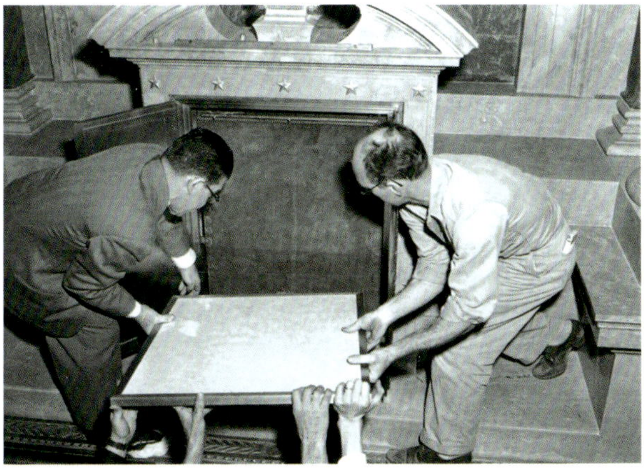

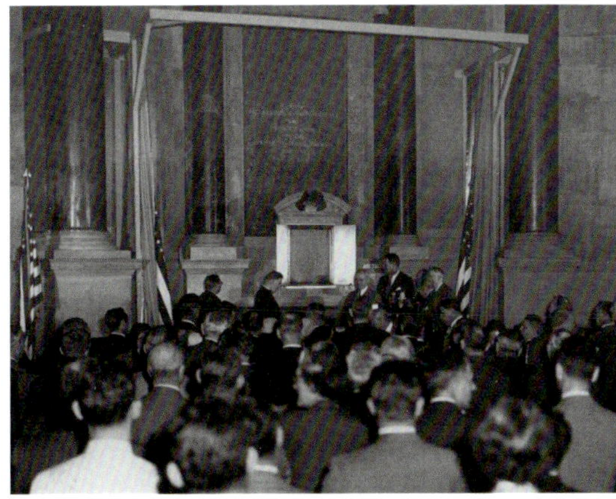

Fig. 5 (left) - Machinist Leroy Morton, left, and carpenter Buck Van Pelt placing the Declaration of Independence in its display case in the Rotunda of the National Archives Building, December 13, 1952, Records of the National Archives and Records Administration, Historic Photograph of National Archives Events and Personnel, NAID: 7657226, ID: 64-NA-1-440.

Fig. 6 (right) - The Shrine Unveiled, December 15, 1952, Records of the National Archives and Records Administration, Historic Photograph of National Archives Events and Personnel, NAID: 12168030, ID: 64-NA-1-455.

Life mural, which began the careers of young artists and organizations planting artistic 'seeds' in the City."[13]

Why does art survive or disappear? Early in my career I would have provided overly simplistic material relying heavily on explanations like "inherent vice" or "environmental conditions" or possibly "poor policy." The answers seemed so obvious then. But this is a partial answer, not a complete explanation. Today I know the actual reason is us. The truth is, objects that survive support the stories the powerful want to tell about themselves and others. Artifacts are physical manifestations of the values, agendas, and narratives often used as projections of power.

December 13, 1952, marked the unveiling of the Declaration of Independence and the Constitution of the United States in the specially designed Rotunda for the Charters of Freedom (figs. 5, 6). At the formal enshrining ceremony on December 15, 1952, President Truman remarked, "We are engaged here today in a symbolic act. We are enshrining these documents for future ages . . . This magnificent hall has been constructed to exhibit them, and the vault beneath, that we have built to protect them, is as safe from destruction as anything that the wit of modern man can devise."[14] This occasion marked just the latest example of the nation deploying state-of-the-art technology of the era to immortalize a document bearing these words: "We hold these truths to be self-evident, that all Men are created equal, that they are endowed by their Creator with certain unalienable Rights, that among these are Life, Liberty, and the Pursuit of Happiness—."[15] Almost half a century later, NASA-aided technology detected micro fissures in the protective enclosure, prompting an assessment and redesign of the encasement.[16]

Great care was taken in the creation of the Declaration of Independence. Timothy Matlack, a clerk in the Pennsylvania State House, was selected as its scribe for his elegant penmanship using iron gall ink on parchment—a technique popular in Europe since the Middle Ages. The durability of parchment was noted centuries prior by Johannes Trithemius in 1490: "handwriting placed on skin will be able to endure a thousand years. But how long will printing last, which is dependent on paper? For if . . . it lasts for two hundred years, that is a long time."[17]

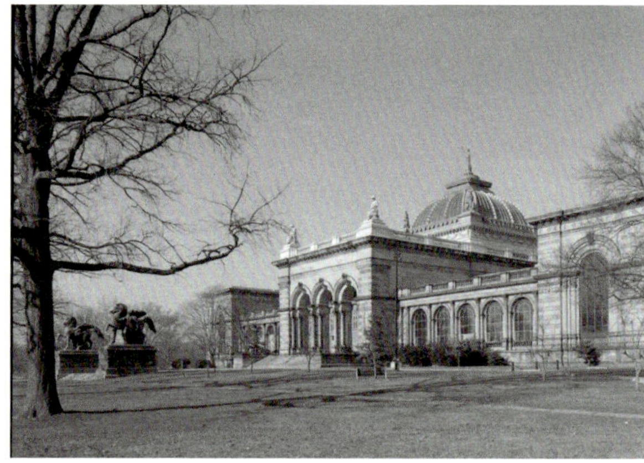

Fig. 7 - Memorial Hall, Philadelphia, built as an art gallery for the 1876 Centennial International Exposition. Photo by the Historic American Buildings Survey, Library of Congress, Prints and Photographs Division, HABS PA, 51-Phila, 265B

After decades of use and handling, the condition of the Declaration of Independence became a cause for concern, prompting the creation of government-sanctioned facsimiles to be safeguarded by the Department of State. Supporting this effort in 1823, the (Washington) *National Intelligencer* observed, "We are very glad to hear this, for the original of that paper which ought to be immortal and imperishable, by being so much handled by copyists and curious visitors, might receive serious injury."[18]

By 1870 a movement was afoot to create a narrative about this country as a leader among the world's nations. Now, only five years after the Civil War, the nation's reach had extended well beyond the original thirteen colonies—comprising an area similar to all of the modern-day United States, save Hawaii and a portion of Eastern Oklahoma, which remained Indian Territory. As reported that year by the *Daily Evening Telegraph*, "The subject of celebrating the centennial anniversary of the Declaration of Independence has been one that has caused considerable debate throughout the country, and now that it has been concluded that an international exhibition is necessary for 1876, the principal cities are naturally desirous that this great event shall transpire within their limits."[19]

Two years later, President Ulysses S. Grant submitted a Special Message to Congress, noting, "There have now been international expositions held by three of the great powers of Europe. It seems fitting that the one hundredth anniversary of our independence should be marked by an event that will display to the world the growth and progress of a nation devoted to freedom and to the pursuit of fame, fortune, and honors by the lowest citizen as well as the highest."[20] Thinking about this enterprise today, one can only marvel at the conceit. The Civil War ended only five years prior and Reconstruction

Era reforms were meeting with violent opposition. During this time period there were thousands of documented lynchings, including thirty-four mass lynchings.[21] After three months on display in the 1876 Centennial International Exhibition (fig. 7), public consternation over the condition of the Declaration of Independence resulted in a joint resolution of Congress forming a commission charged with the restoration of the document.[22] Proving impossible, subsequent generations deployed state-of-the-art technology to prevent further deterioration.

In 1976, the exhibition *Two Centuries of Black American Art* opened for the Bicentennial at the Los Angeles County Museum of Art. This groundbreaking exhibition curated by artist and scholar David C. Driskell, chair of the Department of Art at Fisk University, was the first major historical survey of the Black contribution to the nation's cultural heritage. The exhibition covered the years 1750 to 1950, and featured two hundred works from sixty-three artists, including John Biggers. Reflecting upon this monumental accomplishment in the Introduction to the exhibition catalogue, Rexford Stead, Deputy Director of the Los Angeles County Museum of Art, wrote, "an endless regret is that many black American works have vanished or lack documentation."[23] This was almost fifty years ago, yet these words still apply today. So, today, as the nation prepares for its Sesquicentennial, we need to ask ourselves: What are we doing to safeguard our history?

Seph Rodney

LISTENING TO WHAT THE MURALS ARE TELLING US

The murals that have been acquired, preserved, and documented by the Memorialize the Movement organization seem to me like previously submerged seacraft thrust to the surface of our collective awareness by something momentous. That momentous event was the murder of George Floyd in Minneapolis in May of 2020. A profound tectonic shift occurred with this, which generated massive waves of political and social unrest, judicial prosecution, and public policy changes. That extrajudicial killing of Floyd also generated these plywood protest murals that Memorialize the Movement has conserved, recognizing that they are key historical documents. They are also signs of a collective desire to navigate the subsequent waves and undertows, so we are neither pulled under to be robbed of our breath nor washed out to sea to founder by ourselves.

Rising from complicated circumstances as they do, these murals accomplish several things at the same time. Perhaps primarily they are chronicles that give to those who will live beyond the epicenter of that tumult some sense of what happened and what it means. Additionally, they are aesthetic signs, conveying the perspectives of their artistic authors, who sometimes make representational images, sometimes use only written language, and in other instances combine both. They also represent the thoughts and feelings of an entire community, whose members spontaneously gathered to make them.

As pieces of art, they do certain kinds of work; as linguistic signs, they do other kinds of work, including opening discussions, forwarding arguments, making pleas and

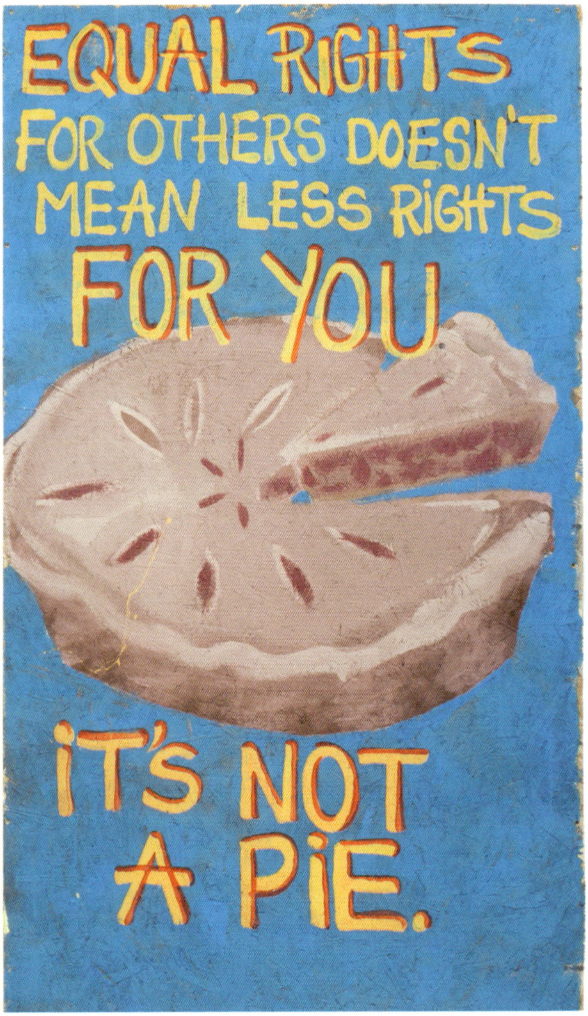

Fig. 1 - Free in Color Arts, Youth Painters, *Equal Rights. . .It's Not a Pie*, 2020, CVS, 1010 W. Lake St., 86 x 48 in.

demands. Examining precisely what they say, and the premises that undergird these statements, we can grasp a good deal of what they mean. Looking at these murals, one of the first aspects that emerges is the prevalence of declarative sentences and phrases.

Generally speaking, in the English language, there are four types of sentences. A sentence is a group of words that conveys a complete thought or set of thoughts and contains a subject and a predicate. The four types of these word groupings are declarative, exclamatory, imperative, and interrogative.

Typically, declarative statements are meant to inform. They issue from the speaker with the intent to impart to the reader or listener information deemed necessary or, at the least, important. Following from this premise, for many of these political billboards, the effort seems to be to enlighten. For example, one mural reads: "Equal Rights for Others Doesn't Mean Less Rights for You. It's Not a Pie" (fig. 1).

This declarative statement recognizes that the members of the dominant culture who systematically organize against the interests of people of color, members of the queer community, and immigrants have a set of politics that are founded in fear, and the speaker wants to negate that fear response by demonstrating that its foundation is unsubstantiated. This message seems particularly directed at those who are the most vehemently opposed to any sort of governmental intervention intended to benefit the underserved groups mentioned above. These right-wing activists subscribe to ideologies such as the "great replacement theory," which was first promulgated by the French author Renaud Camus, who claimed that ethnic French and white European populations are being demographically and culturally replaced by non-white peoples through migration and their demographic

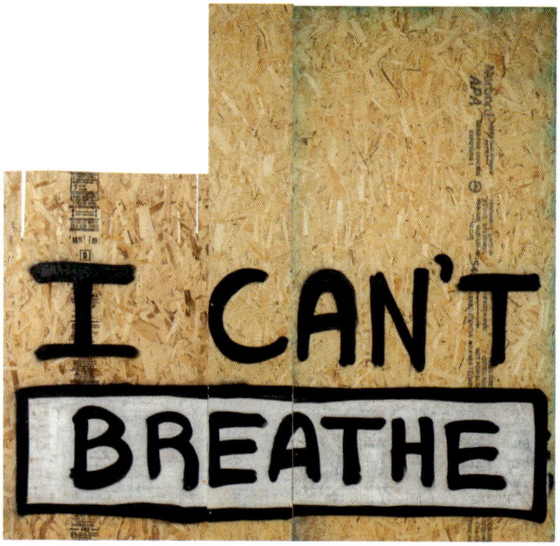

Fig. 2 - Artist Unidentified, *I Can't Breathe*, 2020, 96 x 111 in. approx.

growth within their newly settled countries. For those acolytes, the movement for equal rights via the metrics of race, gender, nationality, and sexuality feels like a zero-sum game, and, in response, this writer means to disarm them of this falsehood.

Similarly, another writer attributes a quotation to Martin Luther King: "True Peace is Not Merely the Absence of Tension; It is the Presence of Justice." This comment seems directed at the voices decrying the eruption of protests across the country in the wake of Floyd's death. In the article "George Floyd Protests: A Timeline," the *New York Times* reports that "protests have erupted in at least 140 cities across the United States, and the National Guard has been activated in at least 21 states," and the reporter acknowledges that some of these protests were violent.[1] Many political actors regarded these demonstrations (rightly, I believe) as representative of the overall struggle to safeguard the lives and liberties of people of color, while others argued that the rallies were invalid because they were accompanied by theft and the destruction of private property. The speaker here suggests that what had seemed like "peace" to some, prior to the nationwide upheaval, was only the slackening of the tensions that persist in a society with a criminal justice system that often treats people of color, prima facie, as if they are suspects, or worse, insurgents. More succinctly, as another mural proclaims: "No Justice No Peace."

These statements are directed to outsiders, to perceived political combatants. In this voice, a mural declares, "until the color of your skin is the target, you will never understand." And this is said less in the spirit of generously prodding the reader toward enlightenment and more in the almost directorial tone of someone pointing out the prerequisites for being able to enact empathic actions that can cross identity boundaries.

More directly, another piece states: "My Skin Isn't My Sin." Here, the appeal is made to another human's ability to recognize that skin color is ultimately not an existentialist feature or a divine judgment—which inveighs against centuries of conspiracy theory that propagated myths claiming that dark-skinned people were descendants of tribes cursed by the Judeo-Christian god. The mural also declares that one's presence in the world as a person of color is not a choice, is not the result of willful action—which is to state what for some is exasperatingly obvious. But its articulation points to one of the foundations of United States popular culture: we believe that people's circumstances are almost always a result of their intentional choosing, even in cases where people are born into wealthy families to benefit from exceptional privilege that they did nothing to earn or merit.

Then there are those statements that mean to sound the alarm, broadcasting that we are in crisis. They are declarative but have an exclamatory feel: "I Can't Breathe." These words come out of a life-altering crisis. They were the last words spoken by Eric Garner after he was placed in an illegal chokehold by a New York City police officer in 2014. They were also uttered by Elijah McClain as he was forcibly detained by police in Aurora, Colorado, in August of 2019, and illegally injected with ketamine by paramedics who were seeking to sedate him. After that dose, he died of cardiac arrest. These words were also reiterated by George Floyd as he lay on the ground, pleading for his life, with police officer Derek Chauvin's knee on his neck. This group of words has served as both a clarion call and an epitaph—these Black men telling us they are drowning in agony and desperate to have someone see them and save them (fig. 2).

I am even more moved by the declarative statements that are addressed to those imagined to be part of the speaker's community. The declarations "We Have a Voice" and "Together We Can" focus on those with whom the speaker has made common cause. They encourage the community to recognize our combined power and urge us to harness it. These sentences are exhortations, battle cries. Crucially, they do not call for violence but for the hard, long-term work of social and political reorganization. They point to what is possible, though they never name what that future reality might be. For some, this vagueness is representative of a kind of cheap, unhelpful sloganeering. But, rhetorically, these sentences give the reader the sense that they struggle within a coalition of like-minded people, and the historical record bears out that collectives and coordinated movements accomplish far more than individuals operating on their own.

Further to this theme, the statement "Black and Brown Bodies Matter Here" is more healing than I could have imagined. It is a kind of promise to care for my life, to record the actions of police officers, to hold them accountable, to document my treatment at their hands, and even in death—if I were to be arbitrarily killed by officers of the state, or anyone else. The promise is also that my death would matter, that people would risk themselves to protest my passing, would commemorate me, simply because I am a member of the community, and my Black life matters. This is a statement of value, of honor, and it is what the wider society is perhaps slowly coming to understand needs to be given to those who die unjustly, because their deaths presage others.

The imperative statements have different aims entirely. These are made to directly compel action. Here they appear as "Performative Allyship Will Not Suffice; Demand Justice." More simply they also intone: "Fight for Justice." These are directed to all readers. These statements say what must be done, without recourse to explaining a historical context, likely because the speaker understands that the alarms are already going off everywhere in the city and township. You can barely hear another person speak over the clanging of bells and sirens (fig. 3).

Amid all that noise, others making statements of command ask us to do the simple task of naming the people who have been lost. A mural reads, "Say Their Names," as in, the names of all the people who have died unjustly. And on the cover of the catalogue in which this essay appears is a sketch by Seitu Jones, who says, in reference to Floyd, "Say *His* Name." To pronounce out loud the name of the person is to honor them, is to invoke them, is to say that they are not forgotten. To do so gives them a kind of extended life when their physical life has been extinguished too soon.

It is critical to point out here that there are few interrogative sentences in these murals. One example asks the reader, "If Not Now, Then When? If Not Us, Then Who?" which seems to be a rhetorical construction. The speaker subtly suggests that the answers given in the question itself are the most valid responses. Therefore "Now" is the only proper time for action, and this action will only be taken up by the activist "Us." Part of the reason for the paucity of questioning is that, having reached the point of calamity that produced these murals, it may no longer feel to these writers and artists that there is time and space for true dialogic engagement. There is a long list of people of color who have recently died at the hands

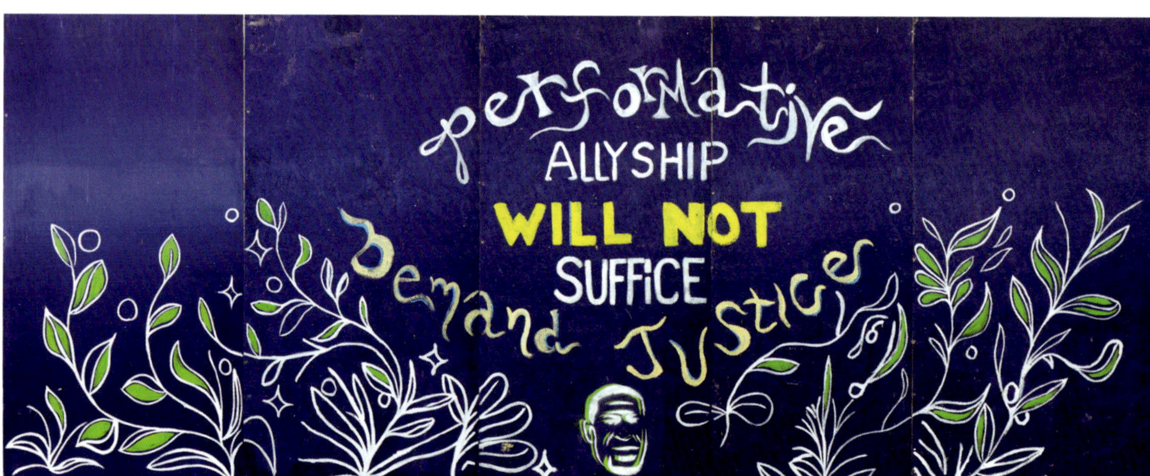

Fig. 3 - Taylan DeJohnette, Patricio De Lara, and Ashley Koudou, *Performative Allyship Will Not Suffice Demand Justice*, 2020, Seward Community Co-op, 96 x 223 in.

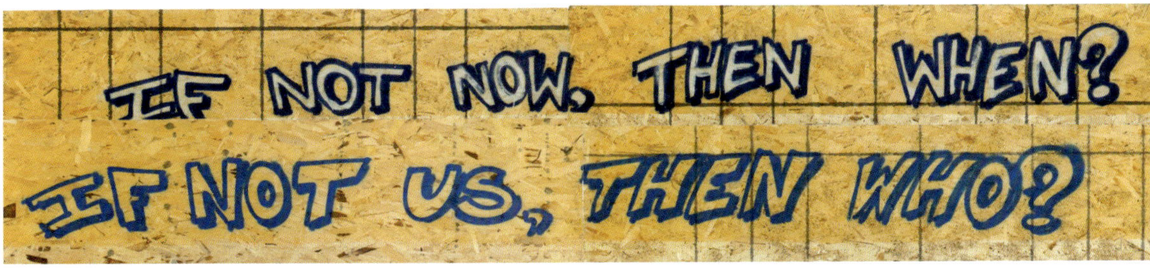

Fig. 4 - Artist Unidentified, *If Not Now, Then When? If Not Us, Then Who?*, 2020, Cafetto Coffee House, 708 W. 22nd St., 40 x 180 in.

of officers of the state in either questionable circumstances, or situations that are blatantly illegal and incontrovertibly dehumanizing: Breonna Taylor, Philando Castile, Tamir Rice, John Crawford III, Sandra Bland, Alton Sterling, Oscar Grant, and on. That another unjustifiable killing may happen tomorrow is both completely expected and utterly disheartening (fig. 4).

Perhaps the scarcity of questioning statements is the most damning message of the murals when considered together. This dearth points to the conviction among these muralists that there are few partners within the law enforcement system or political class available and willing to do the difficult work of allowing themselves to be held accountable to the people they govern, police, and ostensibly protect. A lack of questions indicates less faith in conversation as a tool able to bring about social justice, and perhaps less faith in the usefulness of stepping into another's shoes to see what they see and feel what they feel.

This absence does not bode well for our collective justice work. But we are in a time of crisis and the alarms are clanging and ringing, and it will take some powerful intervention for us to hear each other above the din.

ART AND ARTIFACT
Murals from the Minneapolis Uprising

Location details, current in 2020, are provided where available.

SOUTH MINNEAPOLIS

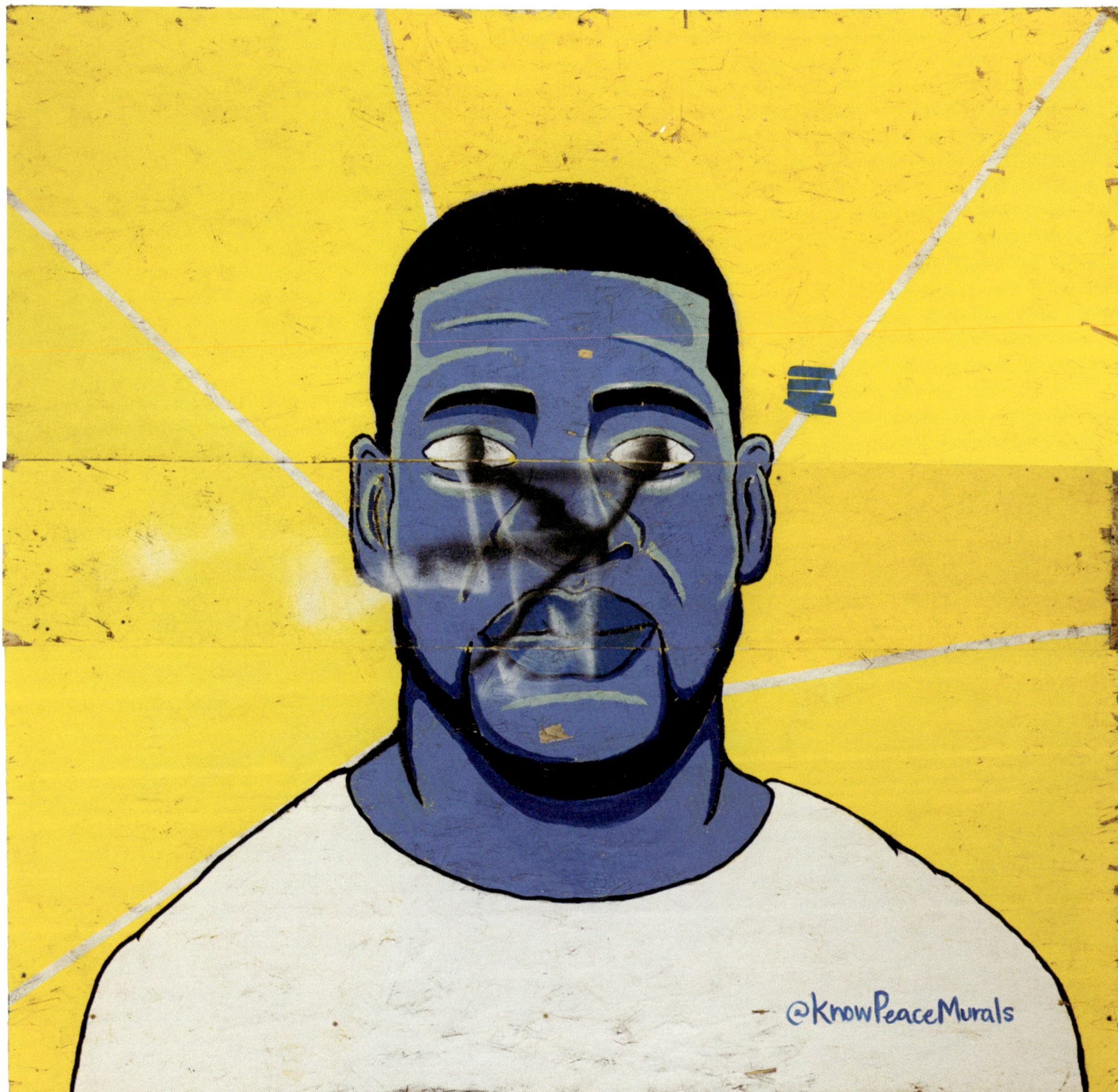

Plate 1

Know Peace Murals, *George Floyd*, 2020

Multiple locations: Vibe Realty and Dogwood Coffee, 96 x 96 in.

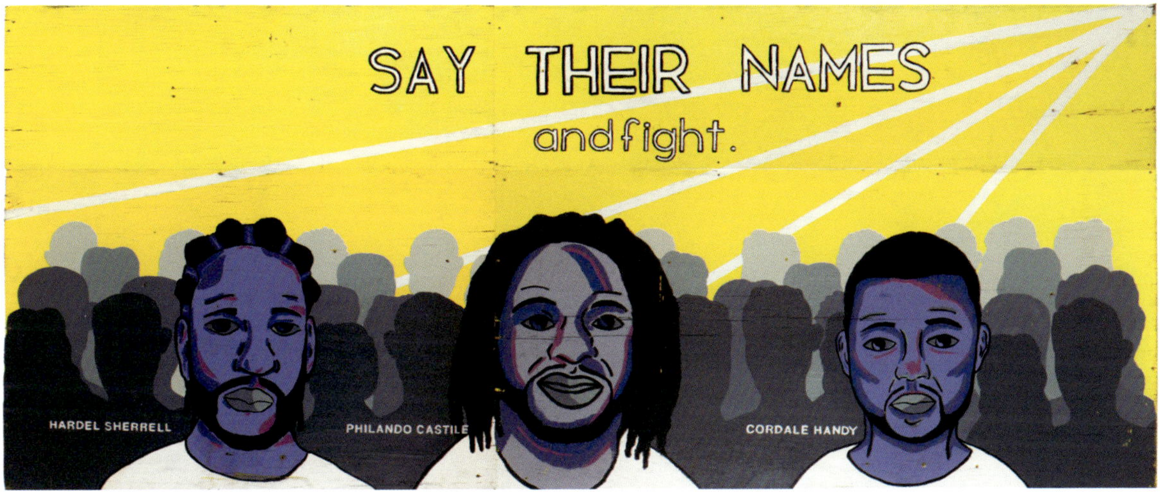

Plate 2

Know Peace Murals, *Say Their Names: Hardel, Philando, Cordale*, 2020
Multiple locations: Vibe Realty and Dogwood Coffee, 48 x 196 in.

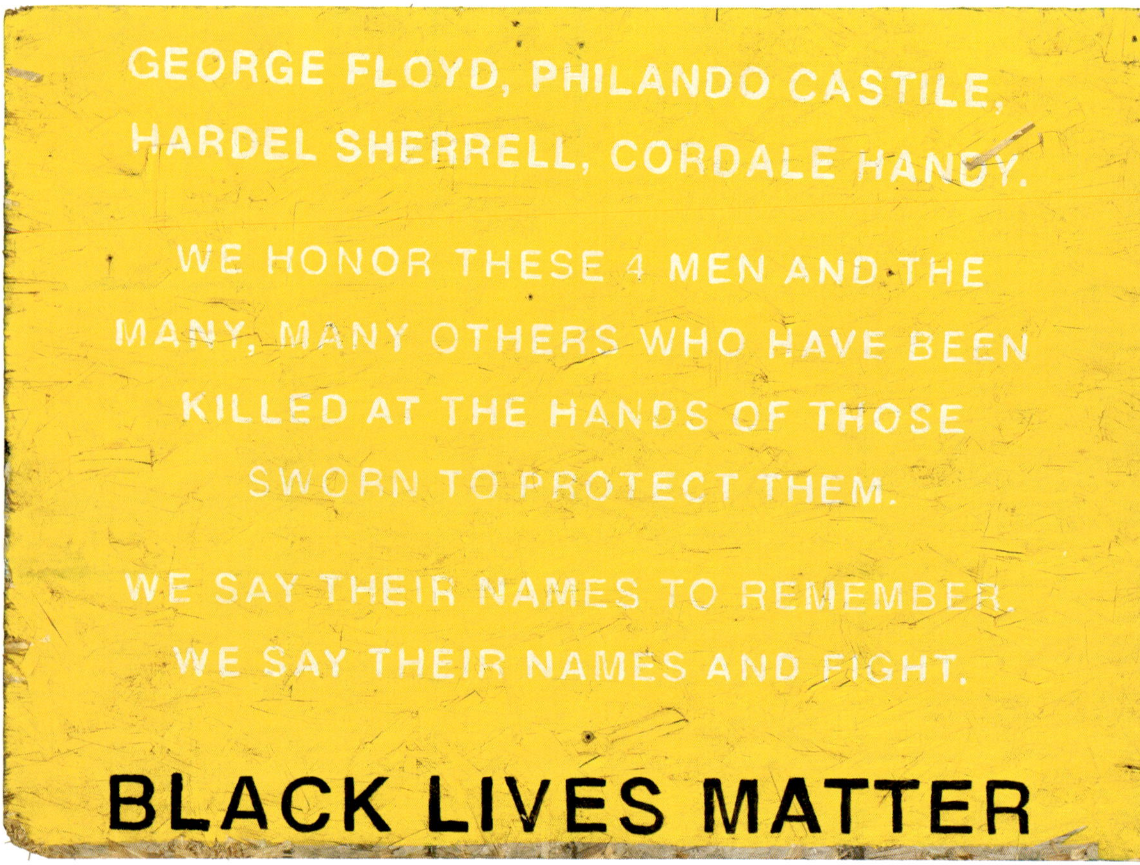

Plate 3

Know Peace Murals, *We Honor These 4 Men*, 2020

Multiple locations: Vibe Realty and Dogwood Coffee, 48 x 62 in.

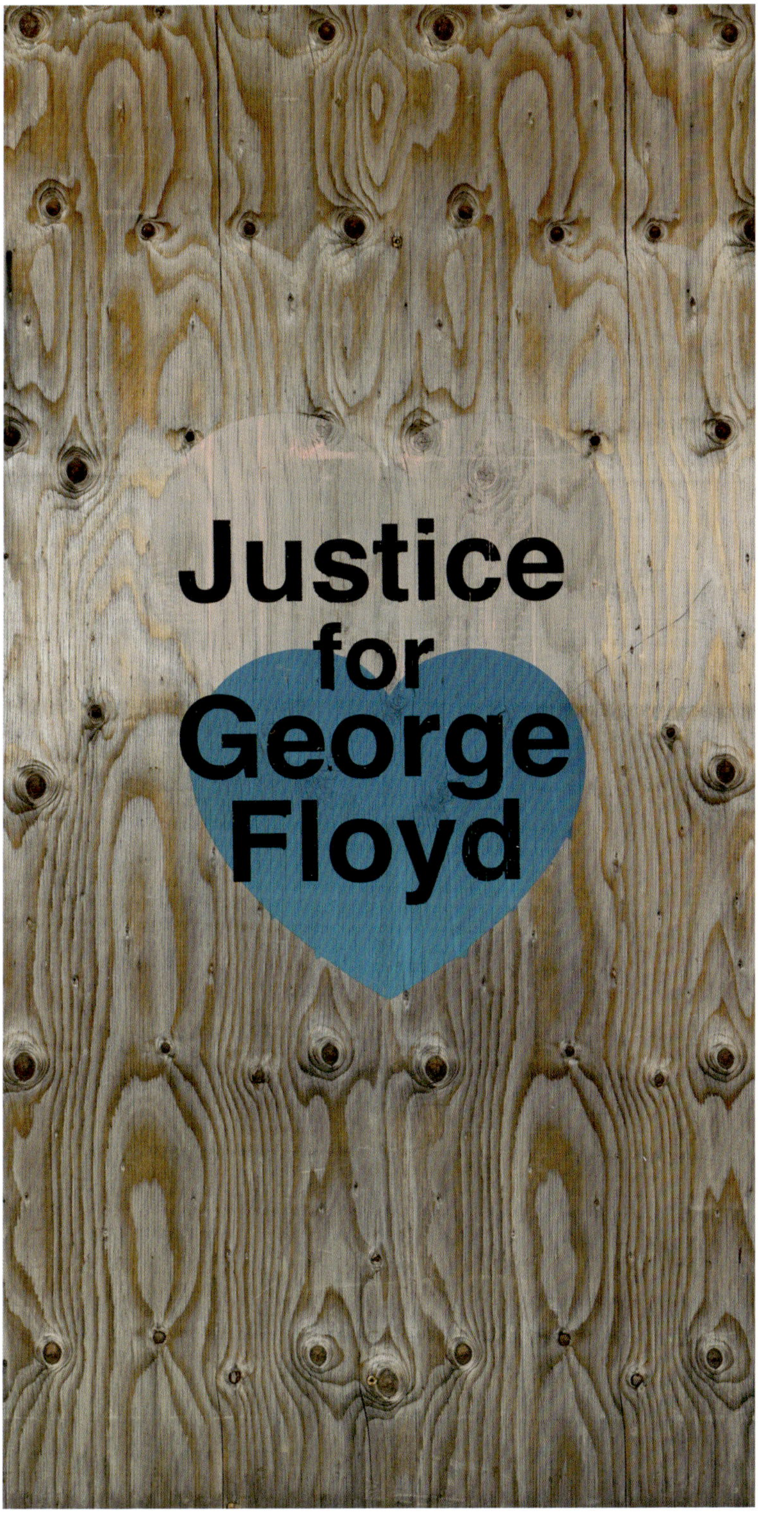

Plate 4
Artist Unidentified,
Justice For George - Blue Heart,
2020, 96 x 48 in.

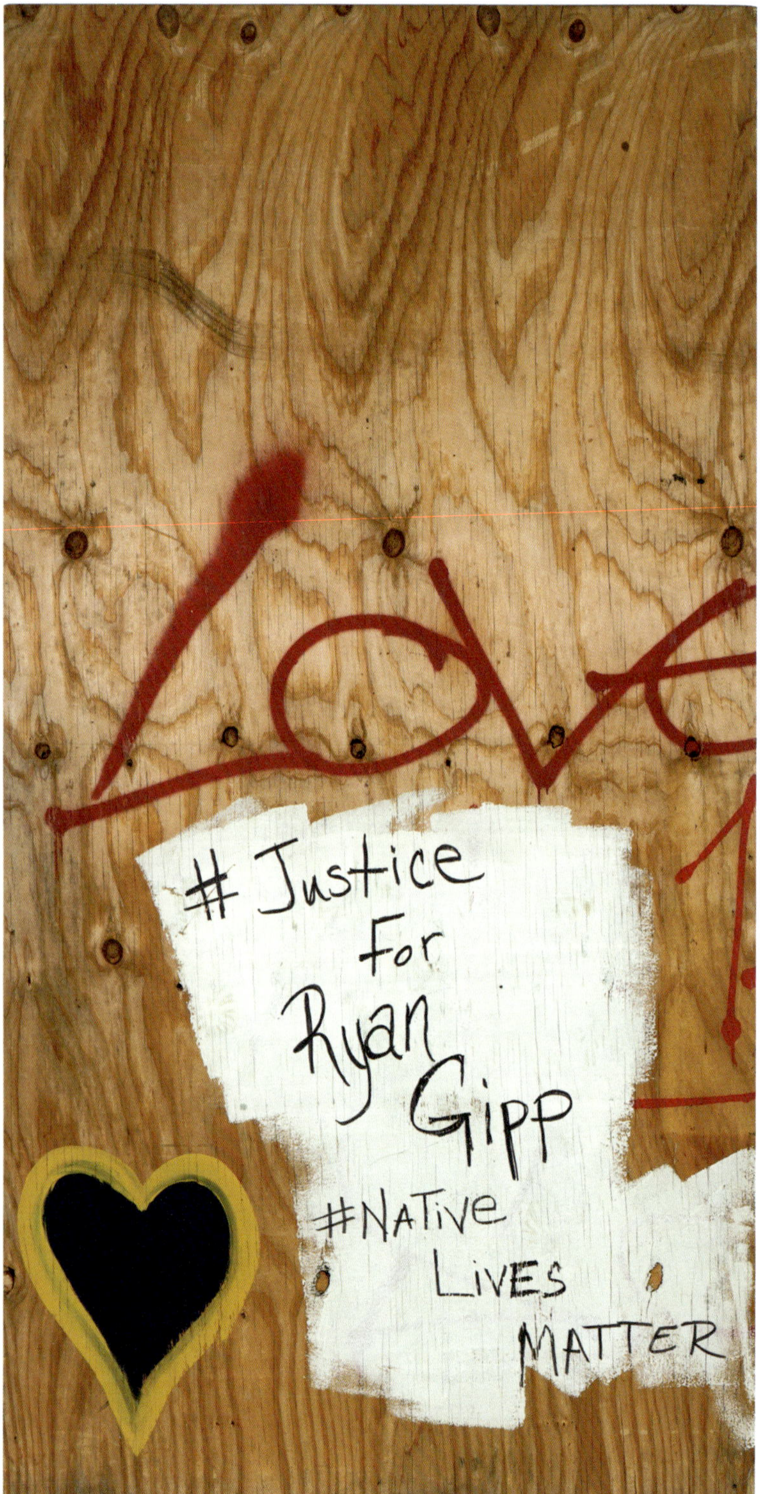

Plate 5

Artist Unidentified, *Justice for Ryan Gipp*, 2020, Minnehaha Wilson Law Group, 3019 Minnehaha Ave., 96 x 48 in.

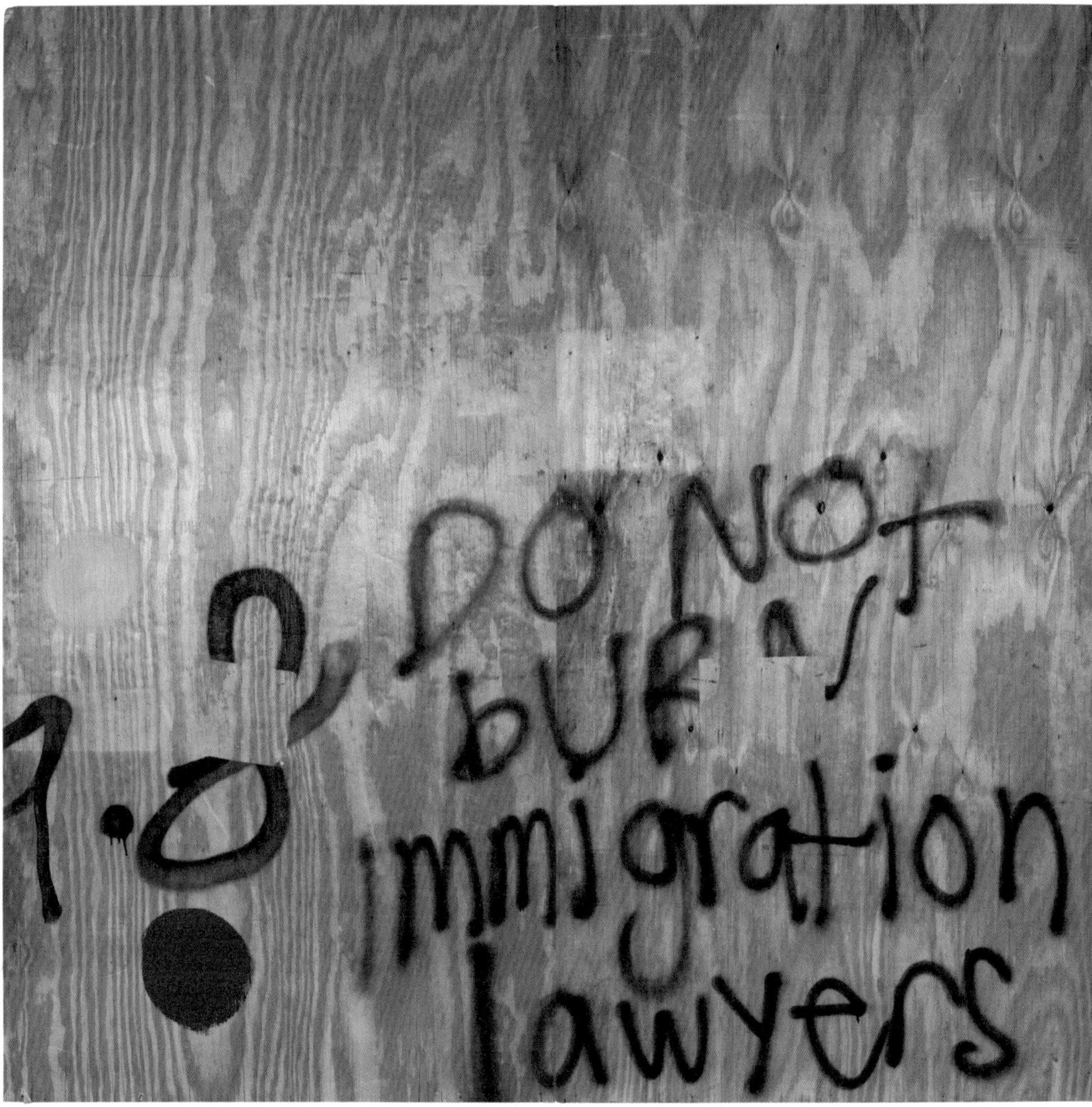

Plate 6

Artist Unidentified, *Do Not Burn, Immigration Lawyers*, 2020
Minnehaha Wilson Law Group, 3019 Minnehaha Ave., 96 x 96 in.

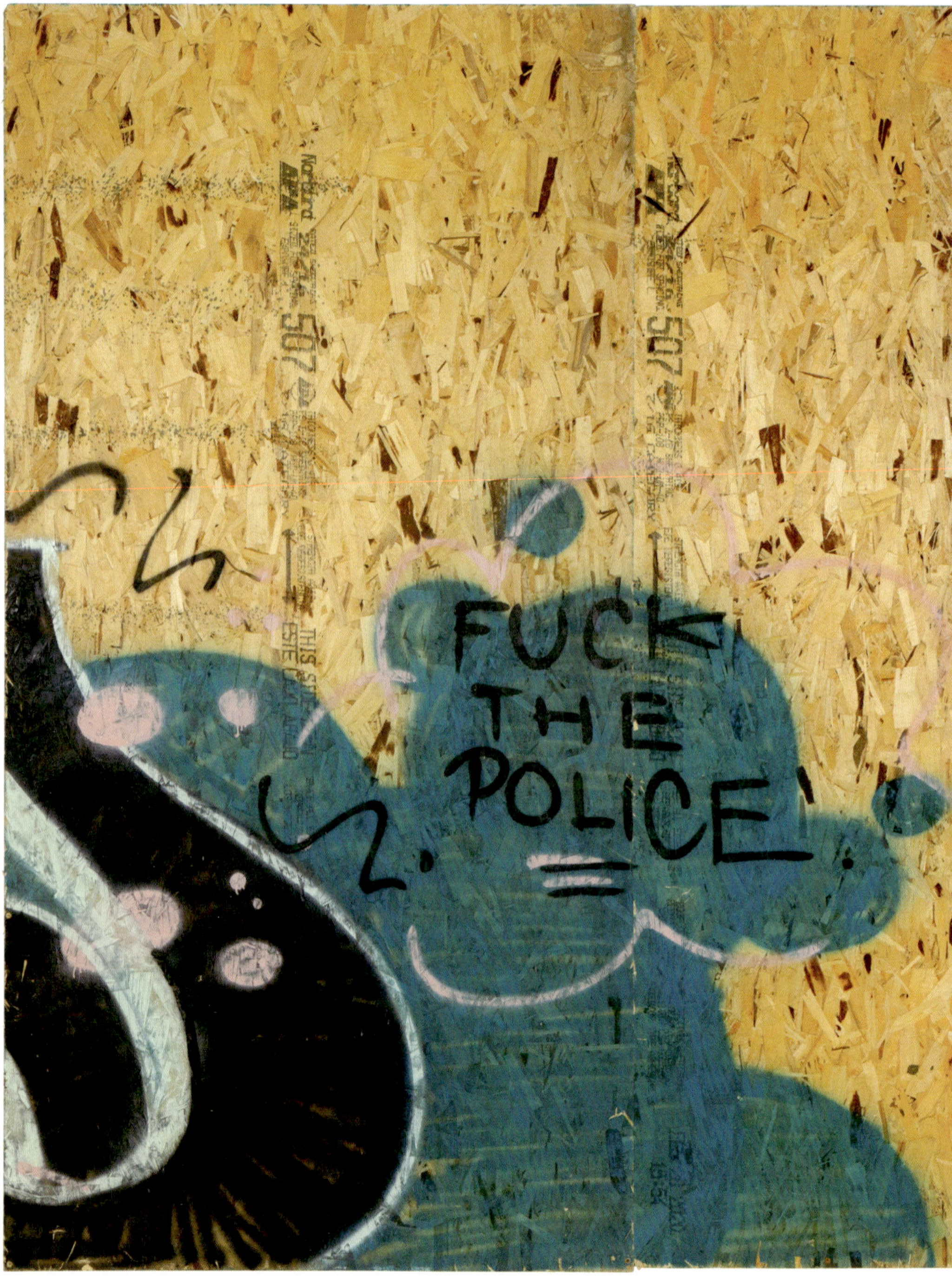

Plate 7

Artist Unidentified, *Fuck the Police*, 2020, 96 x 72 approx.

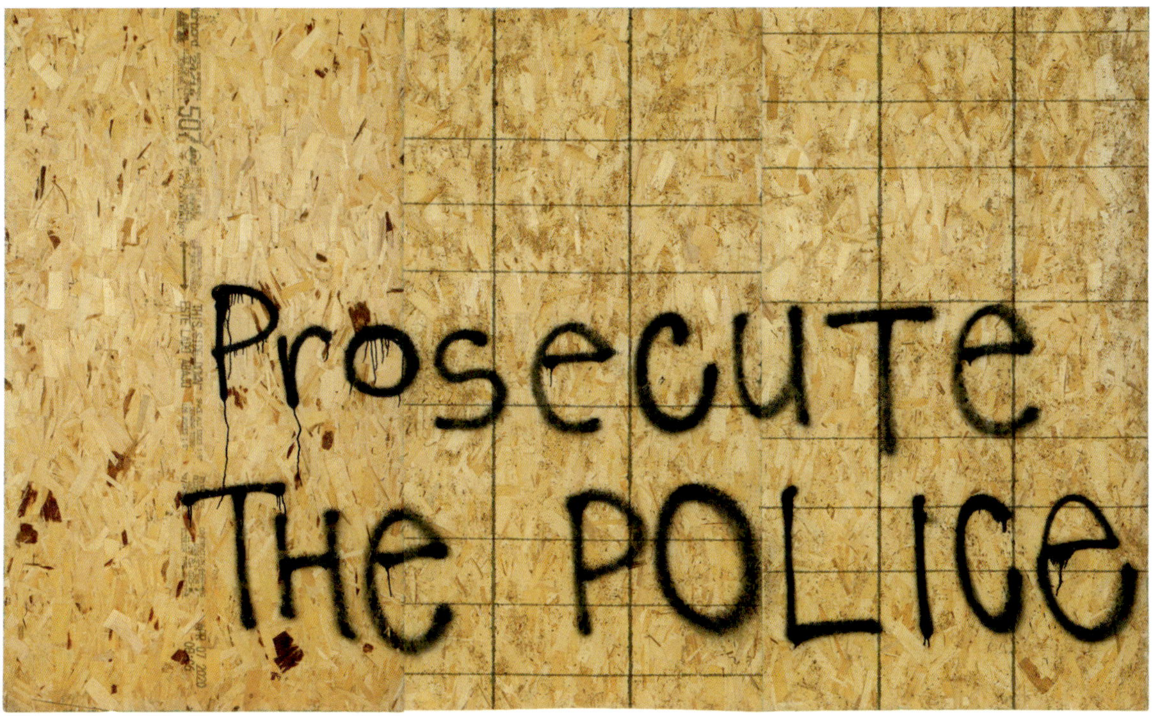

Plate 8

Artist Unidentified, *Prosecute the Police*, 2020, 96 x 144 in.

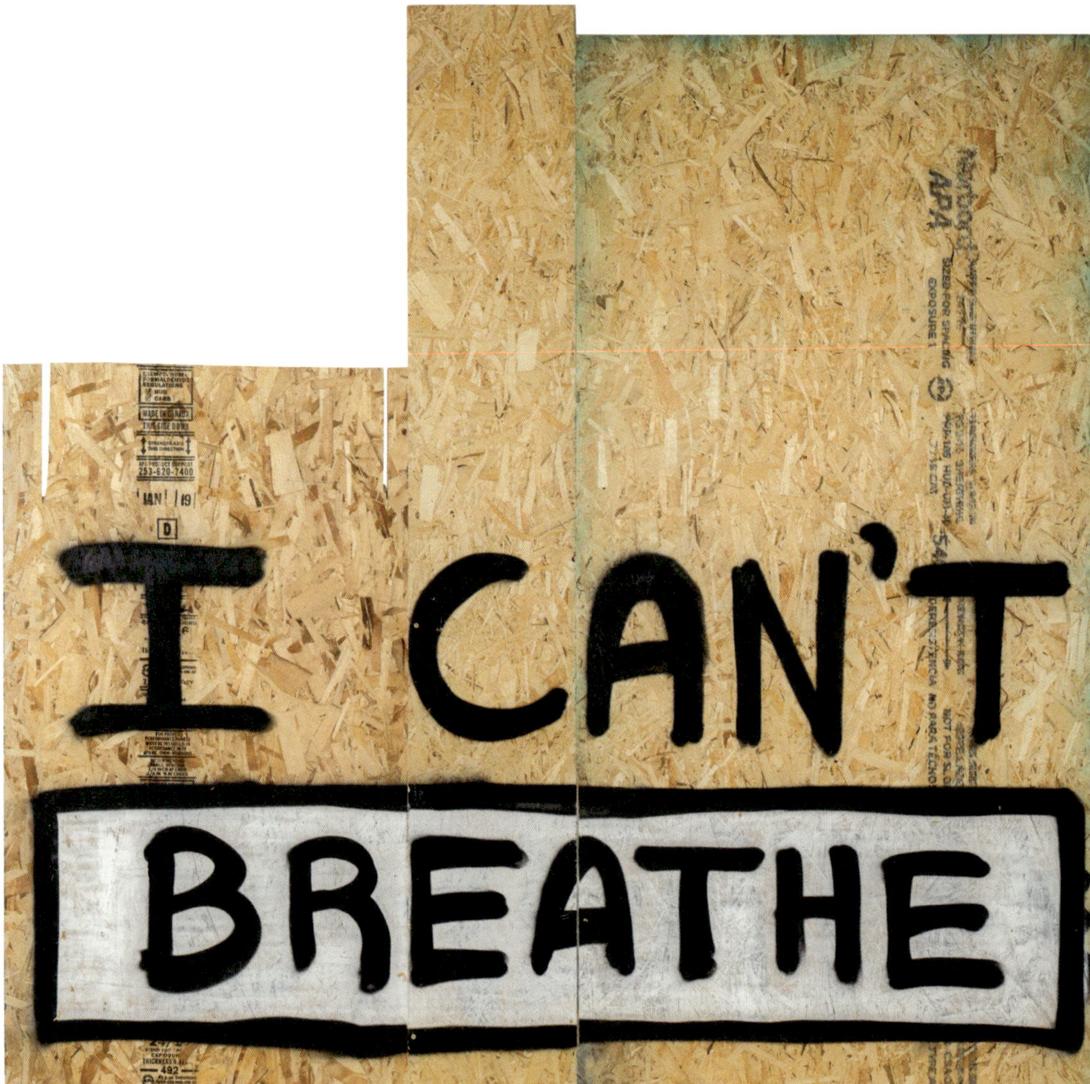

Plate 9

Artist Unidentified, *I Can't Breathe*, 2020, 96 x 111 in. approx.

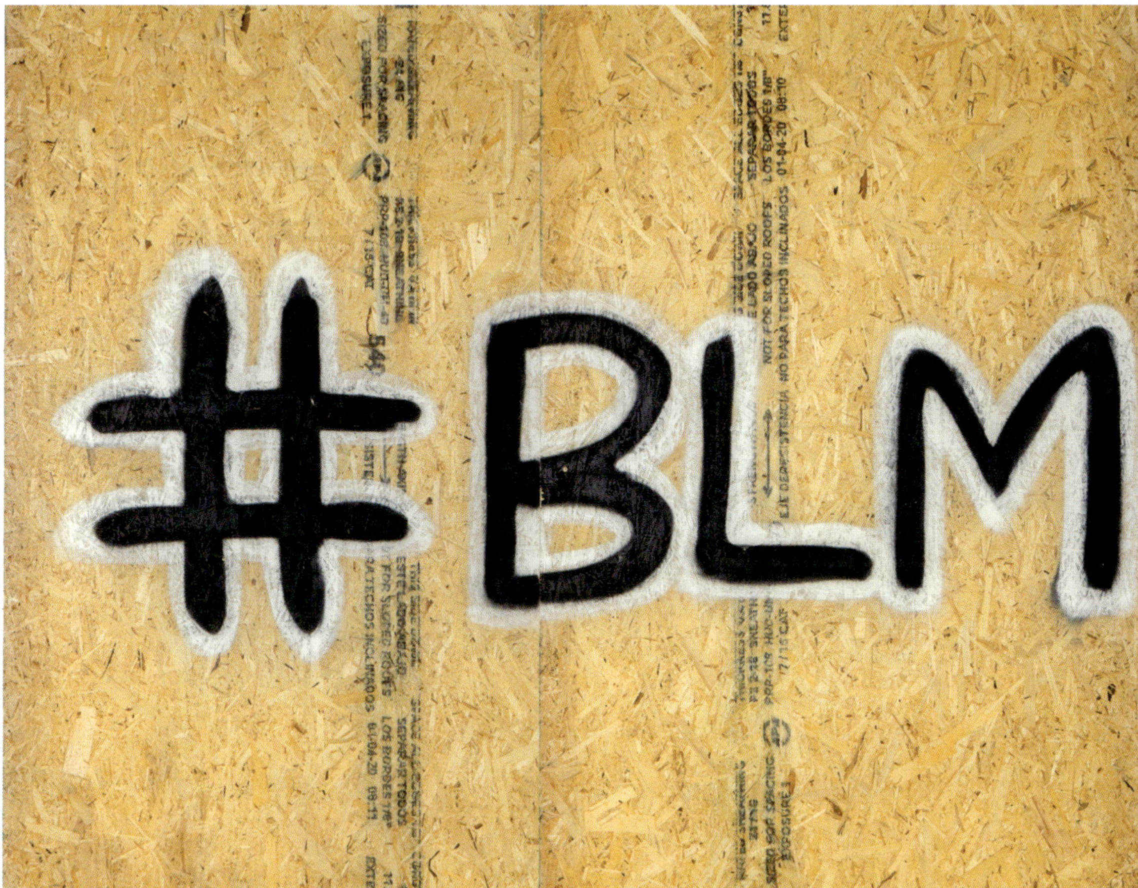

Plate 10
Artist Unidentified, *#BLM*, 2020, 108 x 96 in.

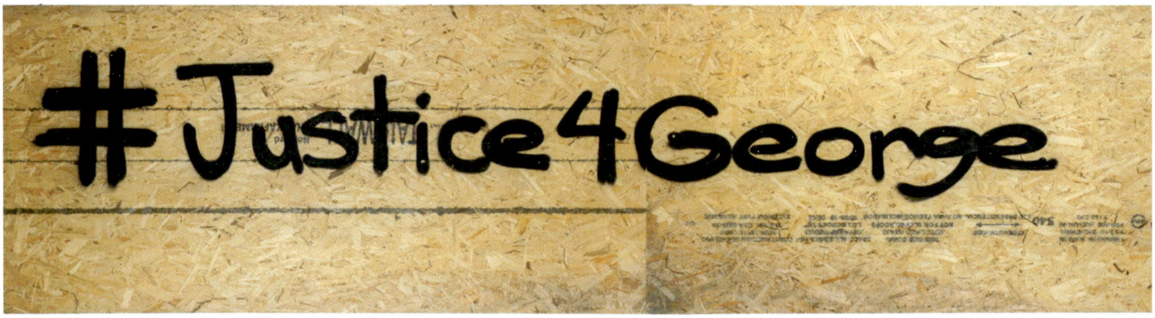

Plate 11

Artist Unidentified, *#Justice4George*, 2020, 48 x 216 in.

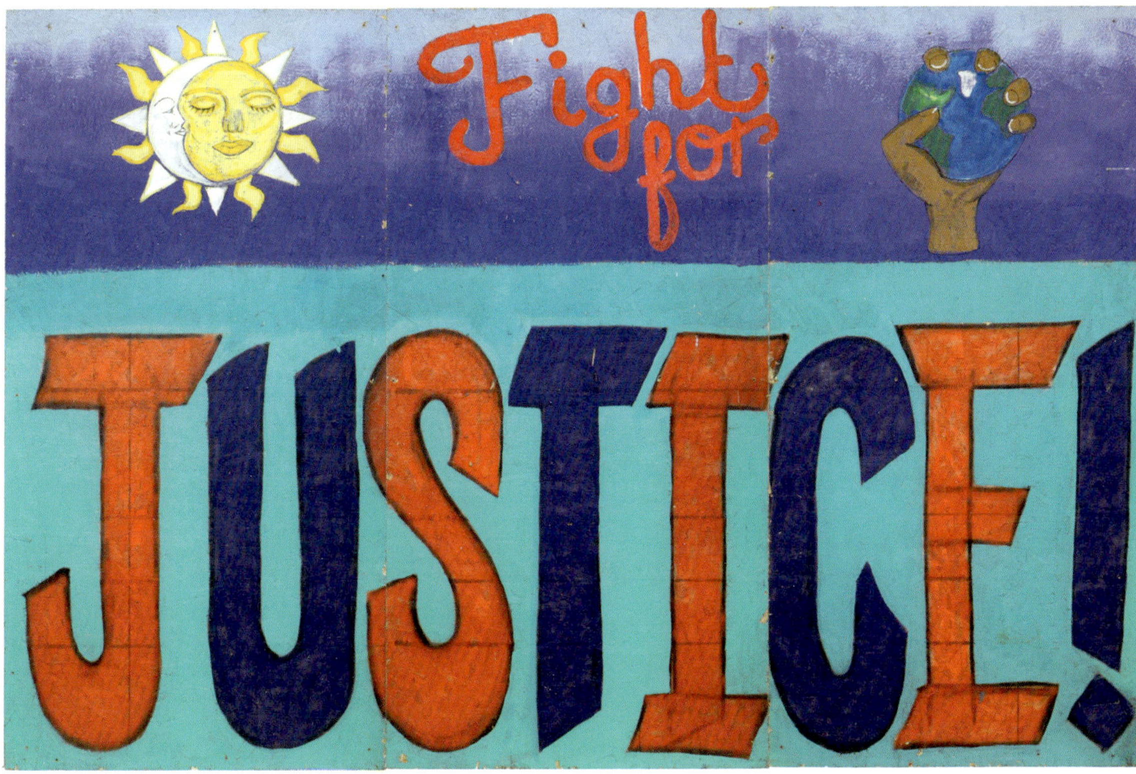

Plate 12

David Chang, Billie White, and Sam Dunne, *Fight for Justice!*, 2020
Seward Community Co-op, 2823 E. Franklin Ave., 96 x 271 in.

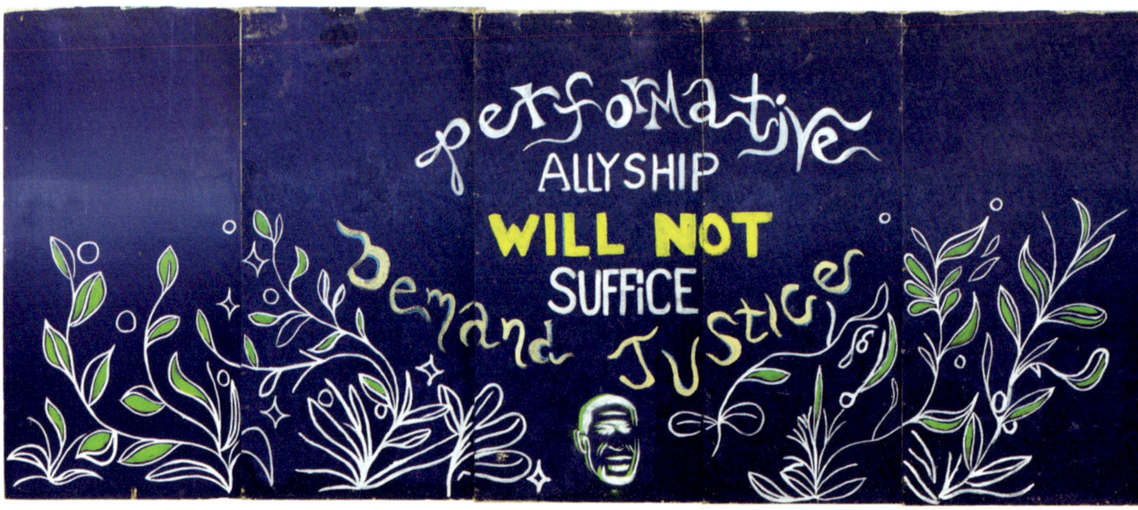

Plate 13

Taylan DeJohnette, Patricio De Lara, and Ashley Koudou, *Performative Allyship Will Not Suffice Demand Justice*, 2020, Seward Community Co-op, 2823 E. Franklin Ave., 96 x 223 in.

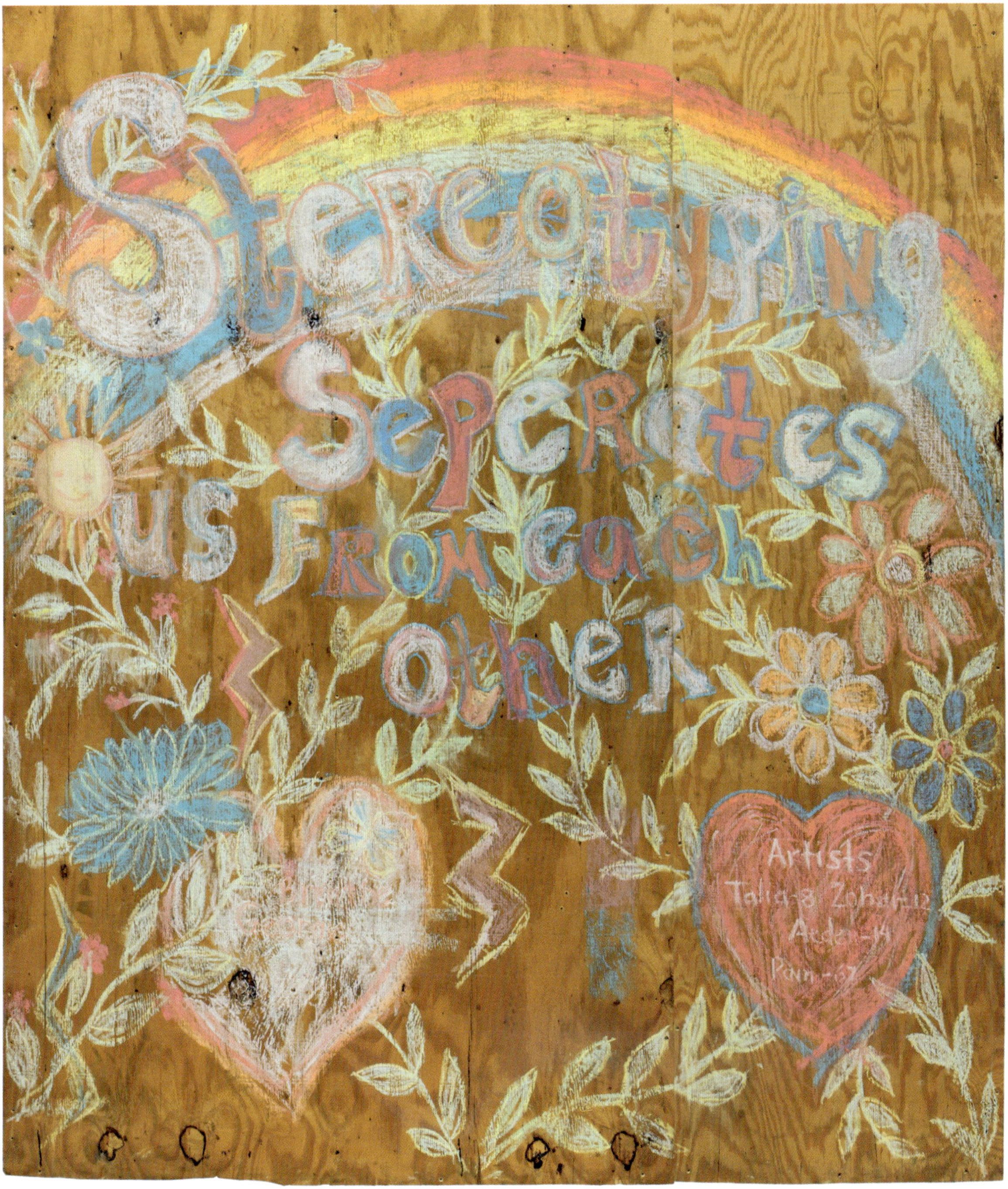

Plate 14

Talia, Zohar, Aeden, Pam, *Stereotyping Separates Us From Each Other*, 2020

Seward Community Co-op, 2823 E. Franklin Ave., 96 x 72 in.

LAKE STREET

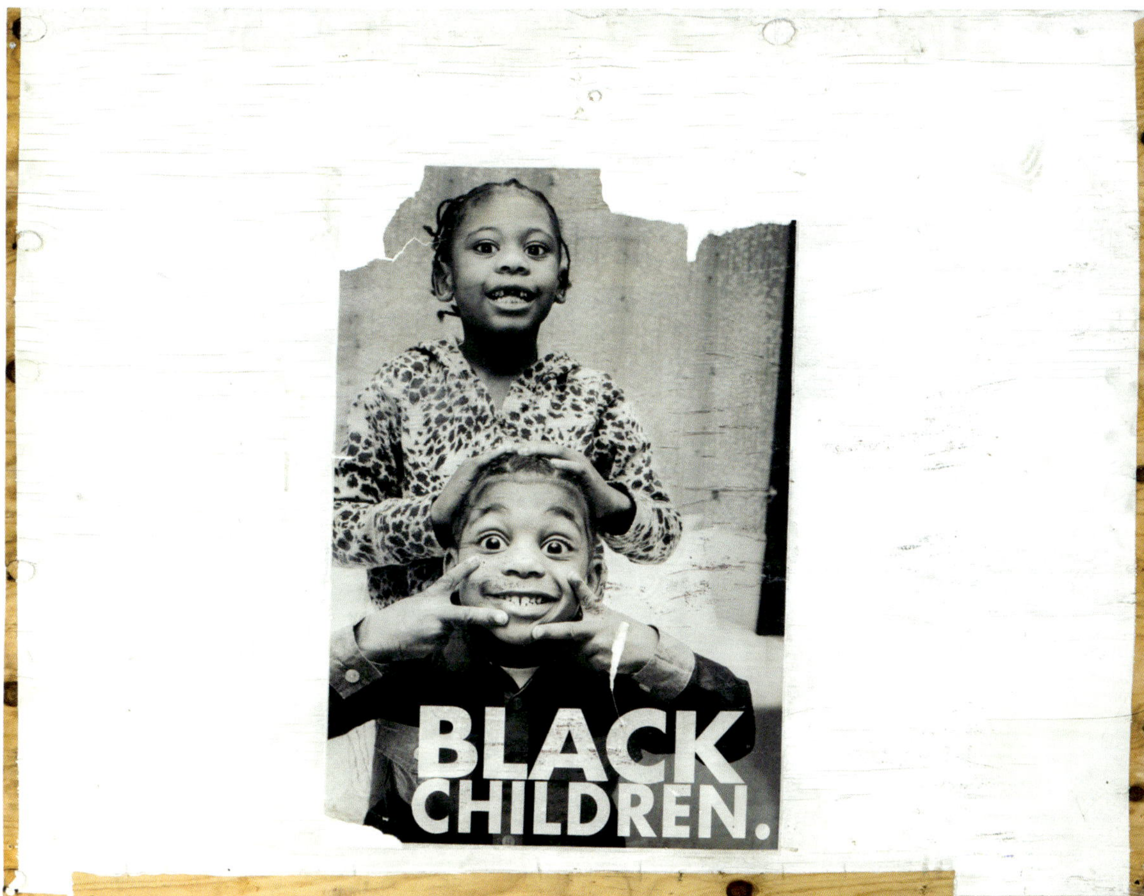

Plate 15

Artist Unidentified, *Black Children*, 2020, 48 x 61 in.

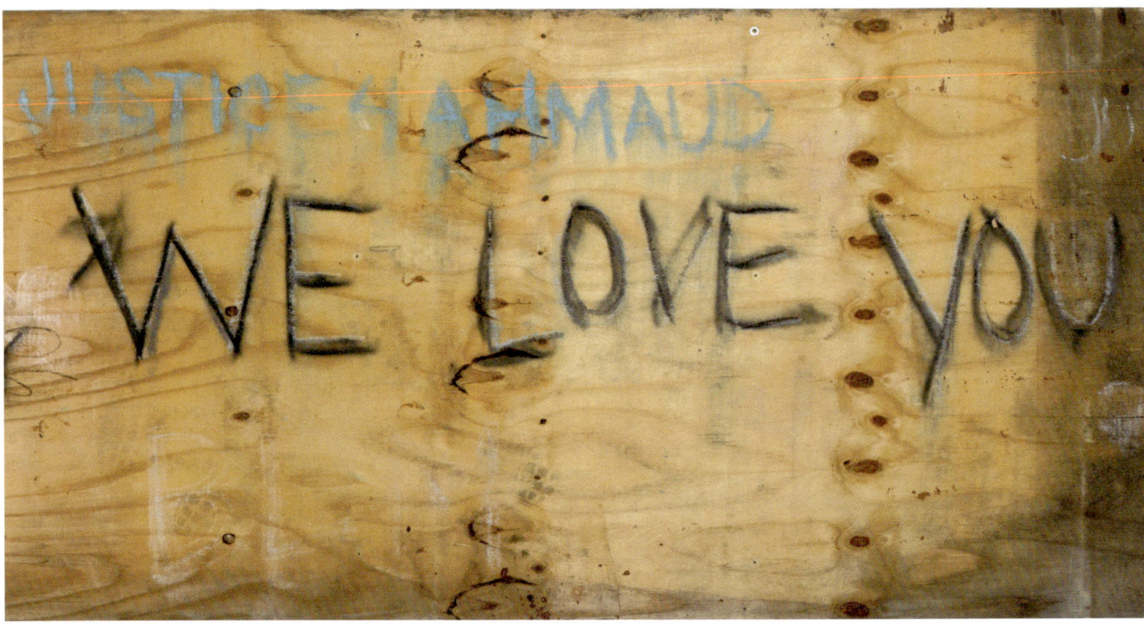

Plate 16

Artist Unidentified, *We Love You*, 2020, 48 x 93.5 in.

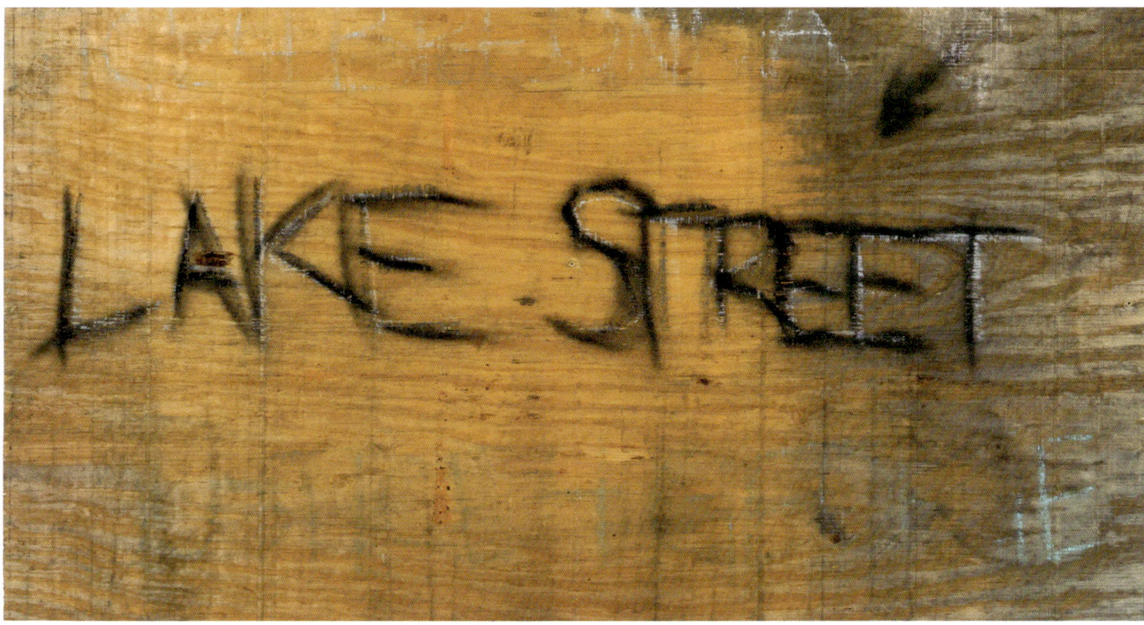

Plate 17
Artist Unidentified, *Lake Street*, 2020, 48 x 64 in.

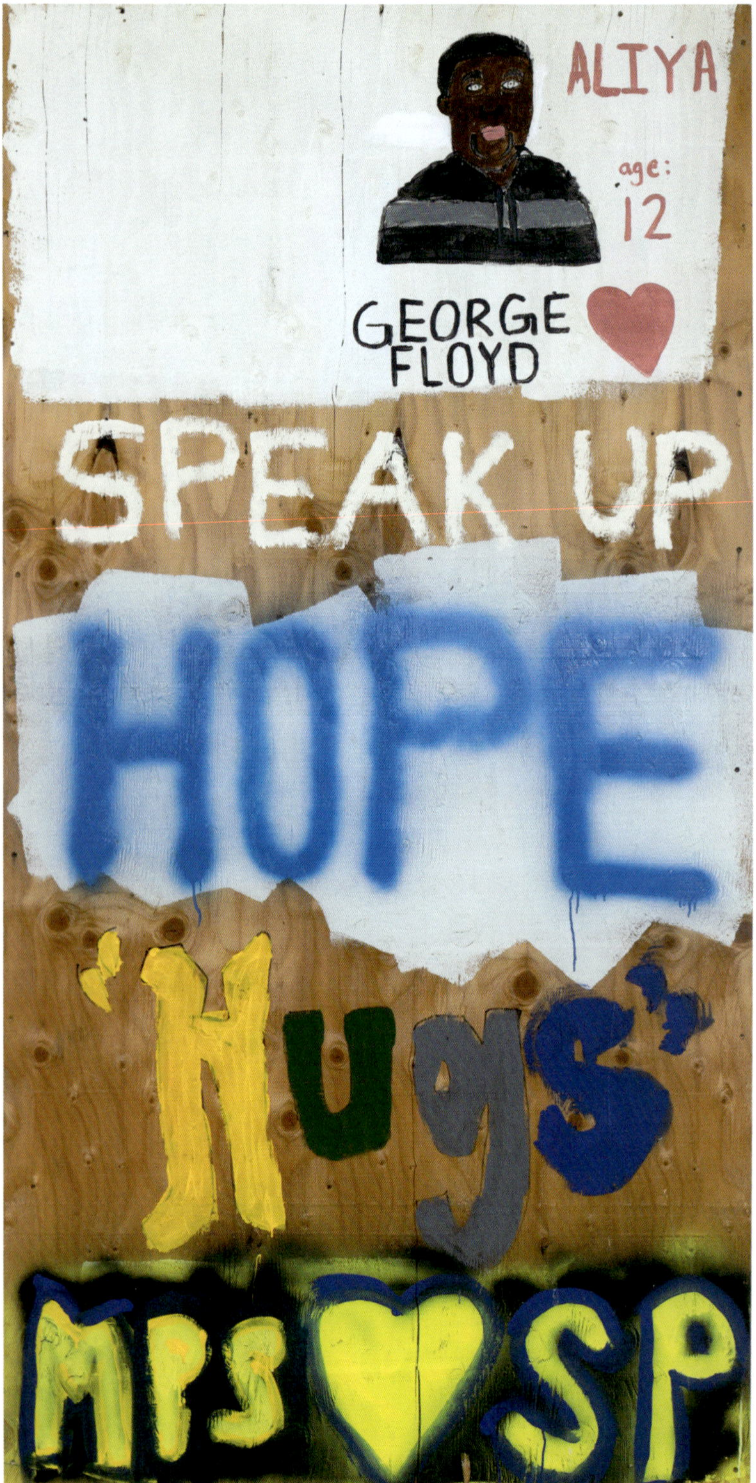

Plate 18

Aliya (age 12), Paint Our Peace, Lake Street Community, *Hope and Hugs*, 2020, Corridor Flats Condominiums/ Aldi Foods, 2929 21st Ave. S., 96 x 48 in.

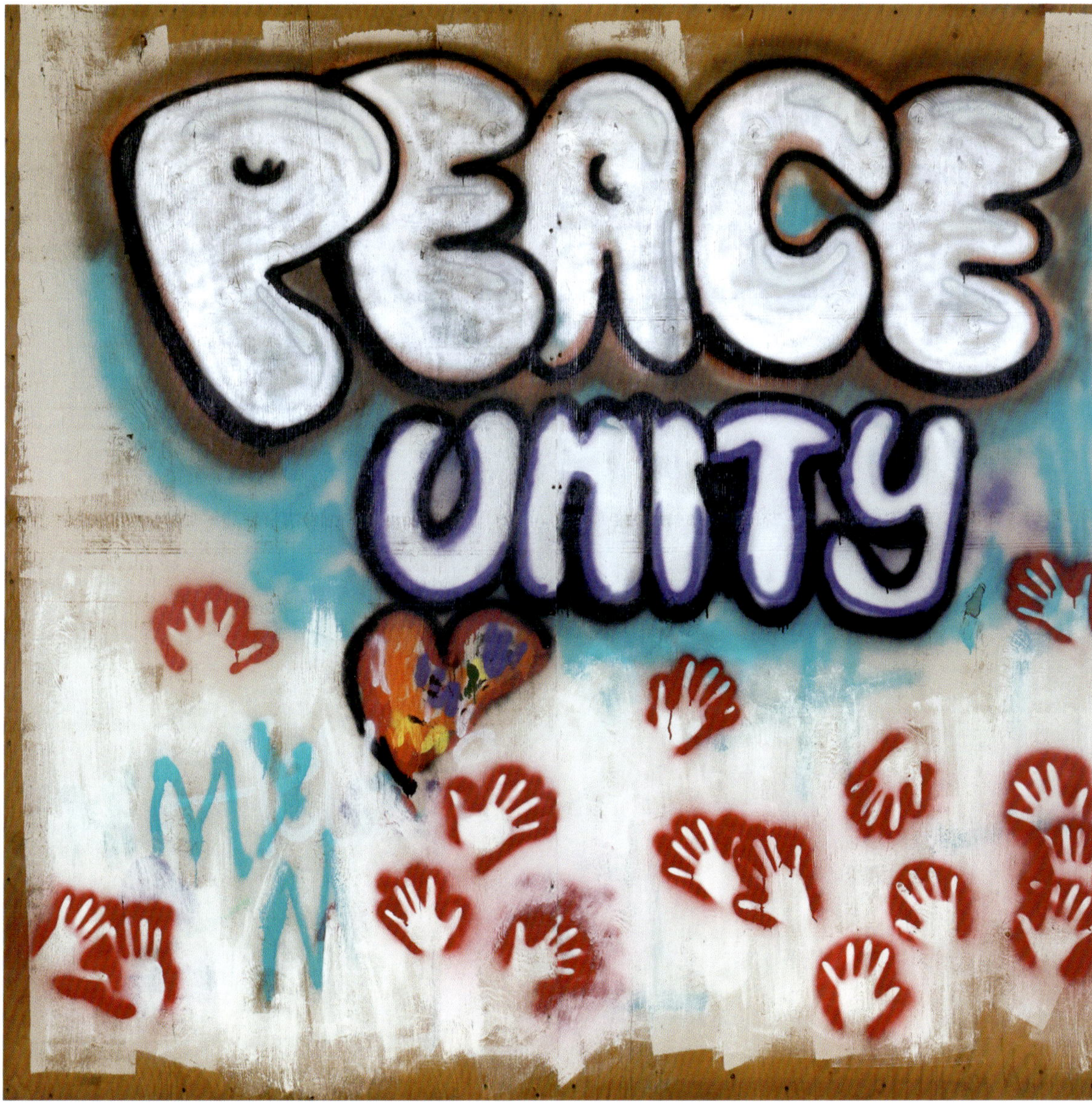

Plate 19

Paint Our Peace, Lake Street Community, *Peace/Unity*, 2020
Corridor Flats Condominiums/Aldi Foods, 2929 21st Ave. S., 96 x 103.5 in.

Plate 20

Paint Our Peace, Lake Street Community, *Don't Abuse Ur Power*, 2020

Corridor Flats Condominiums/Aldi Foods, 2929 21st Ave. S., 72 x 103 in., approx.

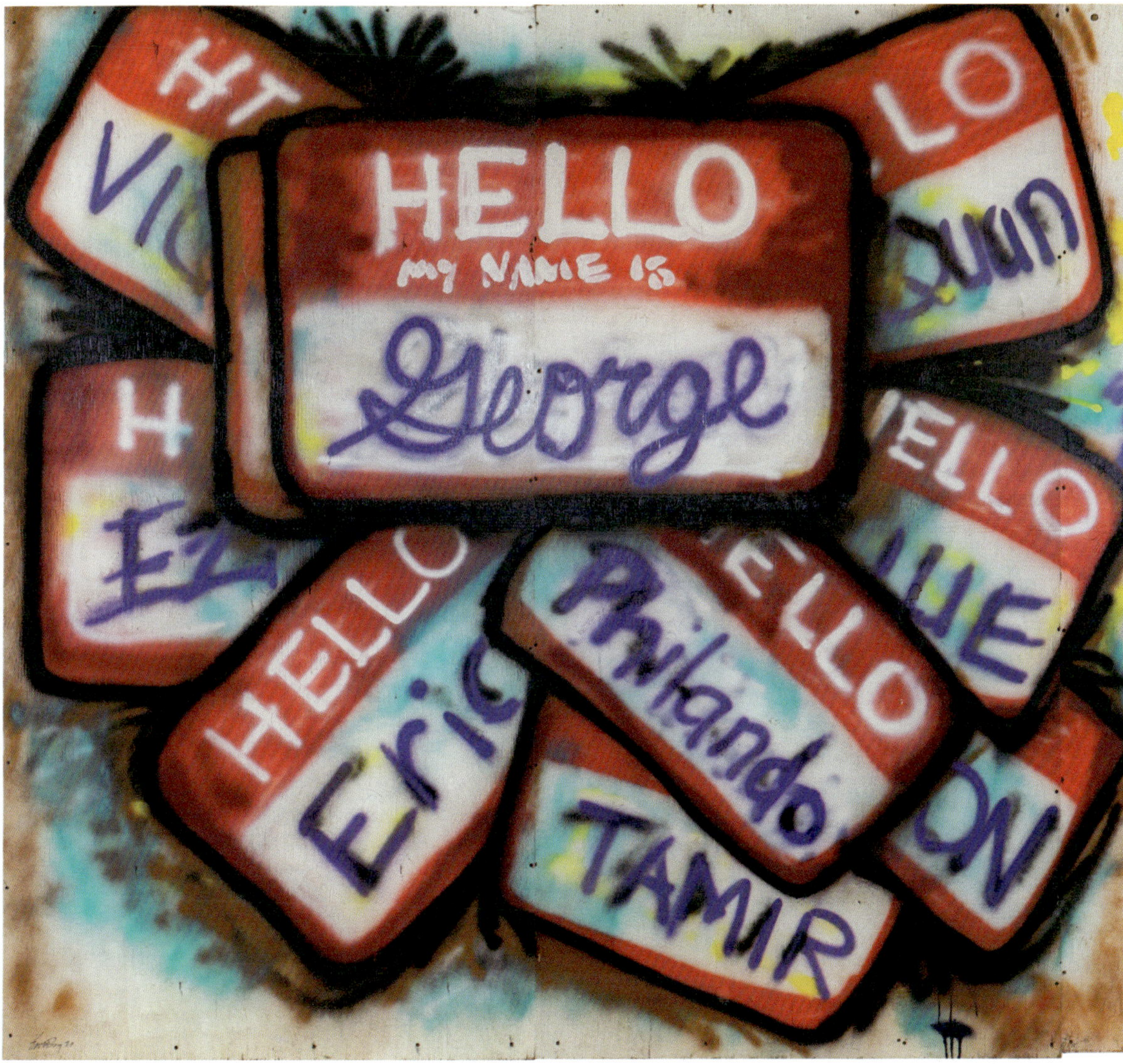

Plate 21

Eric Berg, *Hello, My Name Is*, 2020

Corridor Flats Condominiums/Aldi Foods, 2929 21st Ave. S., 96 x 103.5 in.

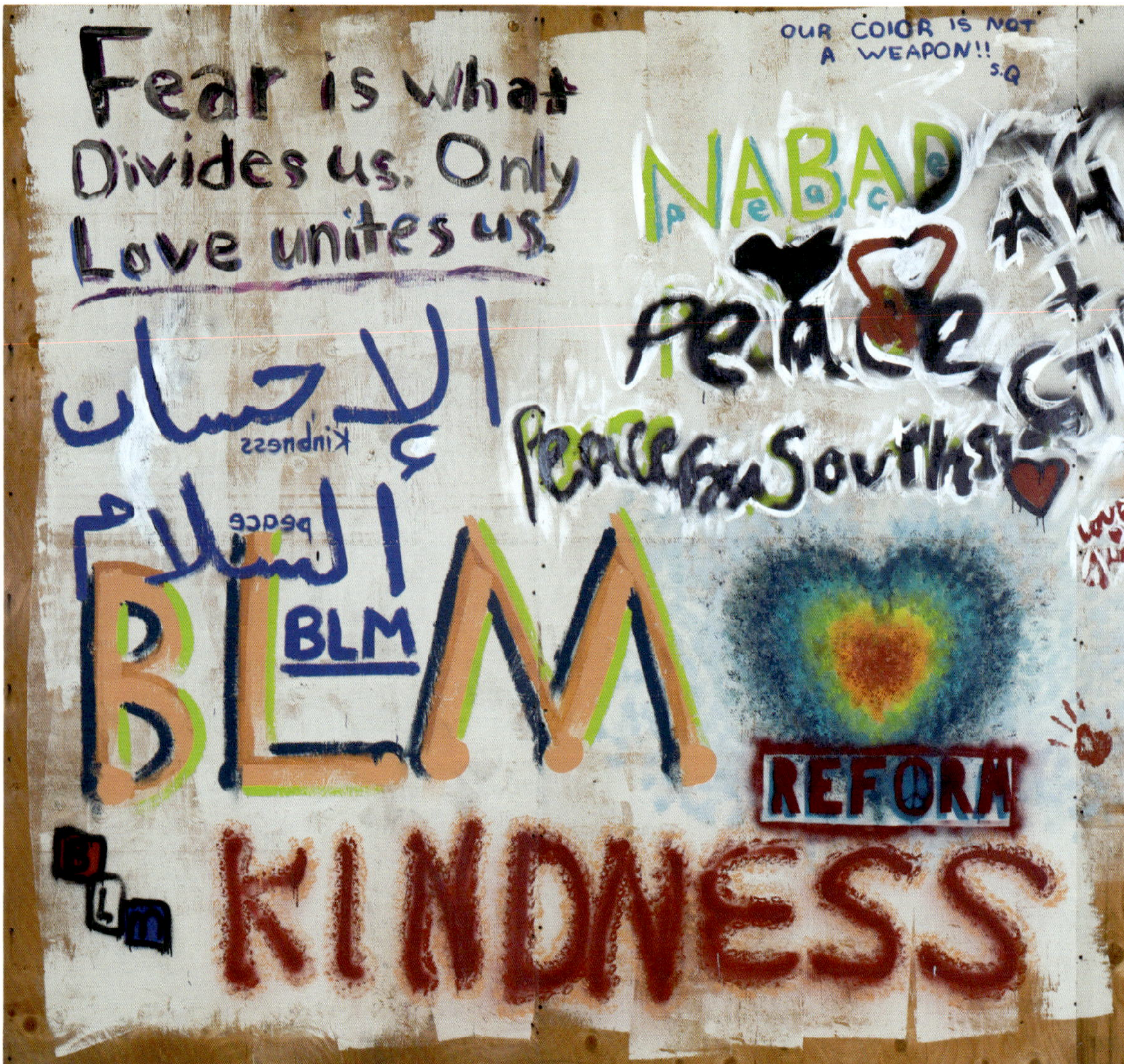

Plate 22

Paint Our Peace, Lake Street Community, *Fear is What Divides Us*, 2020
Corridor Flats Condominiums/Aldi Foods, 2929 21st Ave. S., 96 x 103 in.

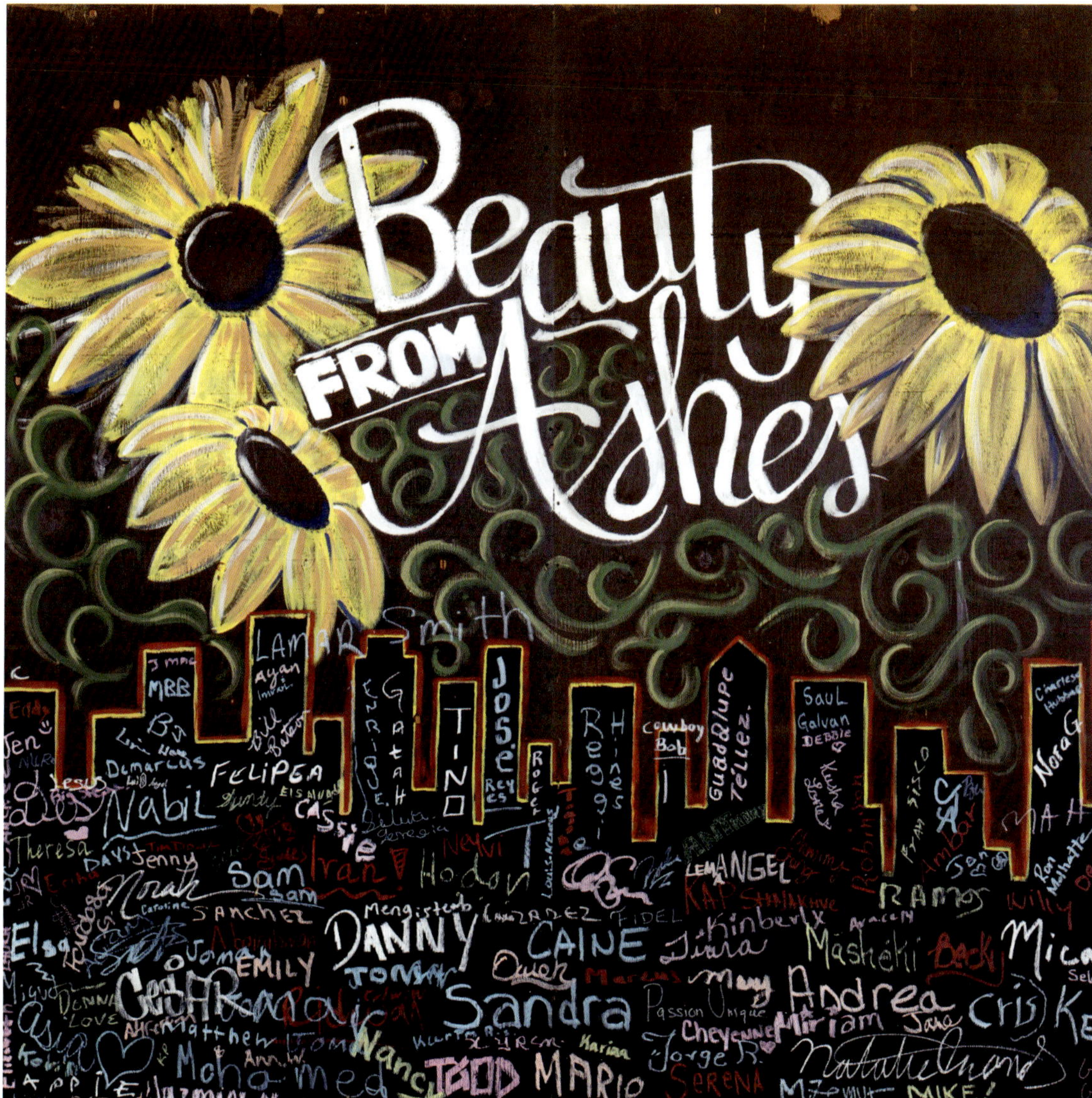

Plate 23

Paint Our Peace, Lake Street Community, *Beauty from Ashes*, 2020

Corridor Flats Condominiums/Aldi Foods, 2929 21st Ave. S., 96 x 103.5 in.

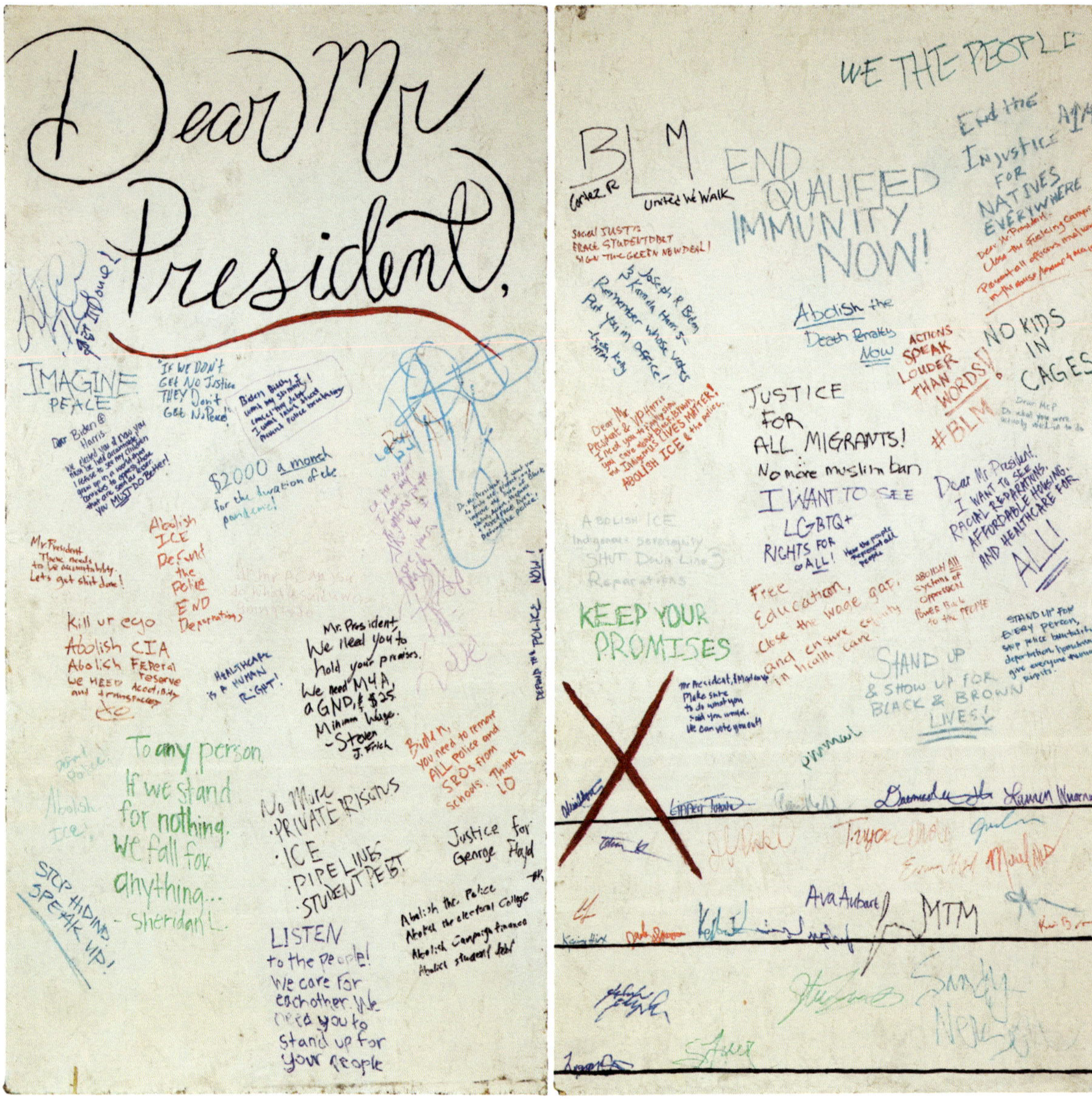

Plate 24

Community painted mural, *Dear Mr. President*, 2021

Made during protest, Target, 2500 E Lake St., Minneapolis, 96 x 96 in.

UPTOWN

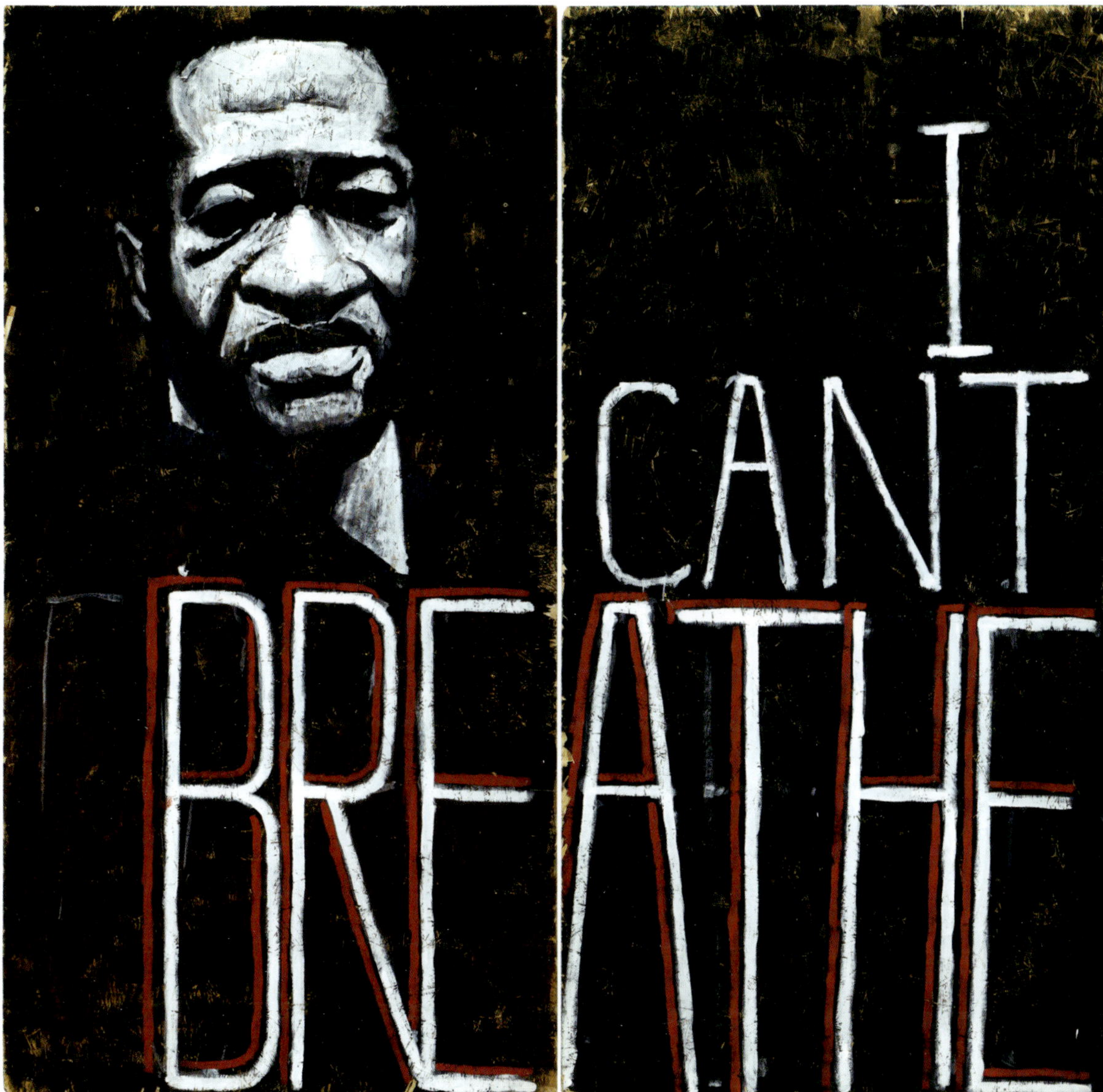

Plate 25

Artist Unidentified, *I Cant Breathe, Portrait*, 2020

Burch Steak, 1933 Colfax Ave. S., 96 x 96 in.

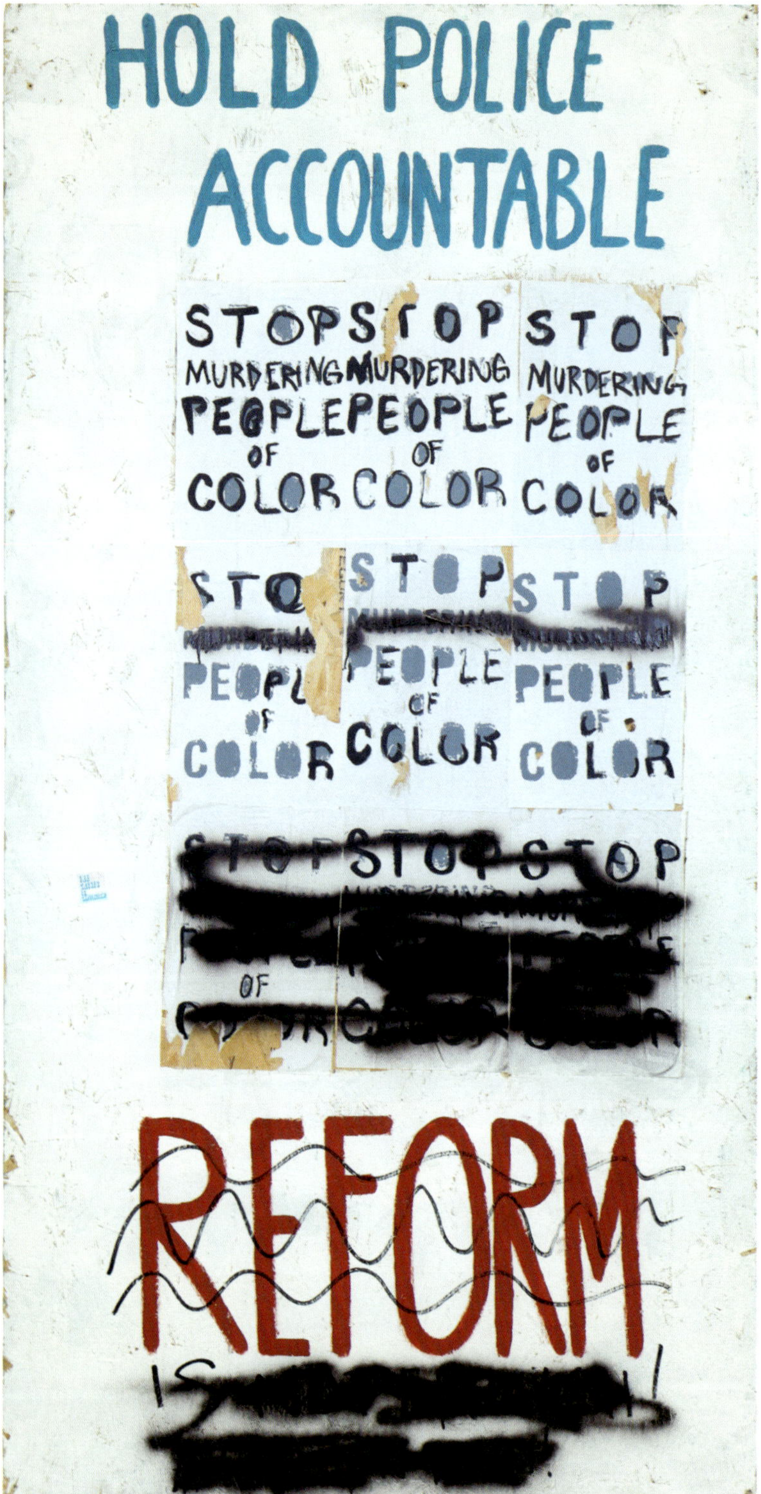

Plate 26

Artist Unidentified, *Hold Police Accountable*, 2020, Burch Steak, 1933 Colfax Ave. S., 96 x 48 in.

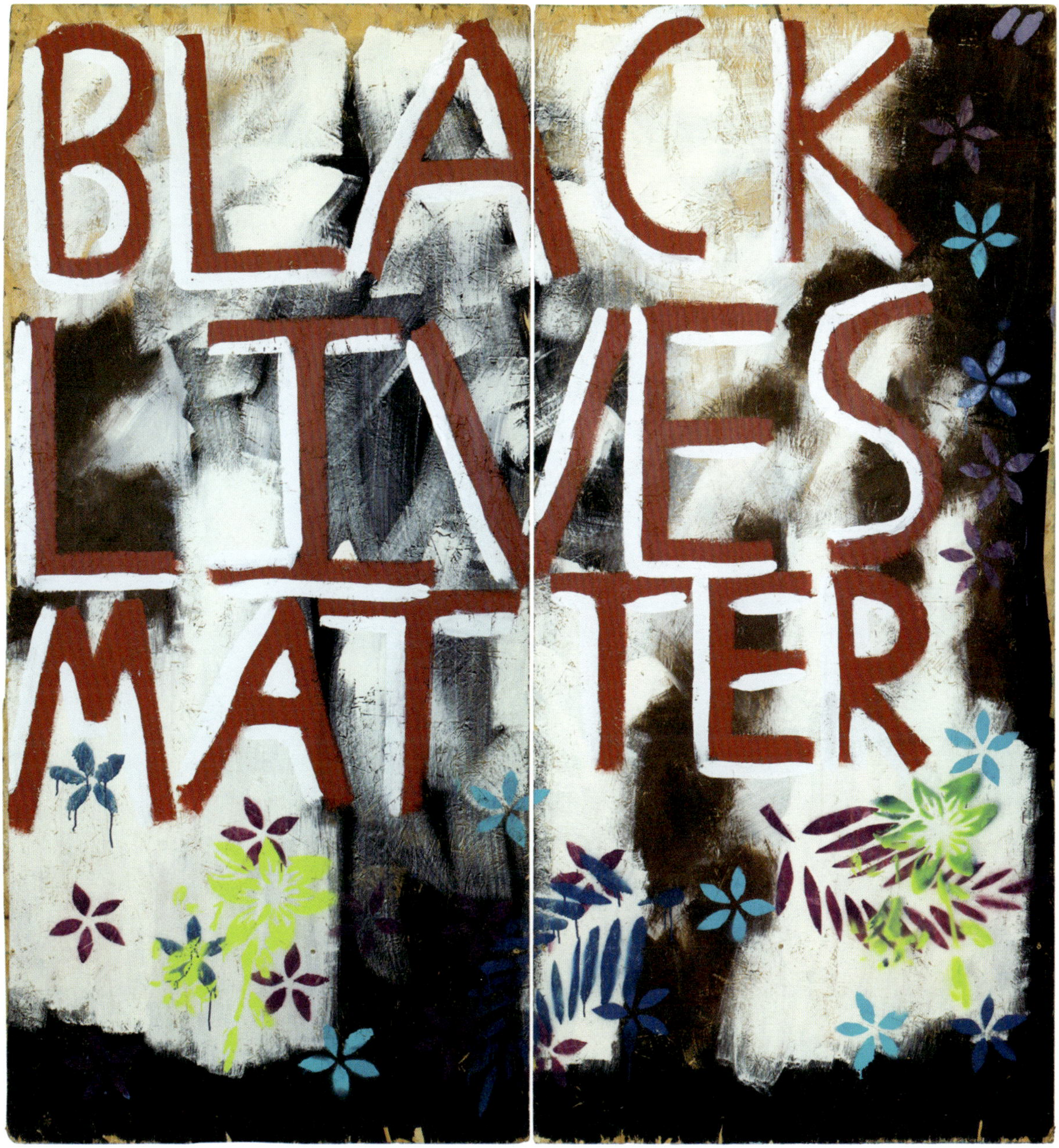

Plate 27

Artist Unidentified, *Black Lives Matter (Red and White)*, 2020

Burch Steak, 1933 Colfax Ave. S., 96 x 96 in.

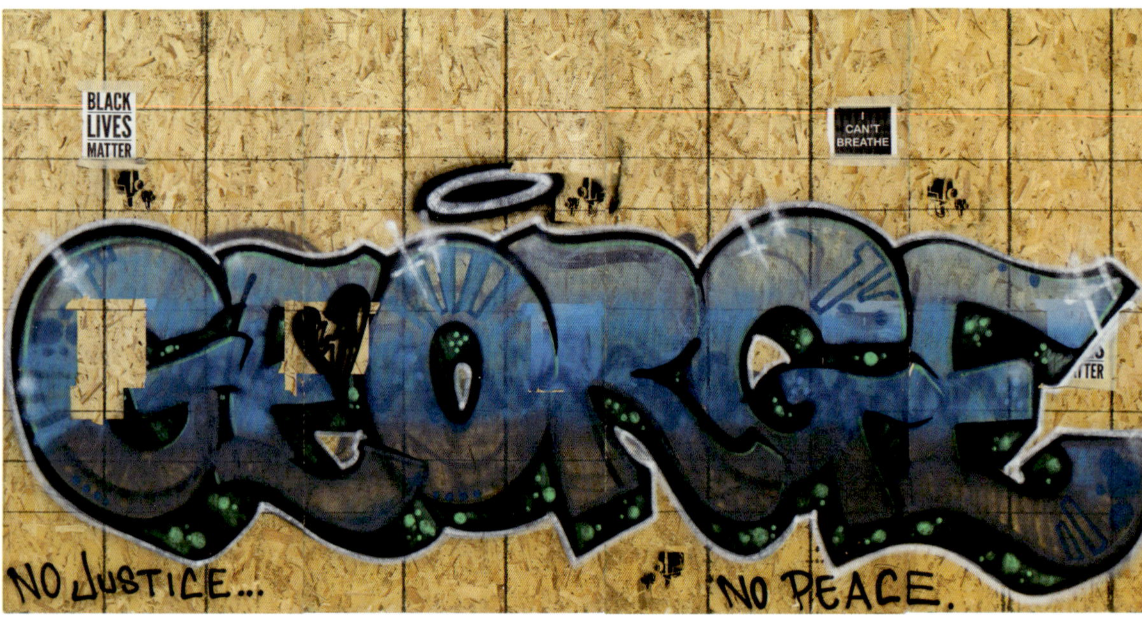

Plate 28

H Kay, *George Floyd, RIP*, 2020

Los Andės Latin Bistro, 607 W. Lake St., 96 x 192 in.

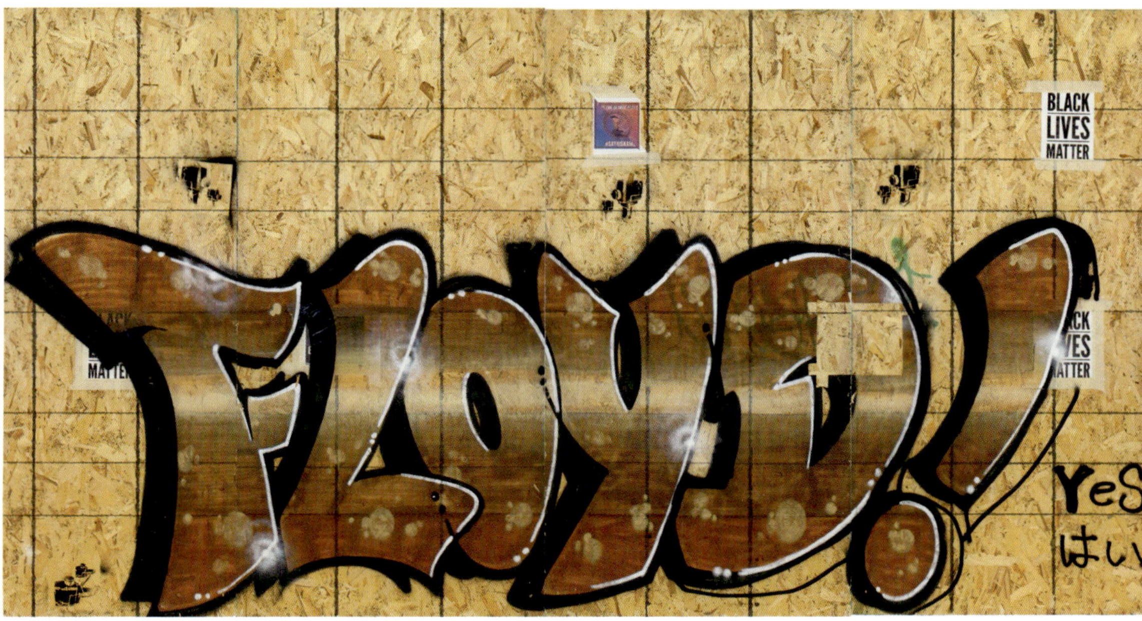

Plate 29

Tom (Jay) Janssen, George Floyd, RIP, 2020

Los Andes Latin Bistro, 607 W. Lake St., 96 x 180 in.

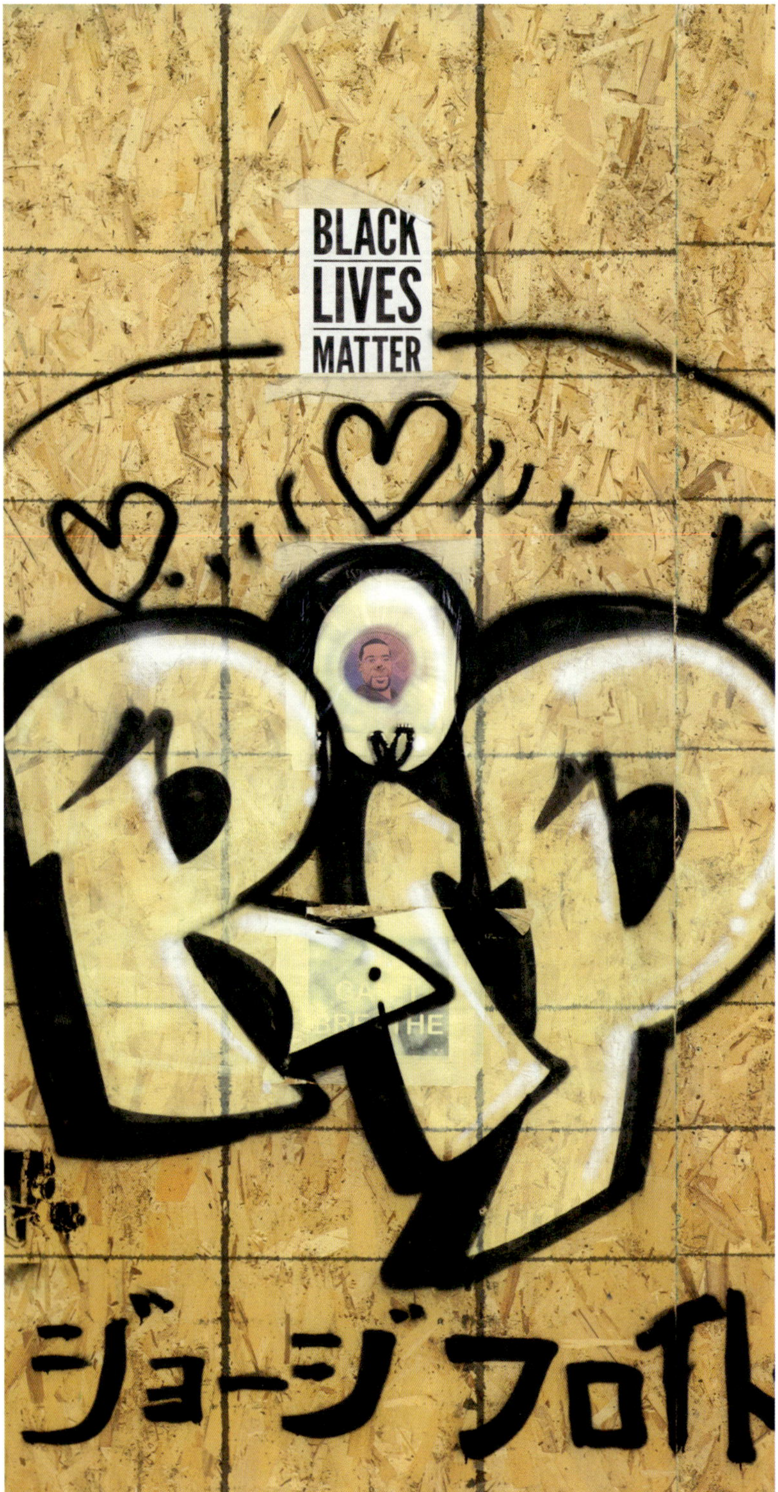

Plate 30

Tom (Jay) Janssen, *George Floyd, RIP*, 2020, Los Andes Latin Bistro, 607 W. Lake St., 96 x 53 in., approx.

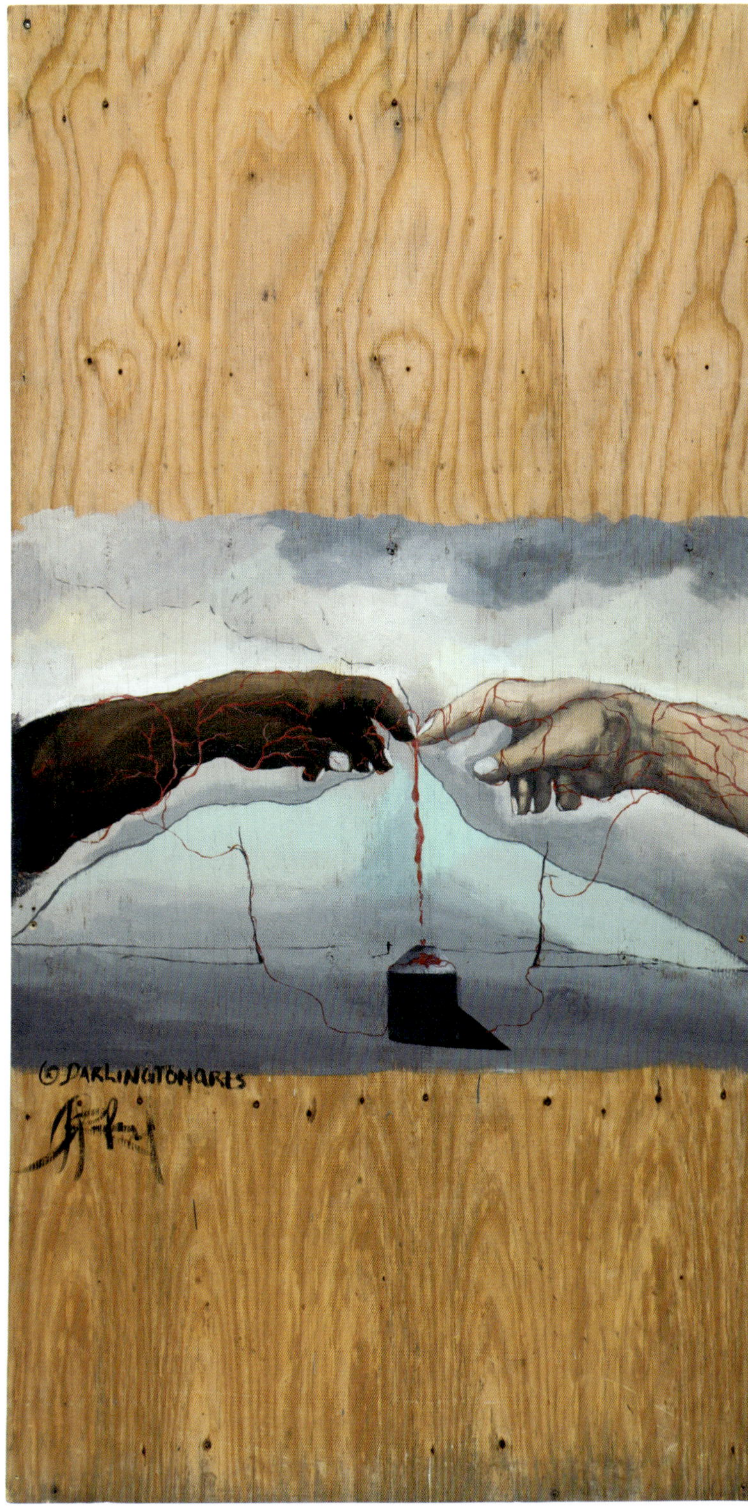

Plate 31
Darlington Panton, *Creation/Connection*, 2020, Urban Outfitters, 3006 Hennepin Ave. S., 96 x 48 in.

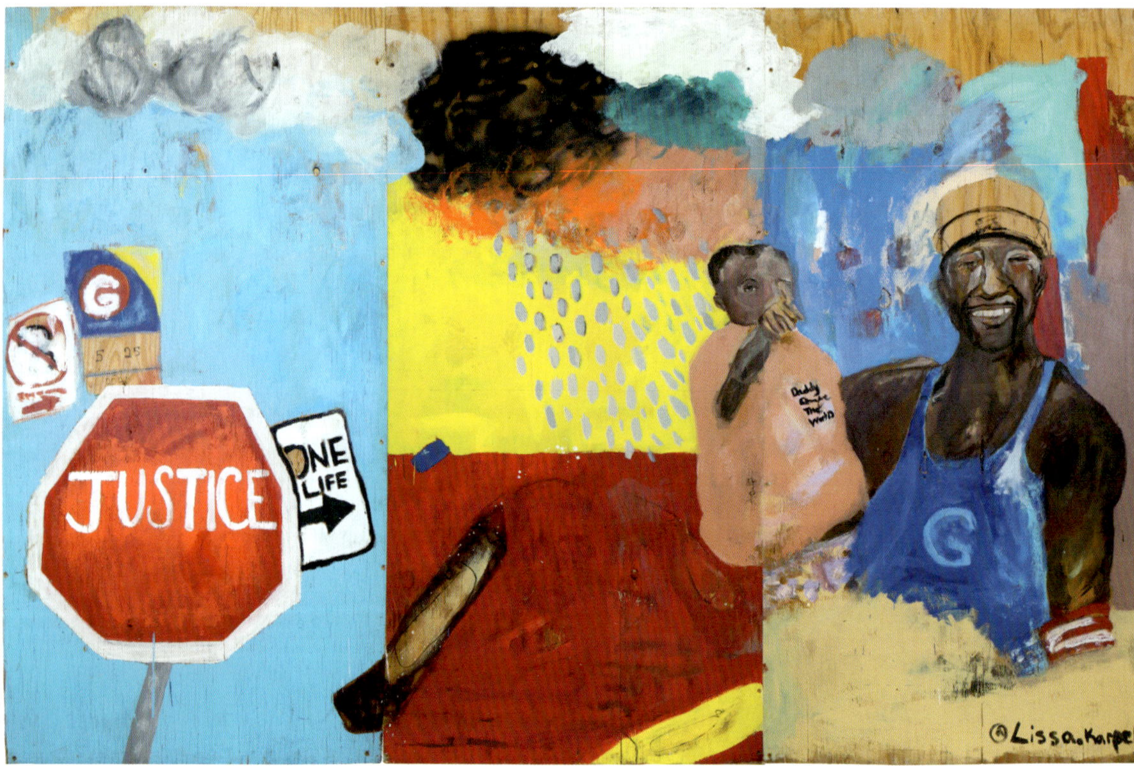

Plate 32

Lissa Karpeh, *Justice*, *Rain Cloud*, *Portrait*, 2020

Urban Outfitters, 3006 Hennepin Ave. S., 96 x 144 in.

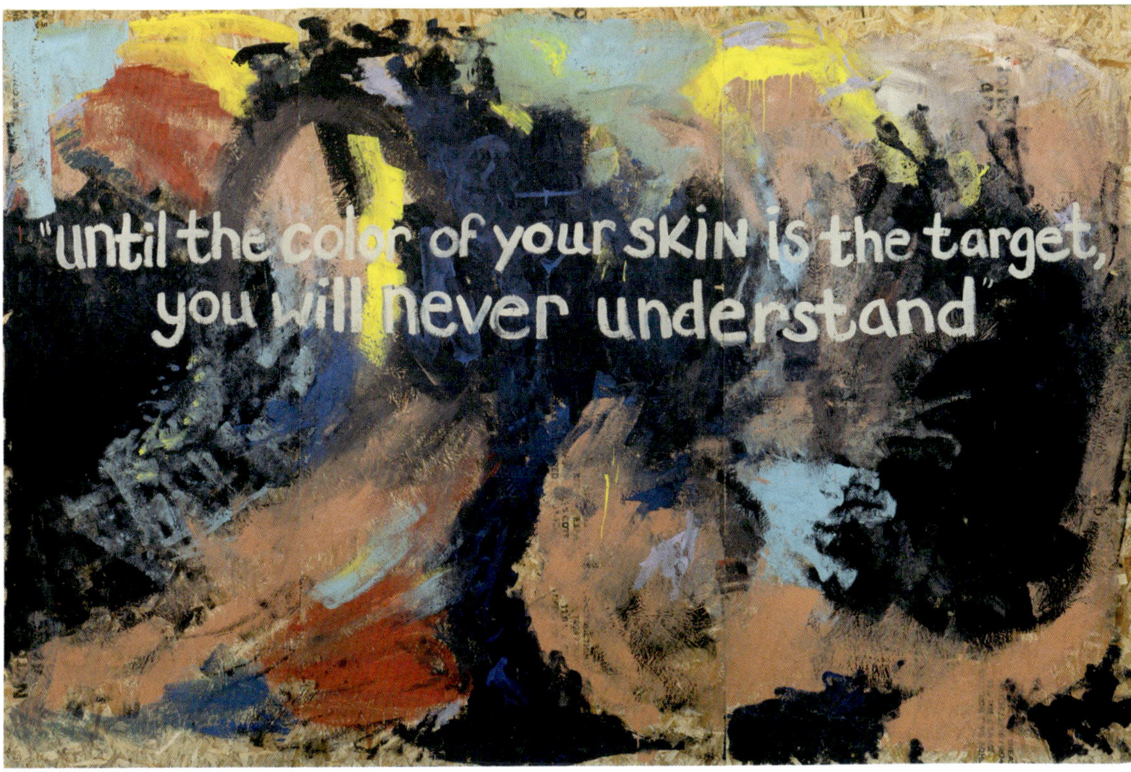

Plate 33

Free in Color Arts, Youth Painters, *Until the Color of Your Skin is the Target*, 2020
CVS, 1010 W. Lake St., 86 x 144 in.

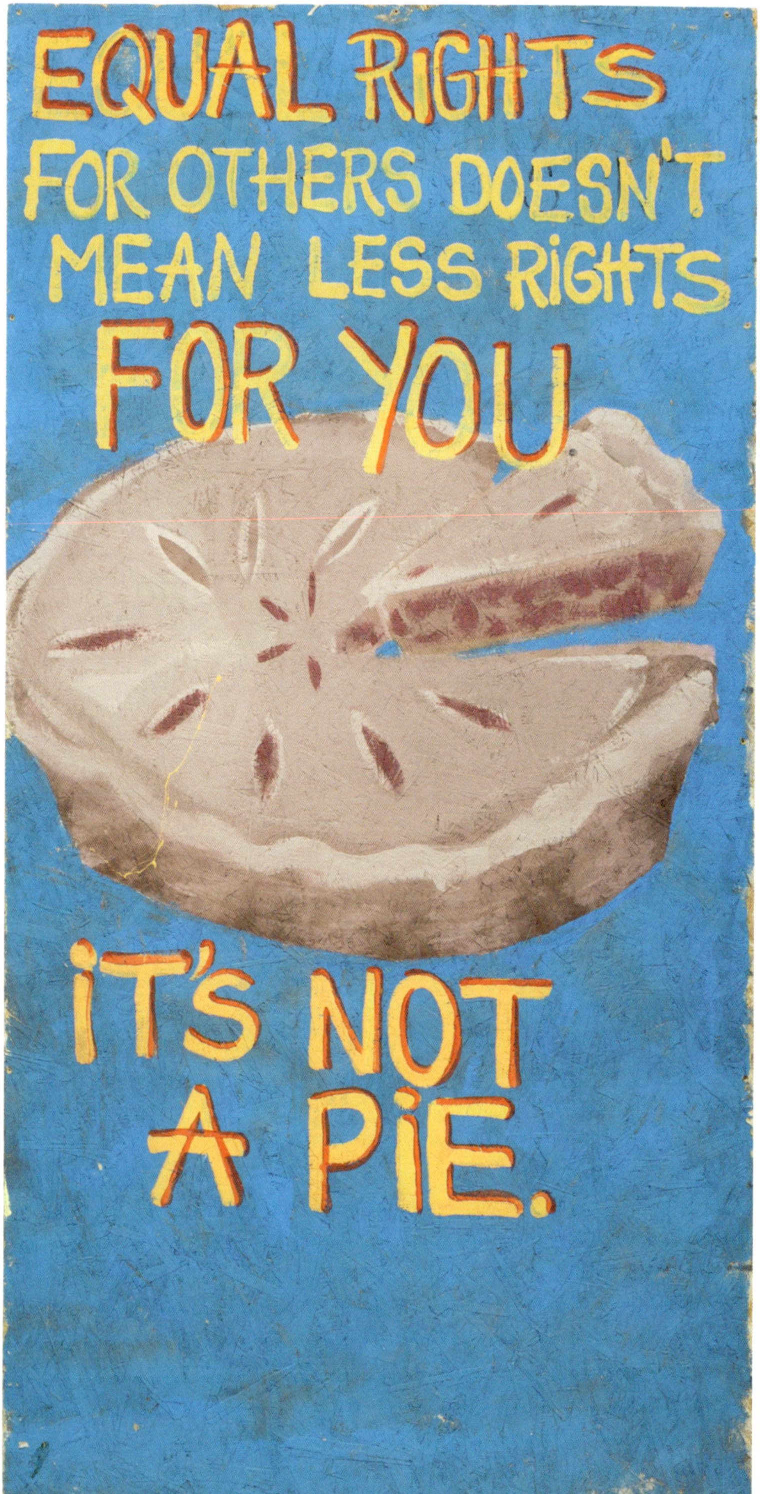

Plate 34

Free in Color Arts, Youth Painters, *Equal Rights. . .It's Not a Pie*, 2020, CVS, 1010 W. Lake St., 86 x 48 in.

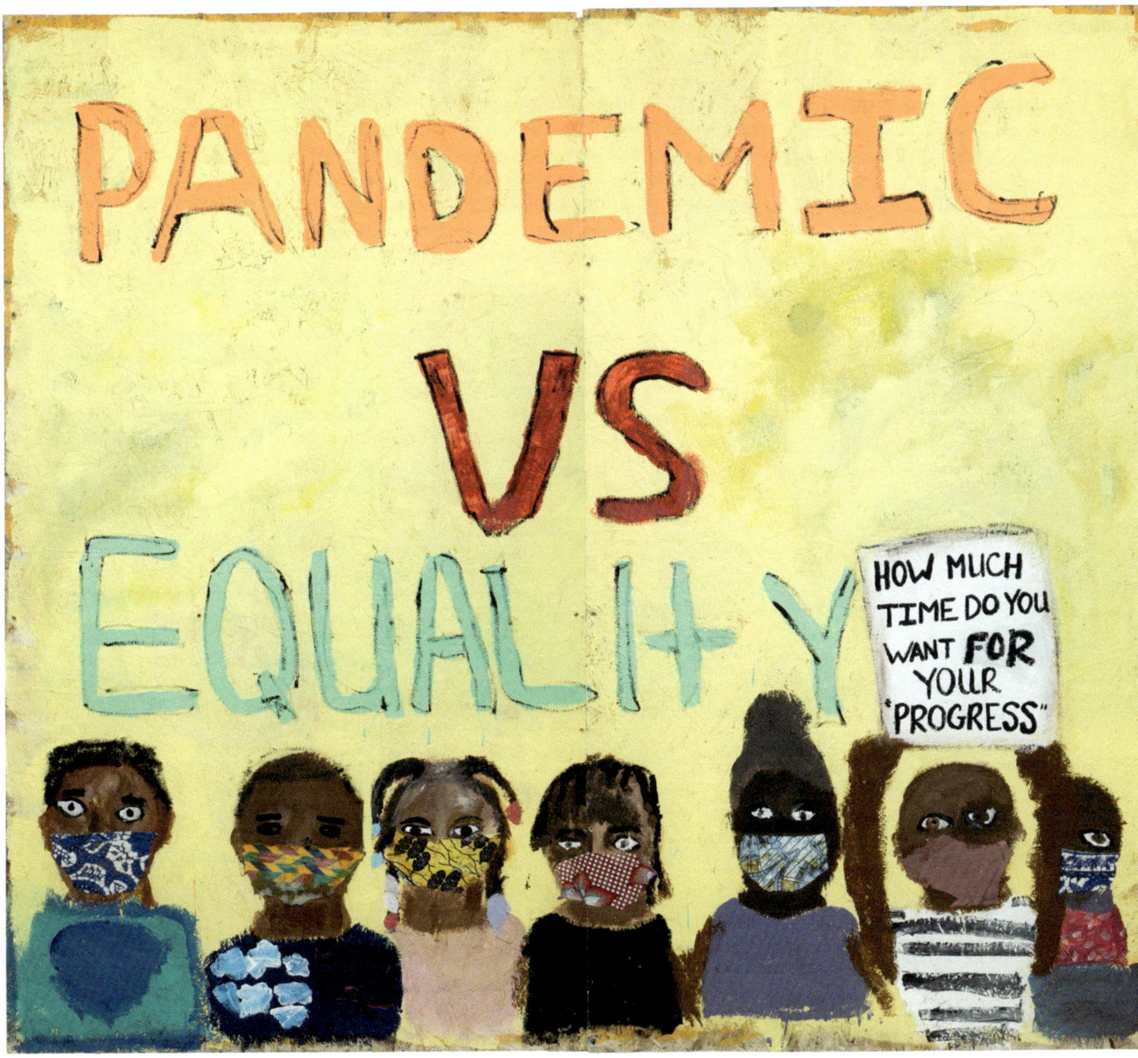

Plate 35

Free in Color Arts, Youth Painters, *Pandemic vs. Equality*, 2020

CVS, 1010 W. Lake St., 86 x 96 in.

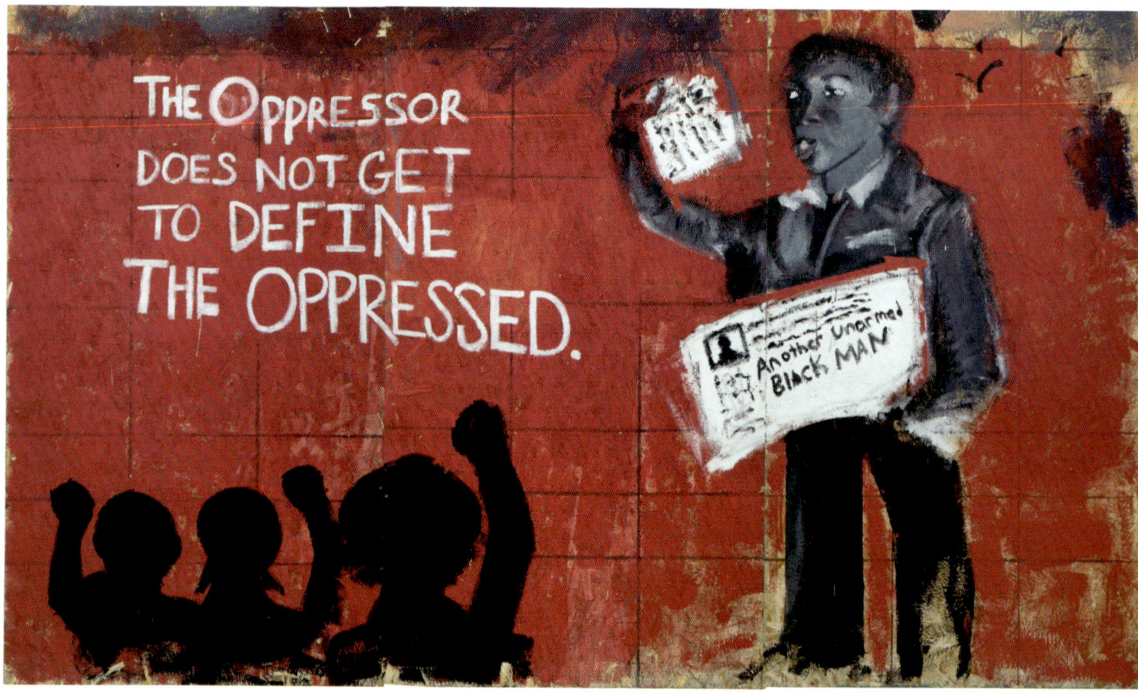

Plate 36

Free in Color Arts, Youth Painters, *The Oppressor Does Not Get to Define the Oppressed*, 2020
CVS, 1010 W. Lake St., 86 x 144 in.

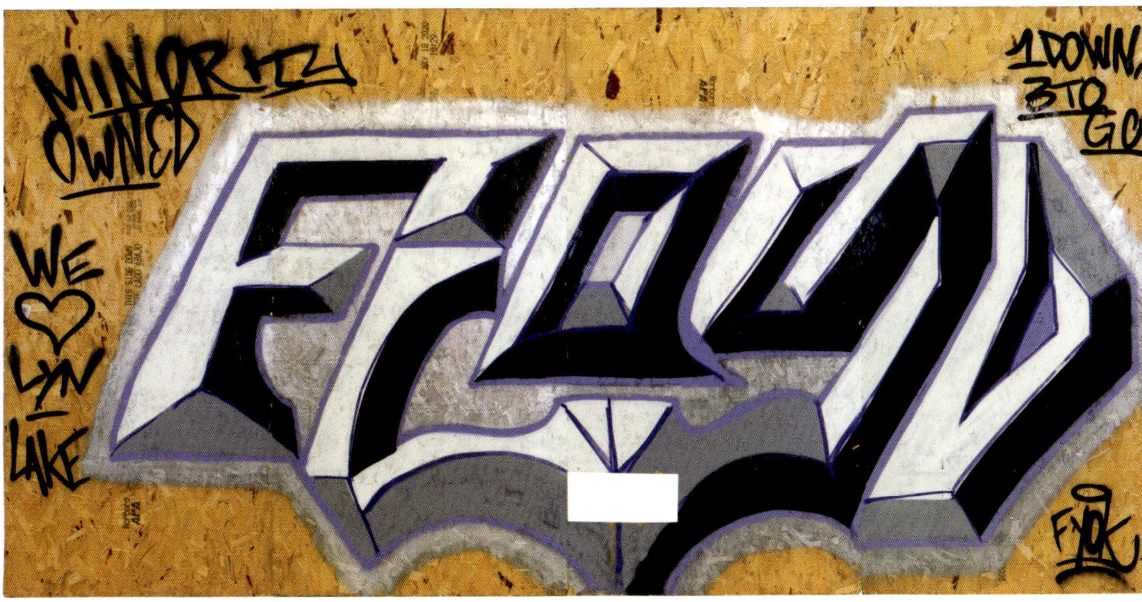

Plate 37

FYOK, *Silver "Floyd"*, 2020

Saigon Uptown Restaurant, 3035 Lyndale Ave. S., 96 x 192 in.

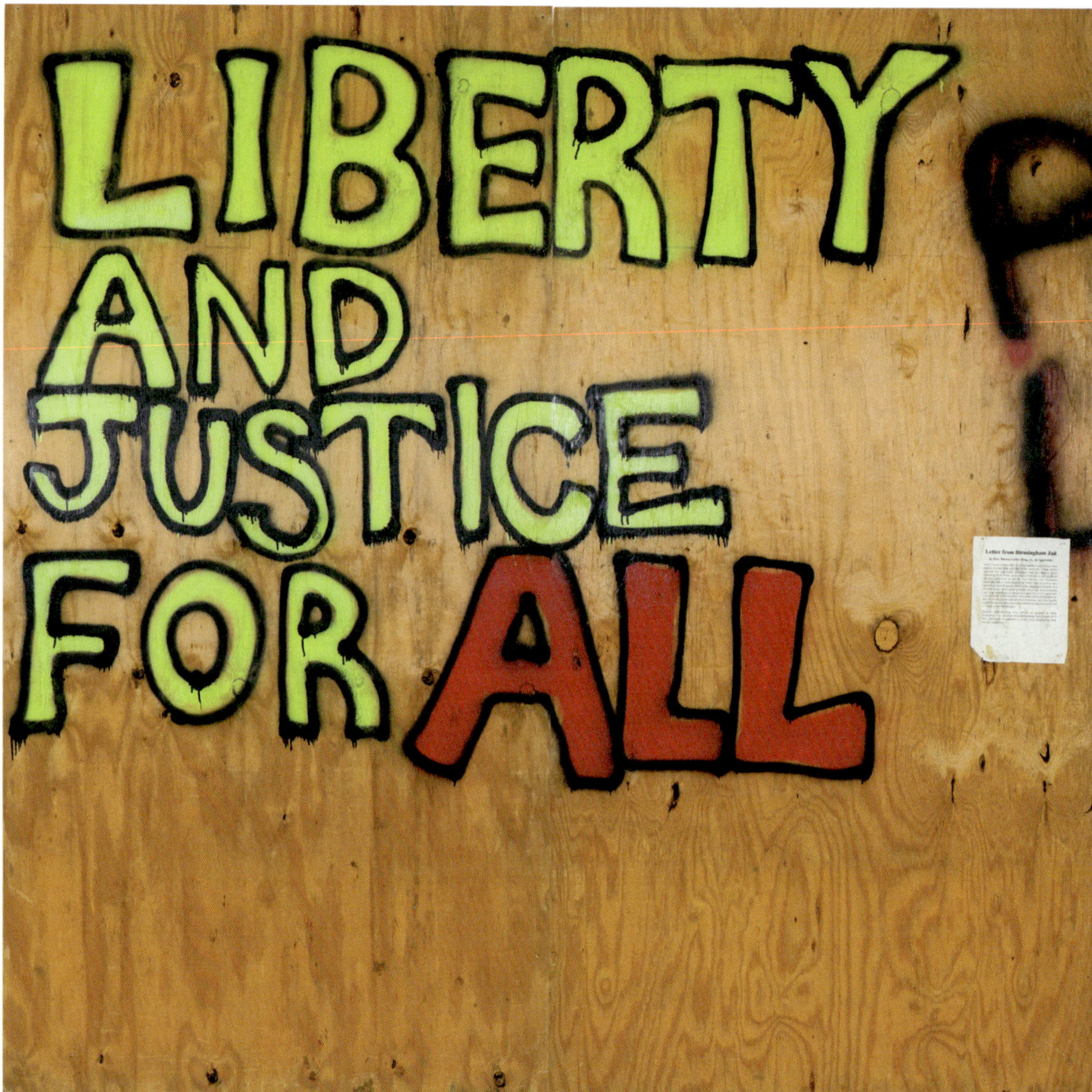

Plate 38

Artist Unidentified, *Liberty and Justice For All*, 2020
Bryant Lake Bowl and Theater, 810 W. Lake St., 96 x 96 in.

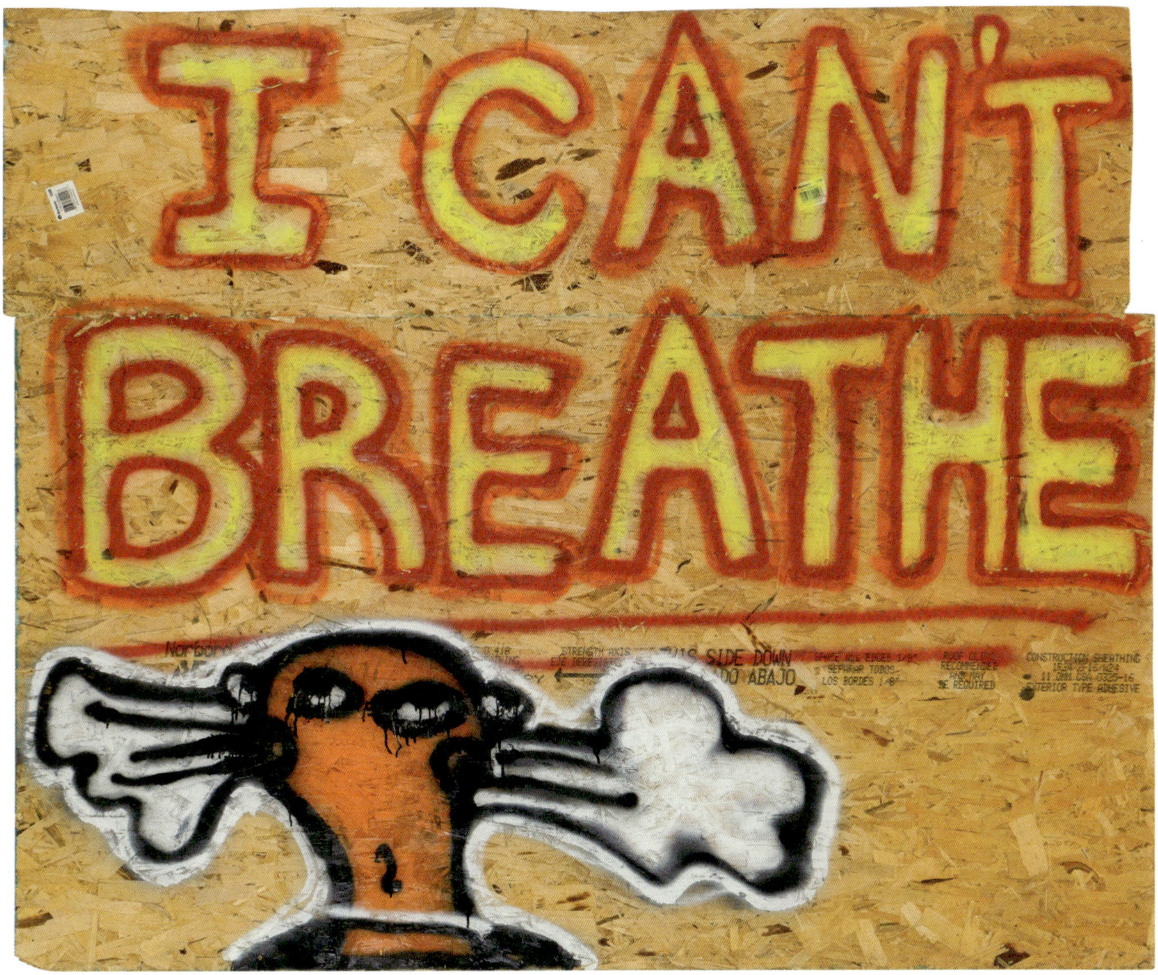

Plate 39

Artist Unidentified, *I Can't Breathe with Orange Character*, 2020

Bryant Lake Bowl and Theater, 810 W. Lake St., 71 x 83 in.

Plate 40
Artist Unidentified,
Justice is Truth in Action, 2020,
Eye of Horus Metaphysical,
910 W. Lake St., 96 x 48 in.

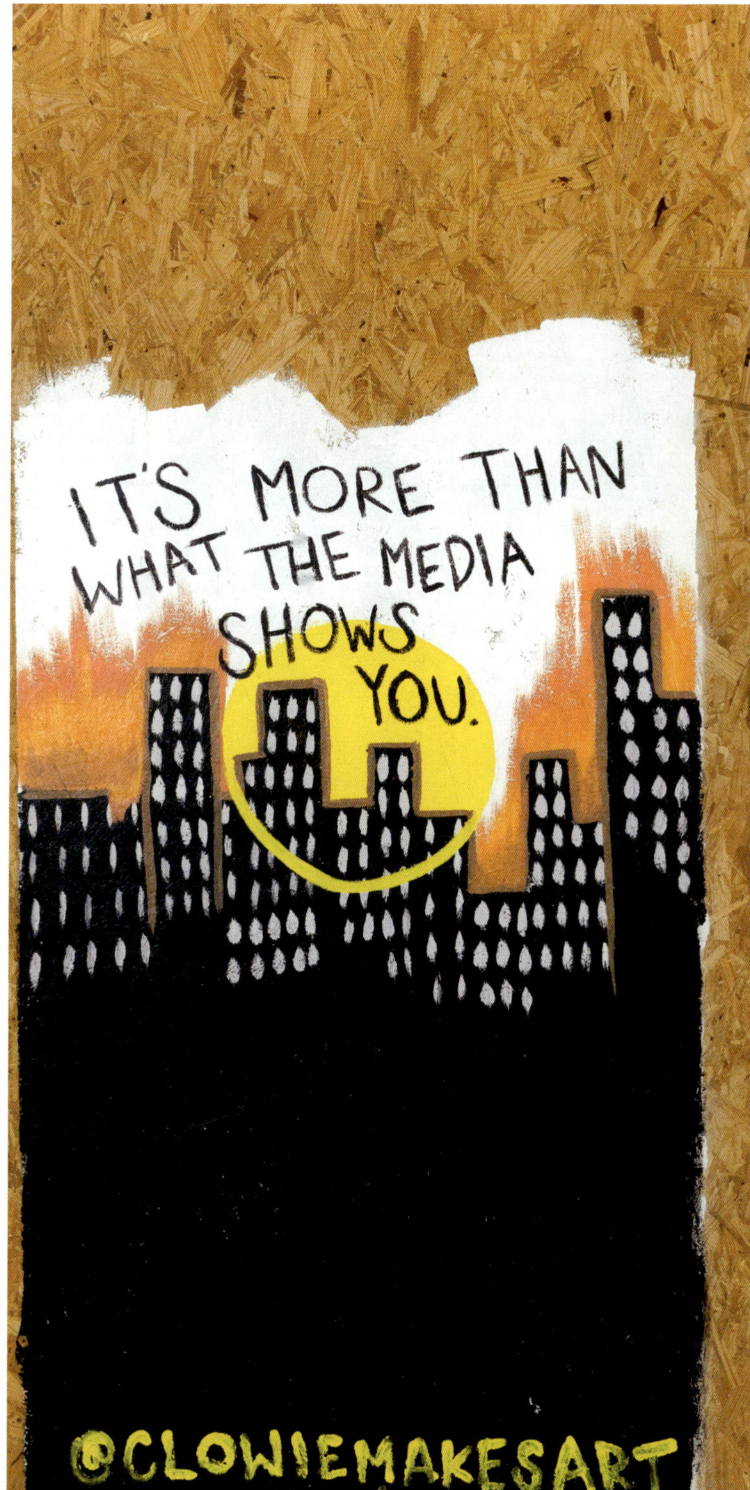

Plate 41

Clowie Makes Art, *It's More Than What the Media Shows You*, 2020, Eye of Horus Metaphysical, 910 W. Lake St., 96 x 48 in.

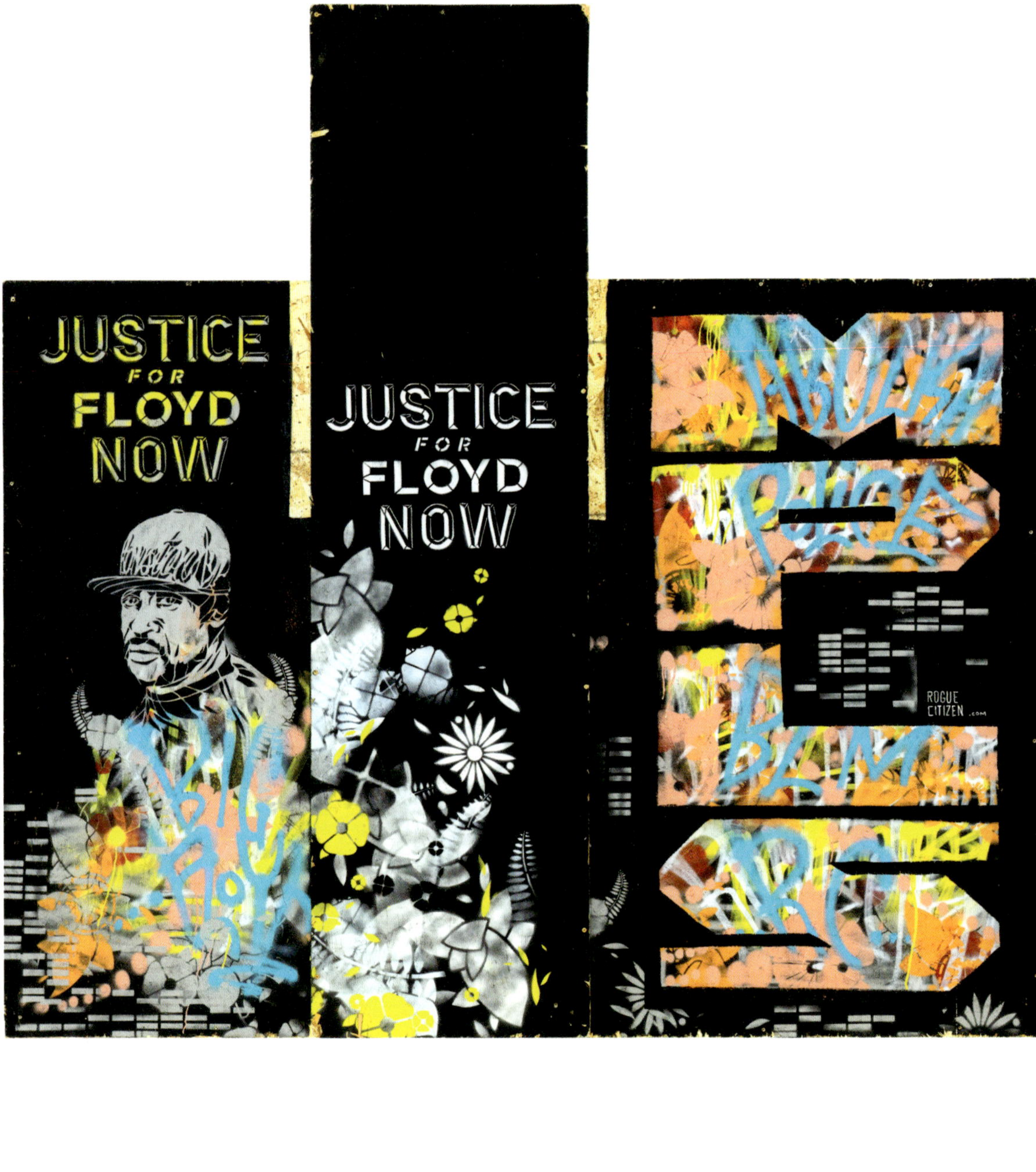

Plate 42

Rogue Citizen, *Justice for Floyd Now*, 2020
3400 Lyndale Ave. S., 96 x 110 in. approx.

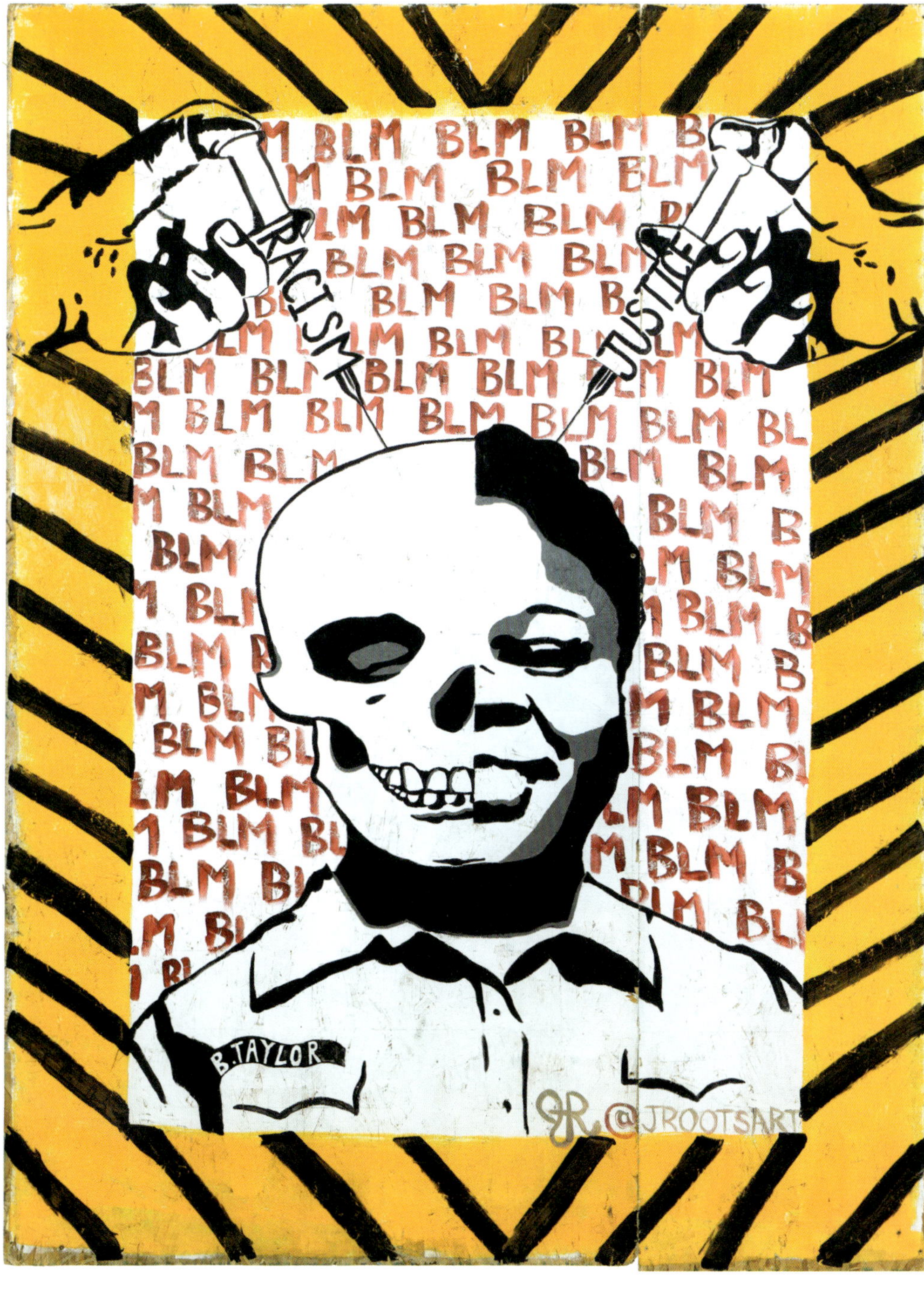

Plate 43

Jordan Roots, *Caution, Racism Kills*, 2020
Brim Restaurant, 2919 Knox Ave. S., 119 x 96 in.

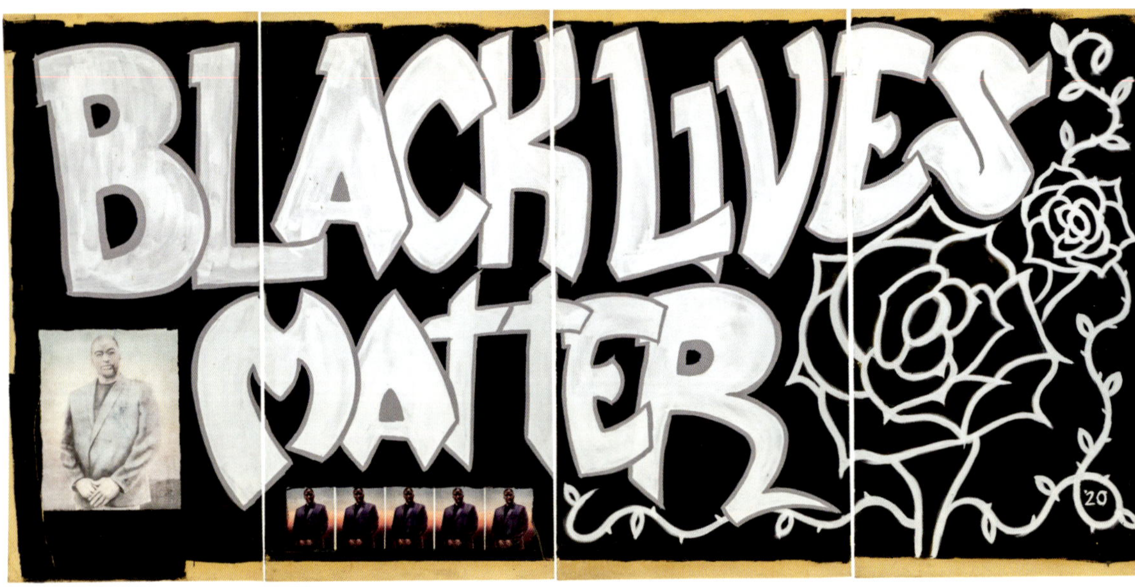

Plate 44

Artist Unidentified, *Black Lives Matter Rose*, 2020

New Bohemia, 800 W. Lake St., 96 x 192

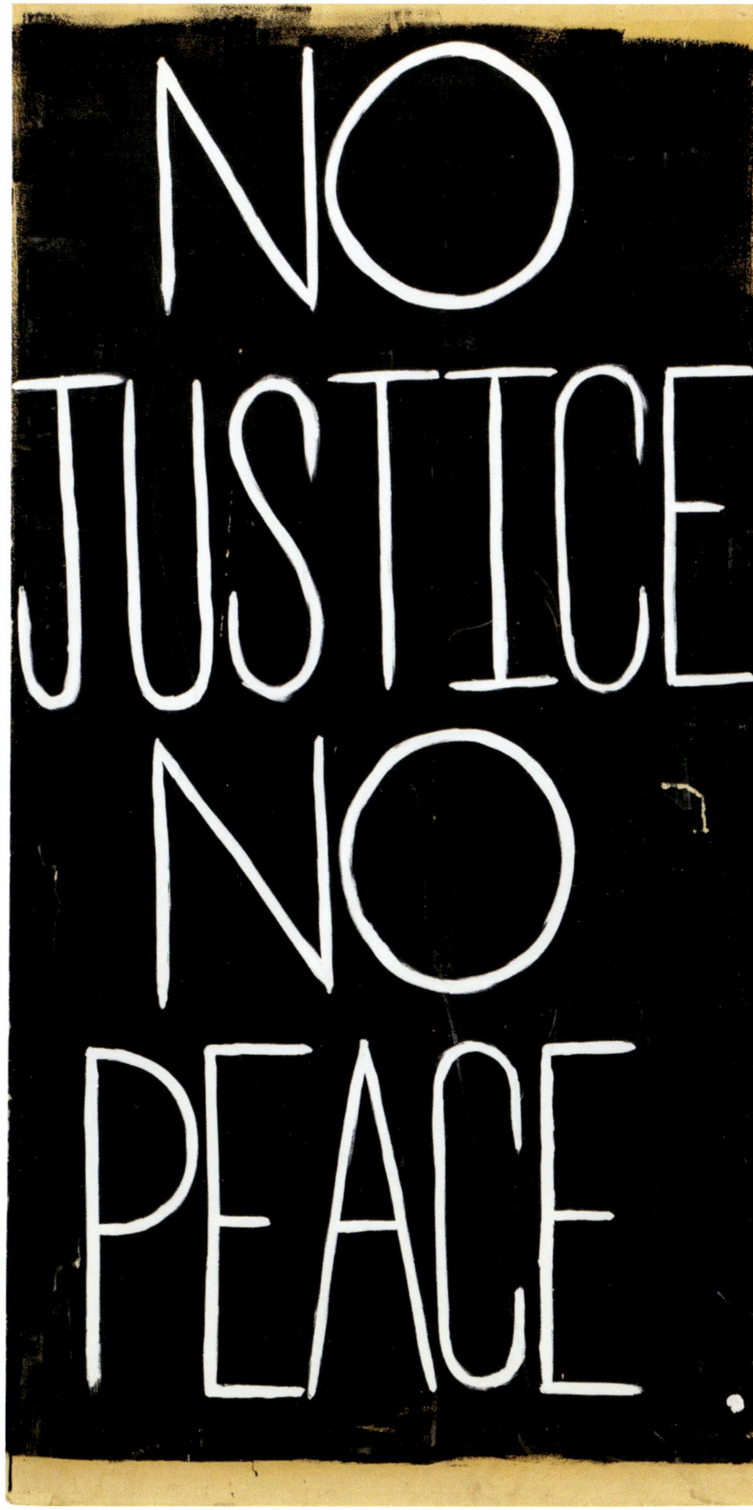

Plate 45

Artist Unidentified, *No Justice No Peace, Black and White*, 2020, New Bohemia, 800 W. Lake St., 96 x 48 in.

WHITTIER

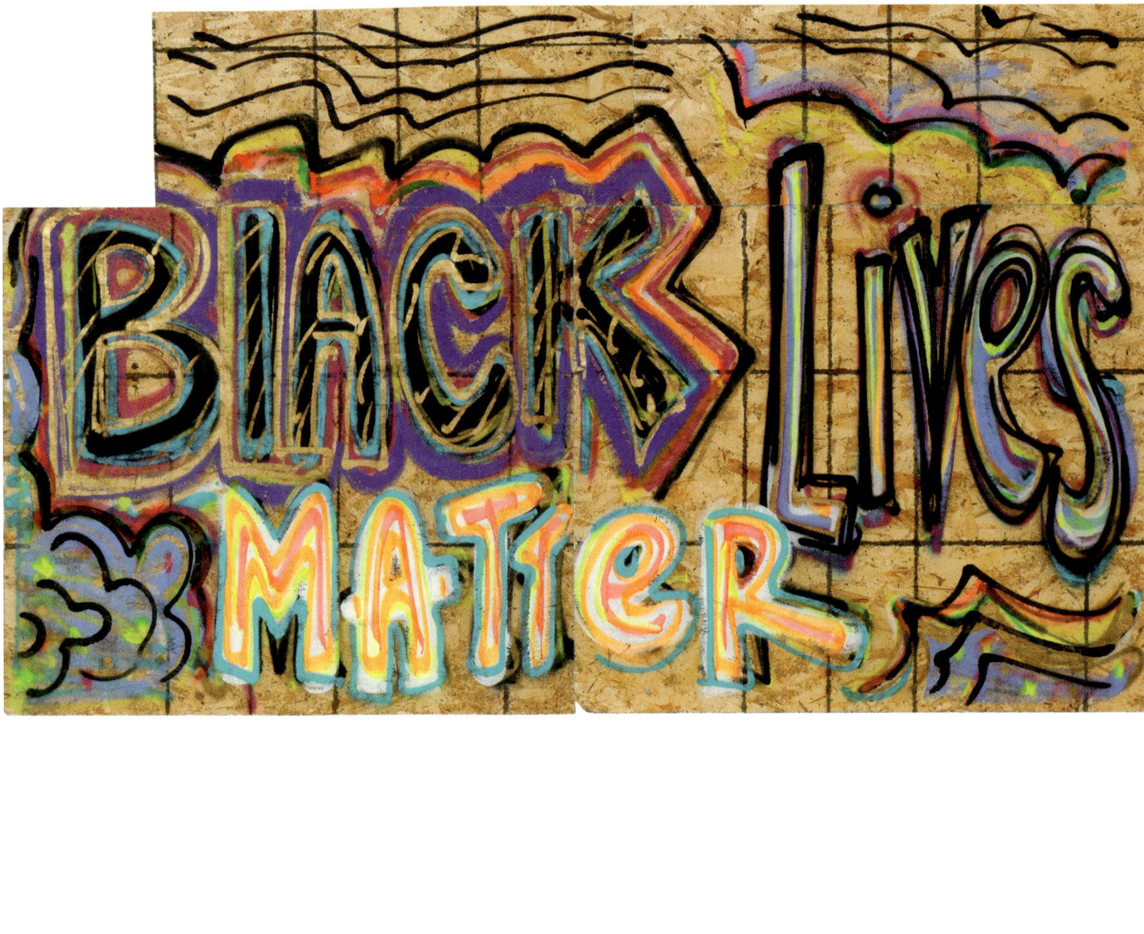

Plate 46

Shaquima Johnson-McSwain, *Black Lives Matter*, 2020

b. Resale, 2613 Nicollet Ave., 67.5 x 108 in. approx.

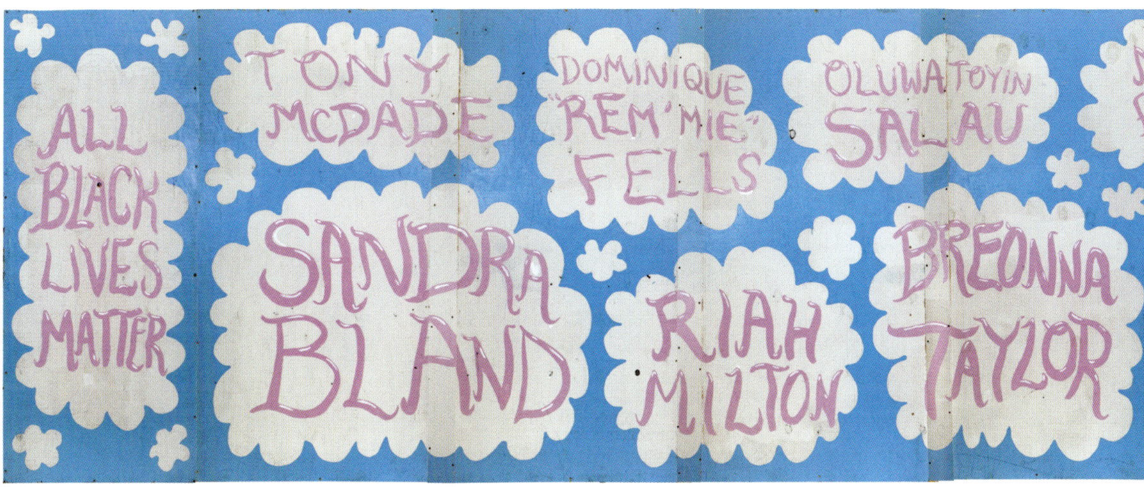

Plate 47

Noah Lawrence-Holder, *In Memory of Black Women and Trans Individuals*, 2020
Curl Power Salon, 8 E. Franklin Ave., 96 x 224 in. approx.

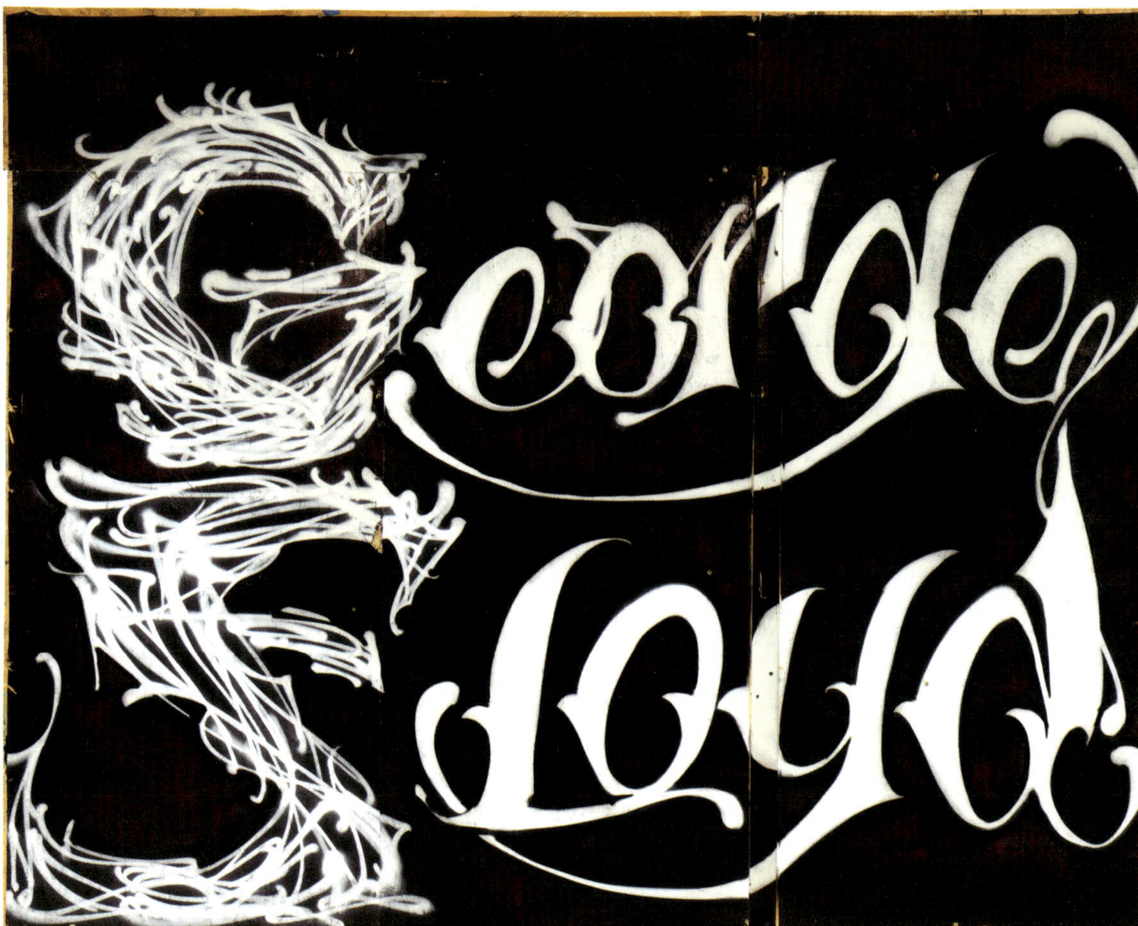

Plate 48

Venser, *George Floyd, Burgundy, Black and White*, 2020
Hum's Liquor, 2126 Lyndale Ave. S., 116 x 146 in.

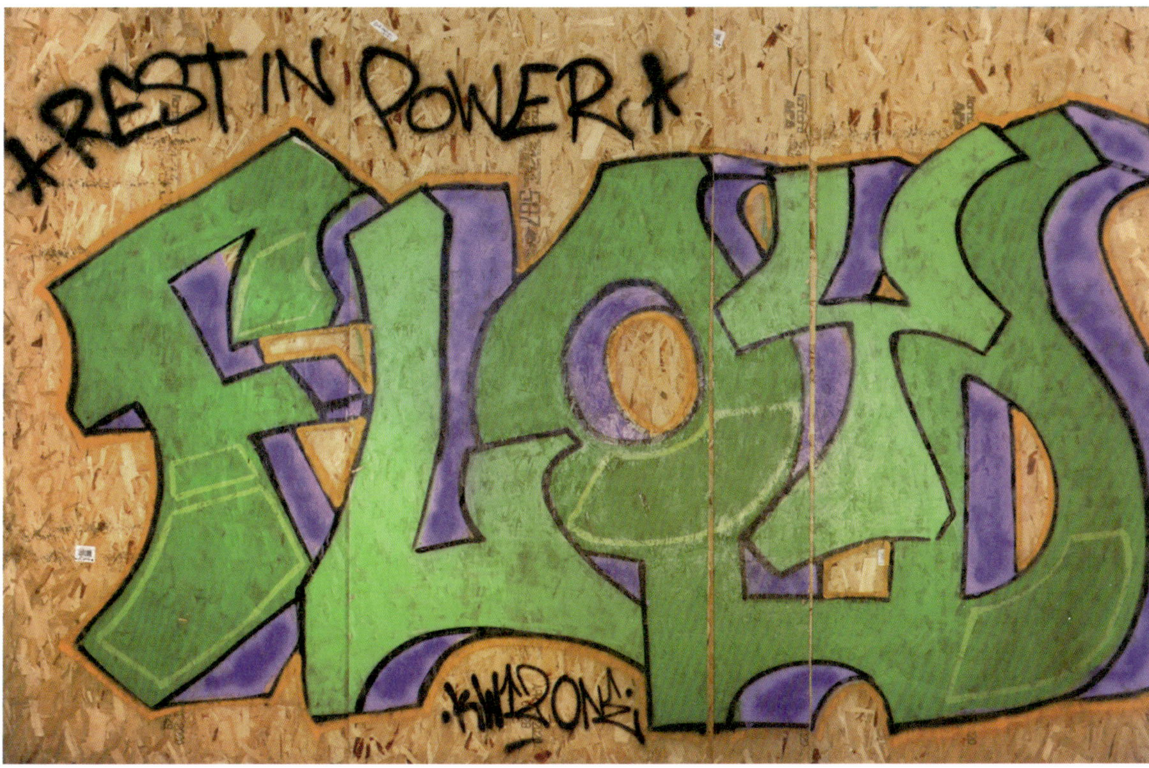

Plate 49

KwizOne, *Rest in Power, Floyd*, 2020

The Bad Waitress, 2 E. 26th St., 96 x 108.25 in.

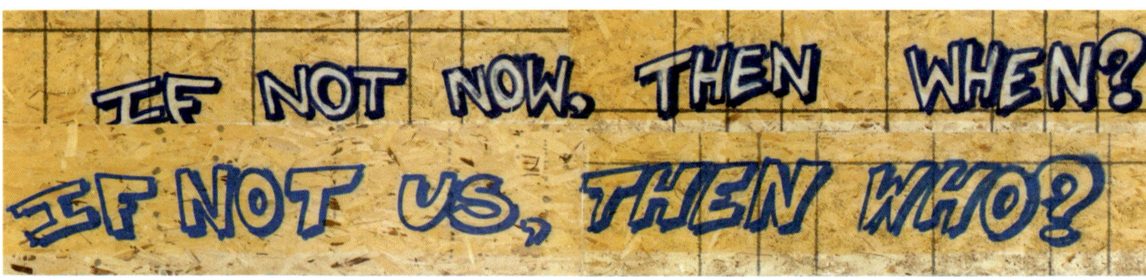

Plate 50

Artist Unidentified, *If Not Now, Then When? If Not Us, Then Who?*, 2020

Cafetto Coffee House, 708 W. 22nd St., 40 x 180 in.

DOWNTOWN

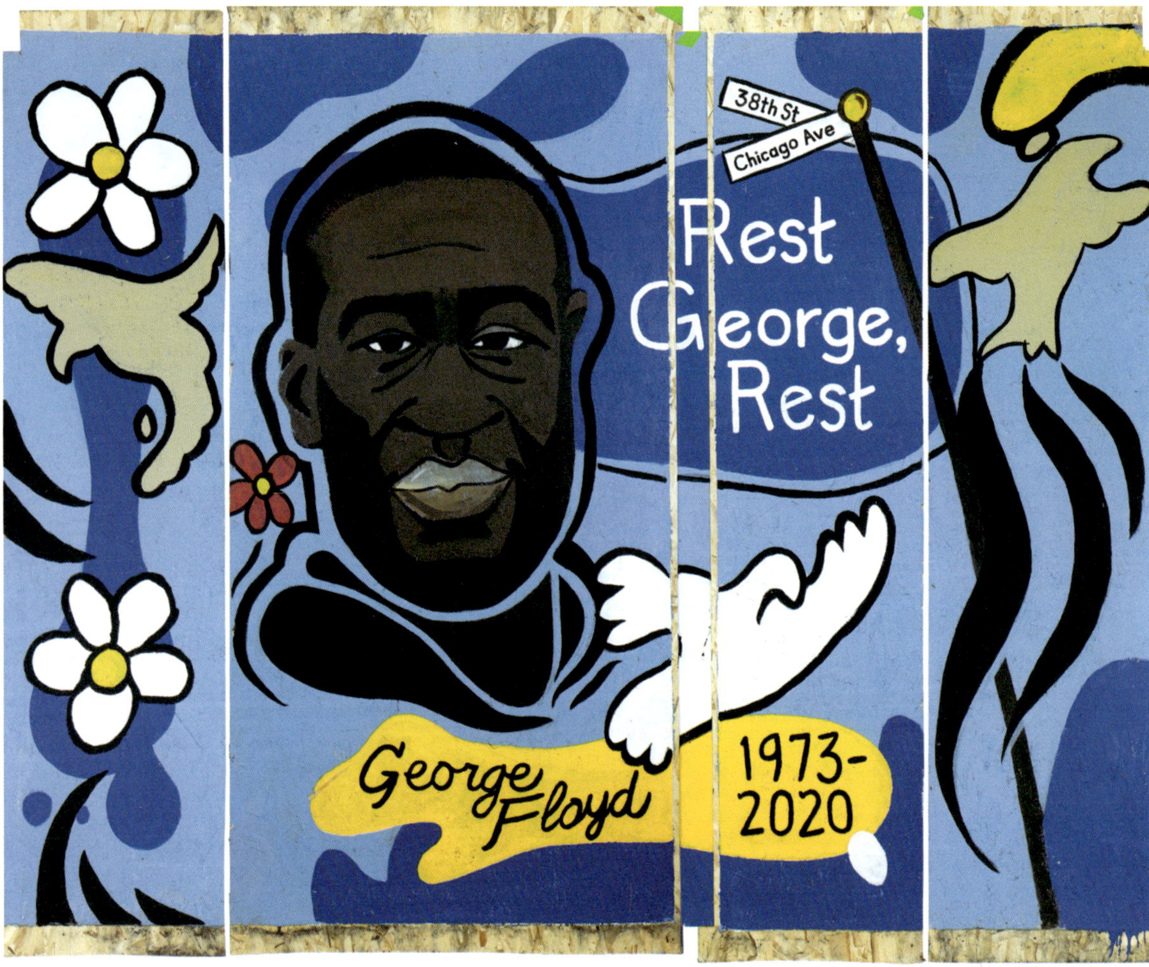

Plate 51

Christopher E. Harrison, *Rest George, Rest*, 2020

Nicollet Mall, 600 Nicollet Ave., 101 x 130.5 in.

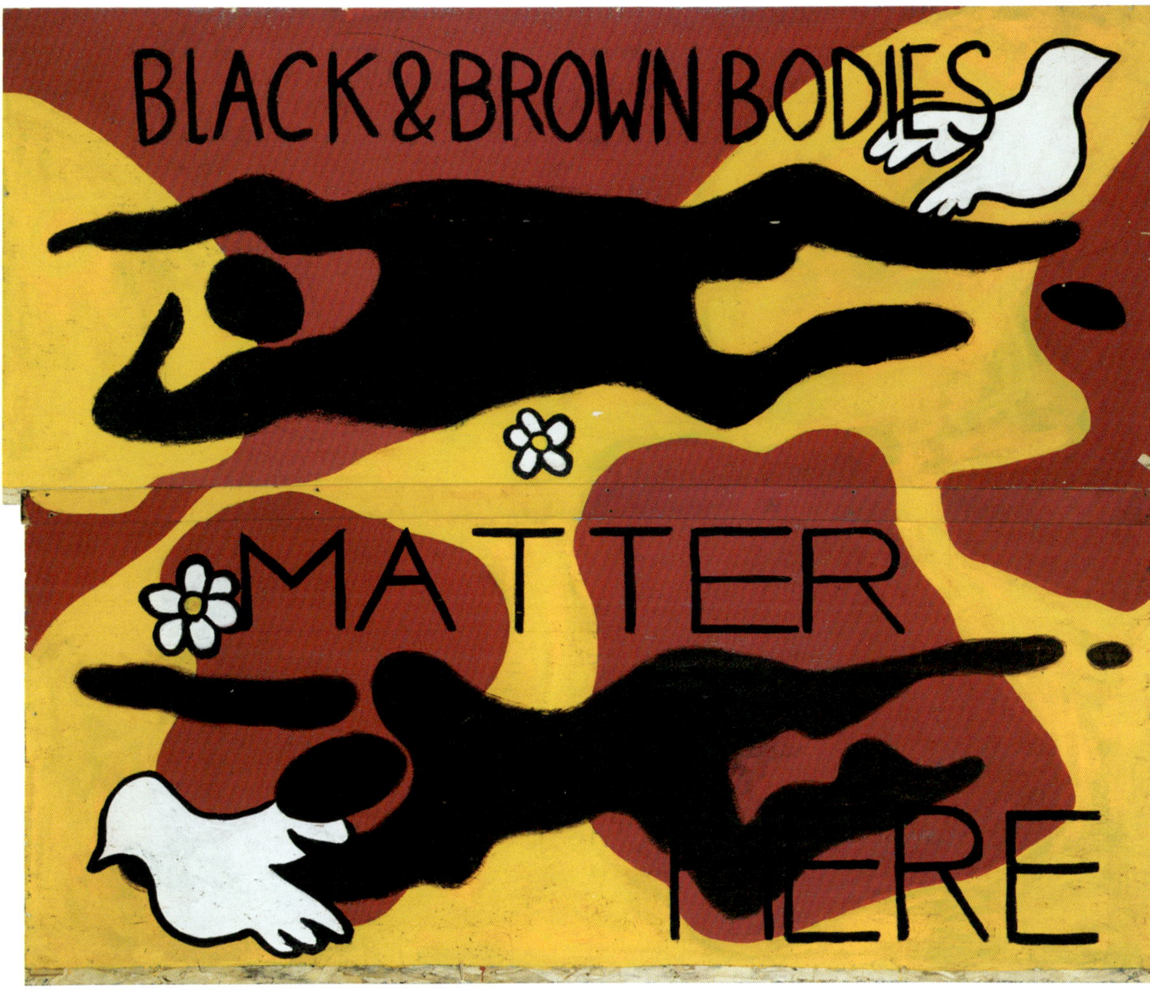

Plate 52

Christopher E. Harrison, *Black and Brown Bodies Matter*, 2020

Nicollet Mall, 600 Nicollet Ave., 100 x 112 in.

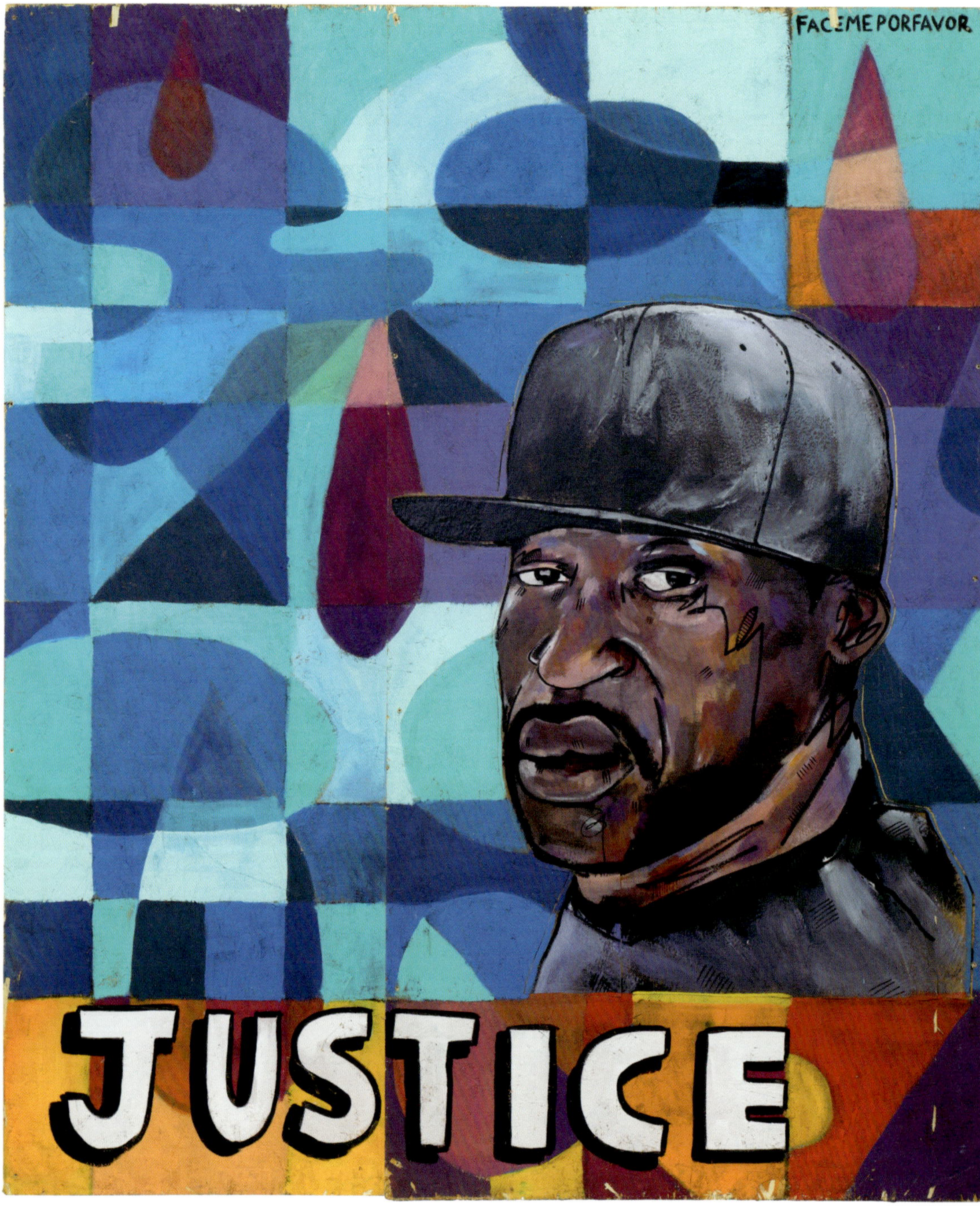

Plate 53

Face Me Por Favor, *Justice, Portrait*, 2020

Segue Coffee, 811 11th Ave. S., 96 x 72 in.

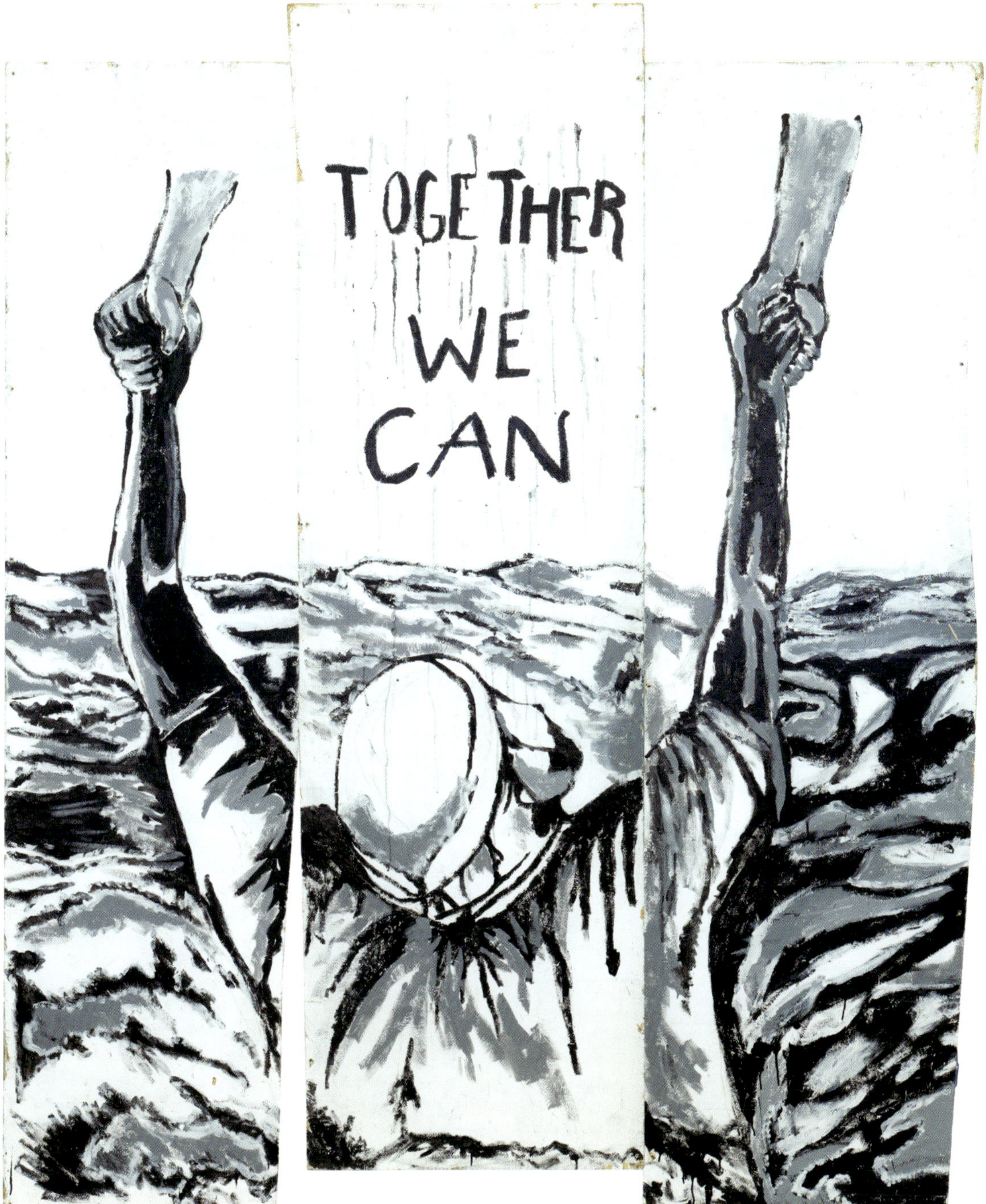

Plate 54

Artist Unidentified, *Together We Can*, 2020

Segue Coffee, 811 11th Ave. S., 96 x 81 in.

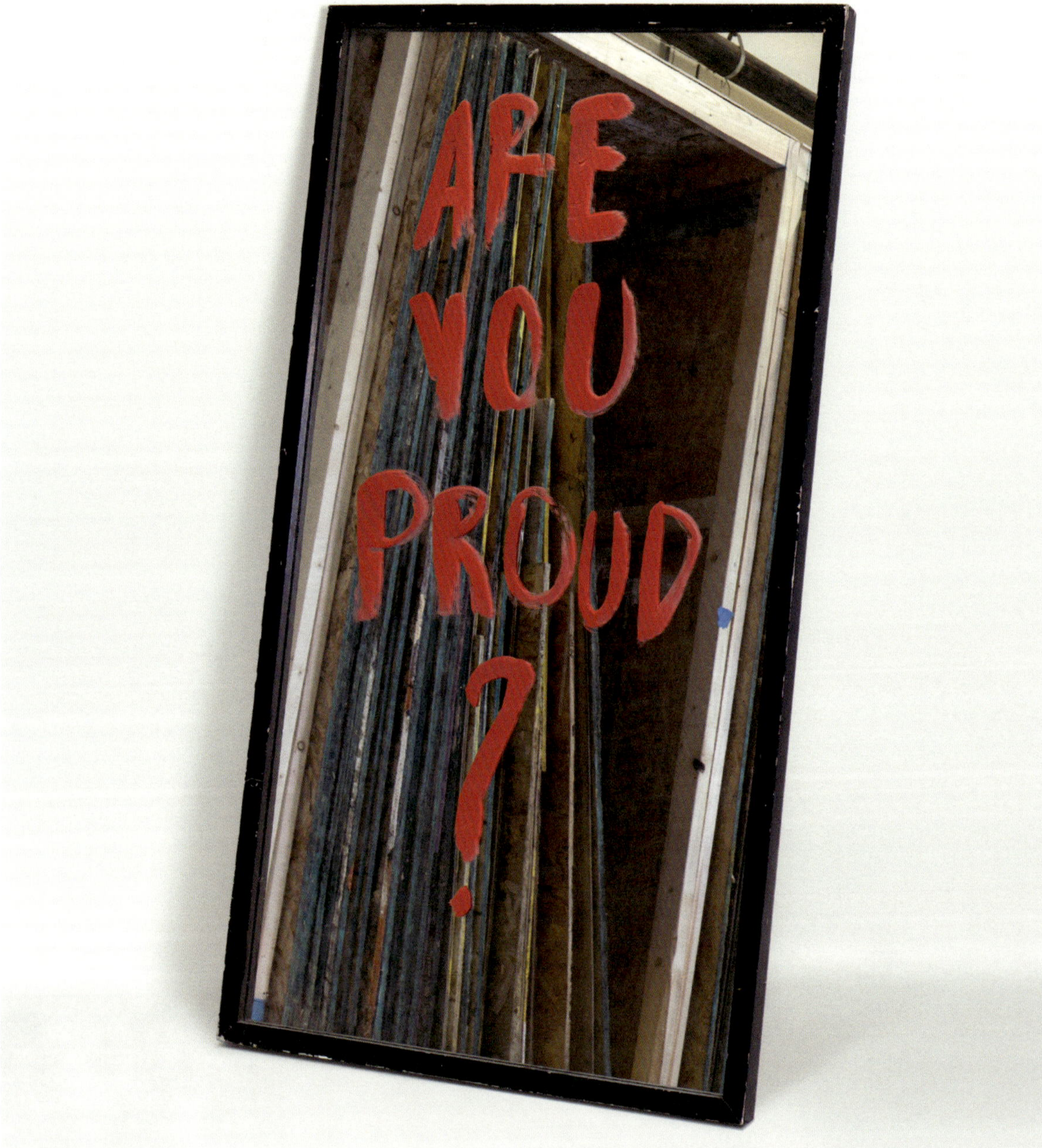

Plate 55

Visual Black Justice, *Are You Proud?*, 2021

Mural on mirror (front), made during protest at trial of Derek Chauvin, 62 x 32 in.

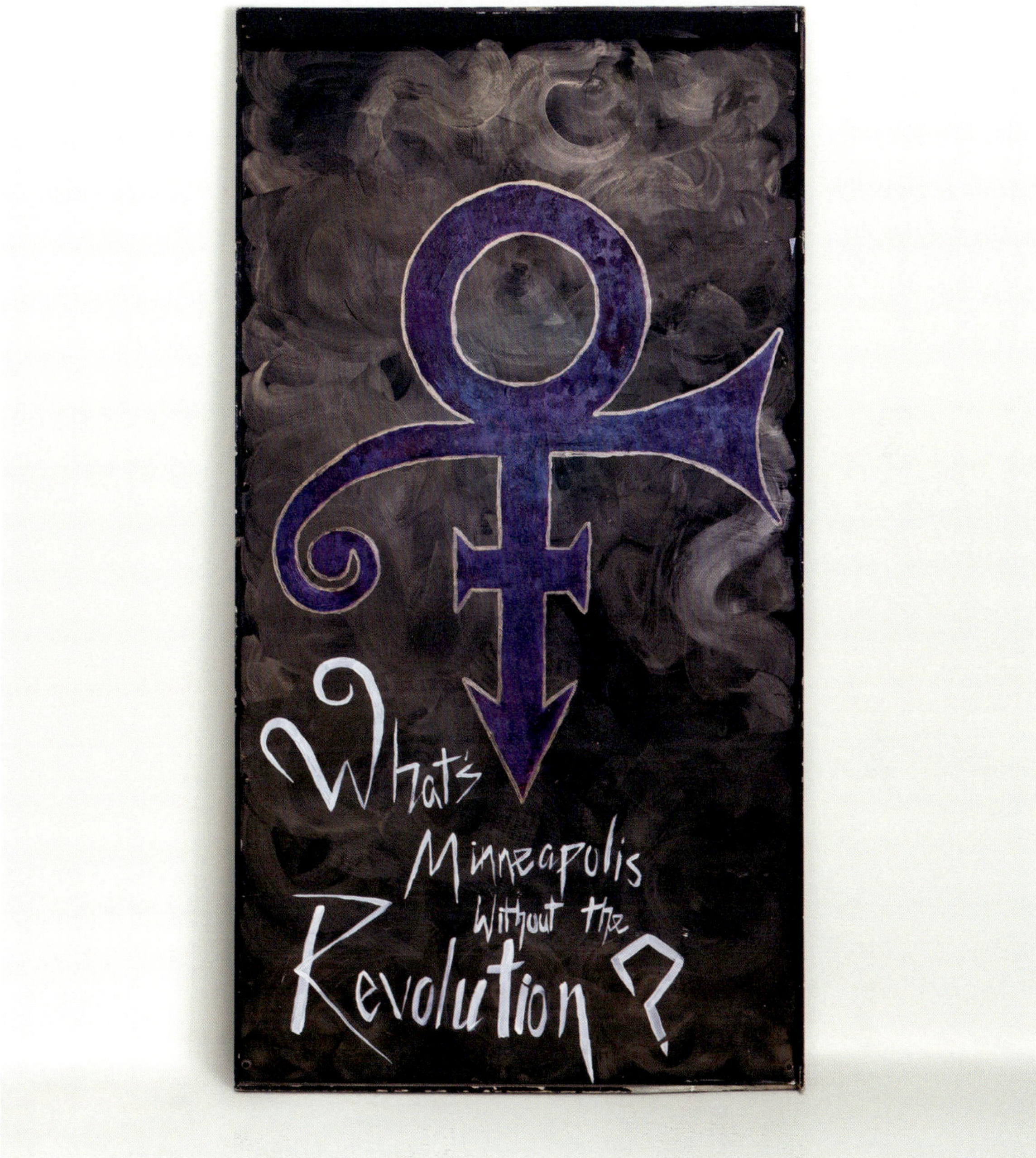

Plate 56

Visual Black Justice, *What's Minneapolis Without the Revolution?*, 2021
Mural on mirror (back), made during protest at trial of Derek Chauvin, 62 x 32 in.

NORTHEAST MINNEAPOLIS

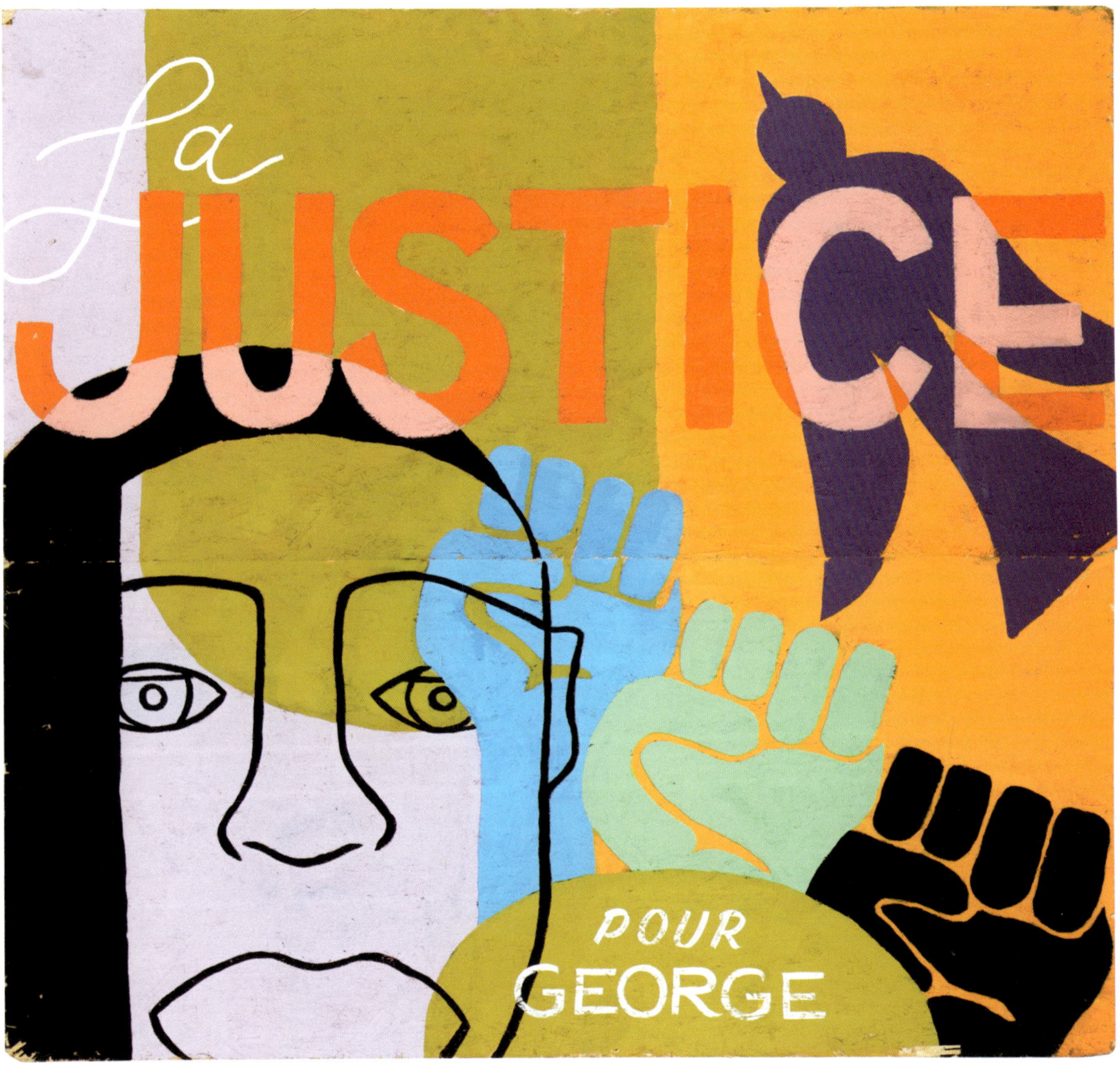

Plate 57

'Sota Letters Co, *La Justice Pour George*, 2020

Cou Cou Minneapolis, 1306 4th St. N.E., 96 x 96 in.

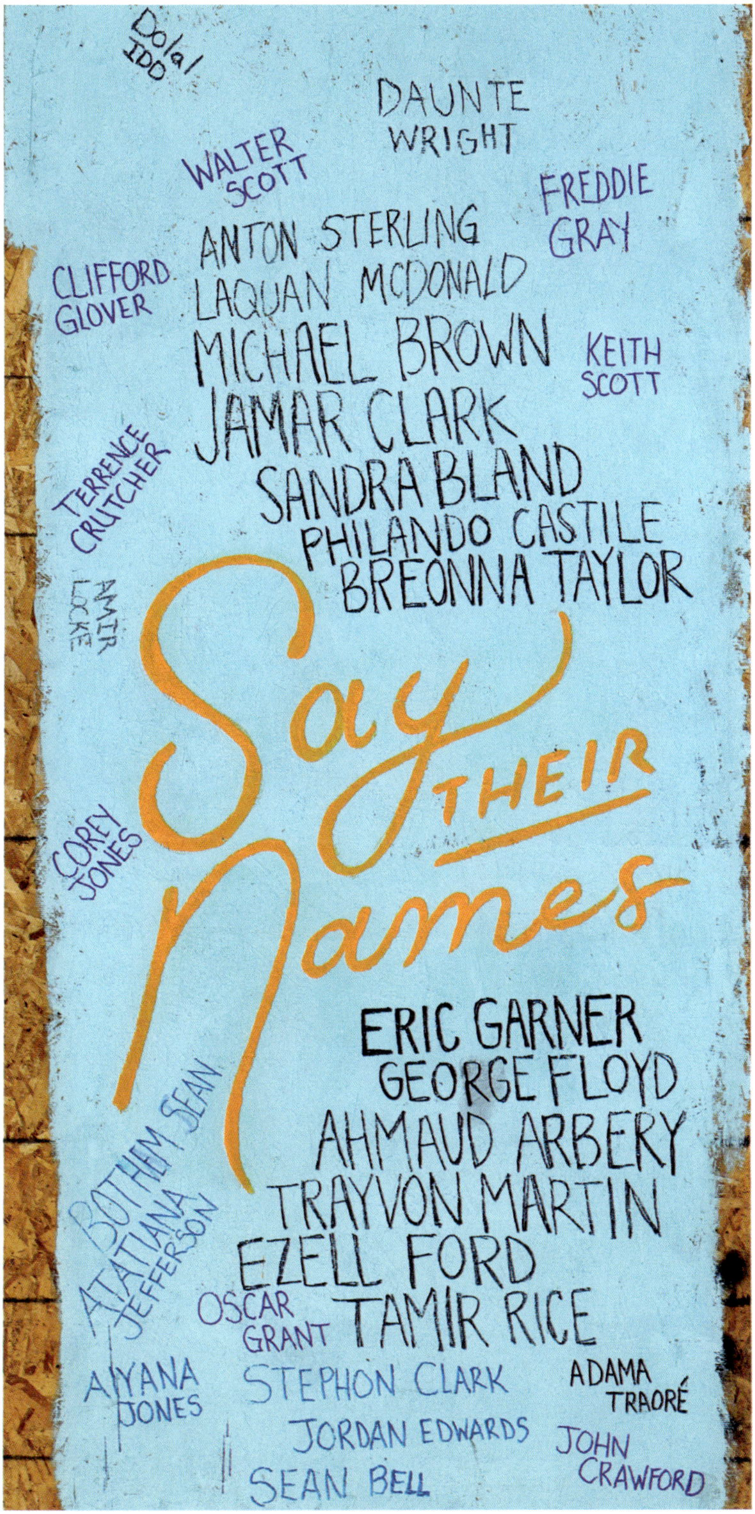

Plate 58

'Sota Letters Co, *Say Their Names*, 2020, Cou Cou Minneapolis, 1306 4th St. N.E., 72 x 42 in. approx.

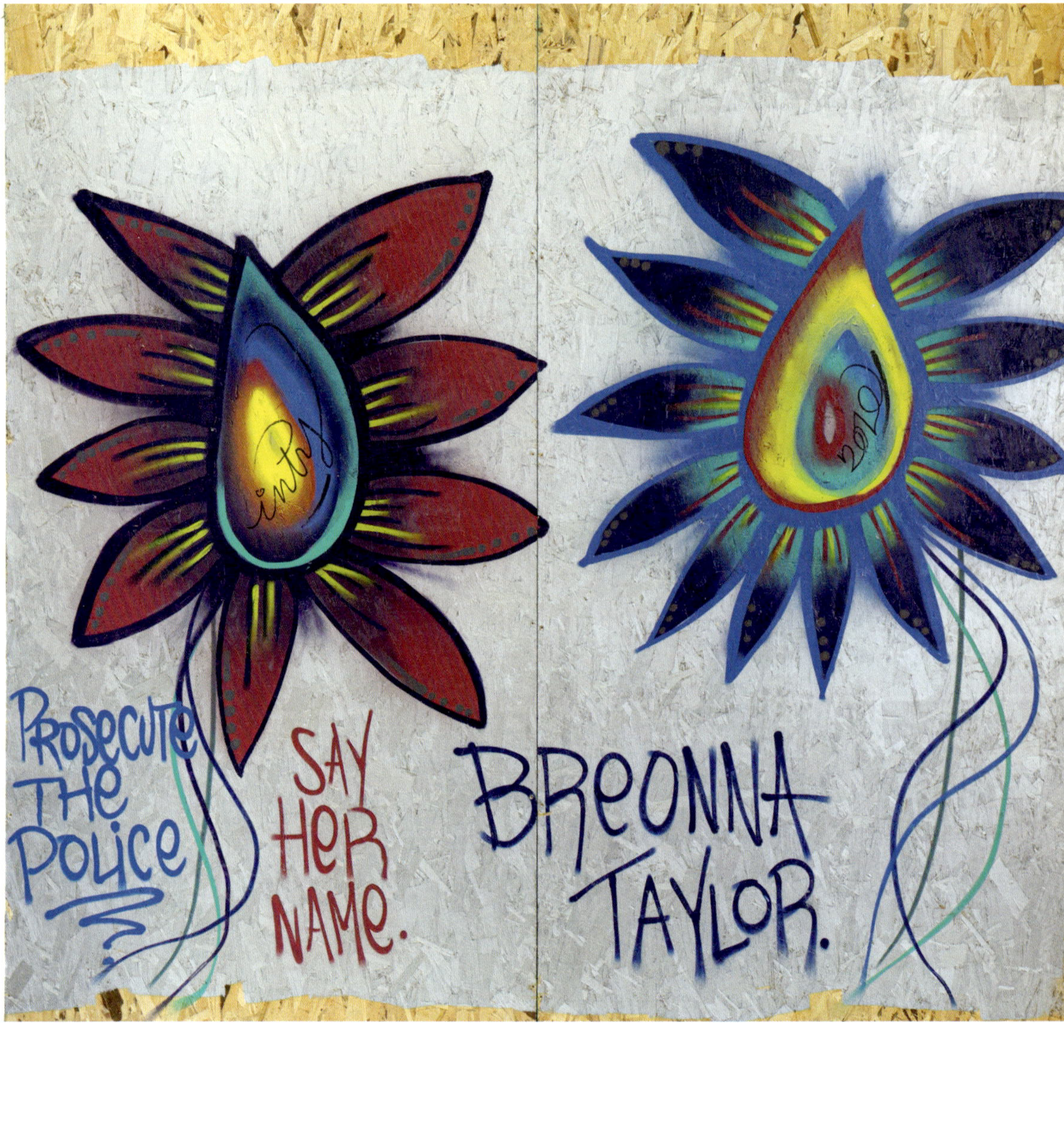

Plate 59

Intra, *Say Her Name*, 2020

Eastside Food Co-op, 2551 Central Ave. N.E., 96 x 96 in.

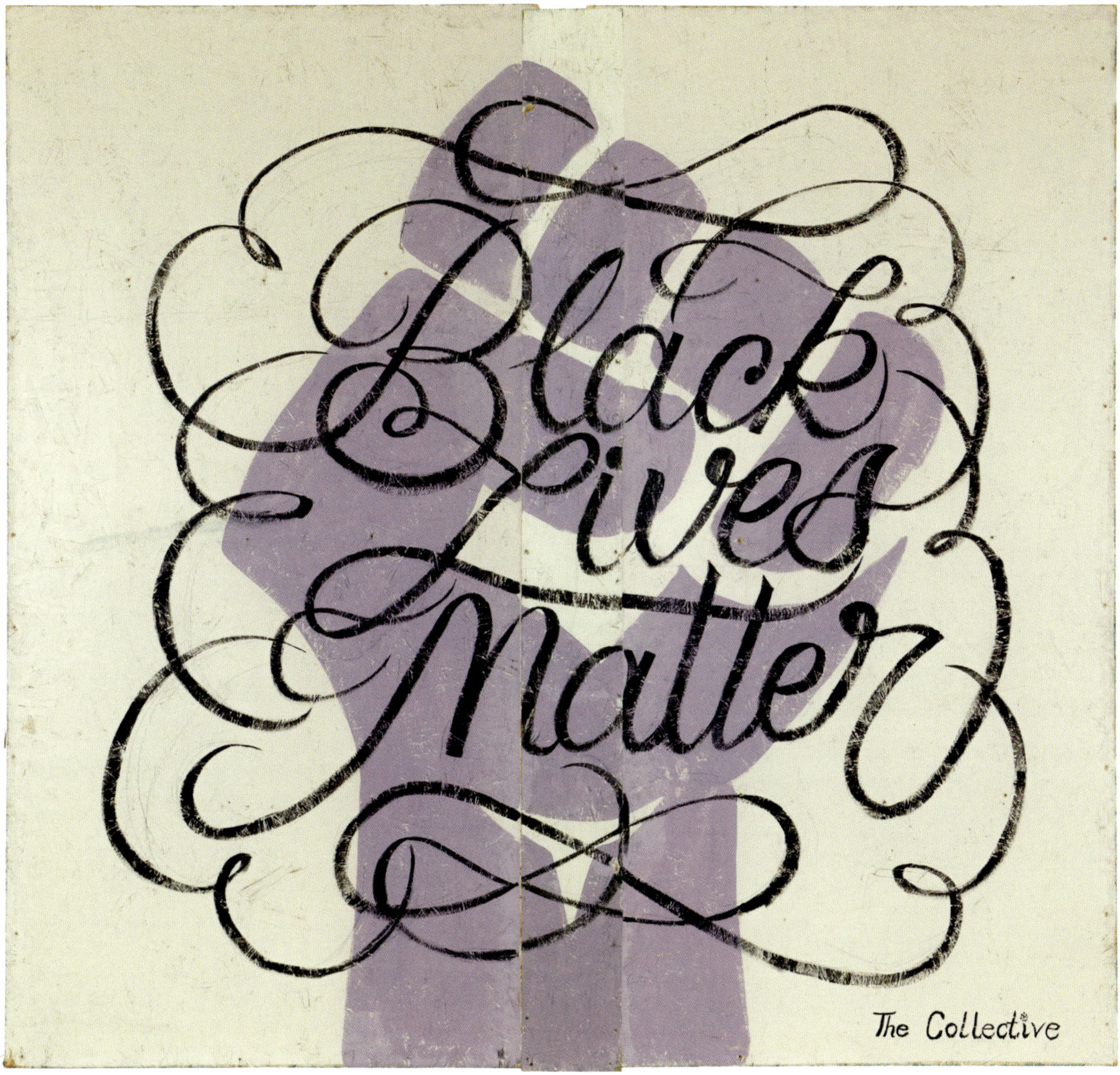

Plate 60

The Collective, *Black Lives Matter (Purple Fist)*, 2020

Denny Kemp Salon, 605 Central Ave. N.E., 96 x 100 in. approx.

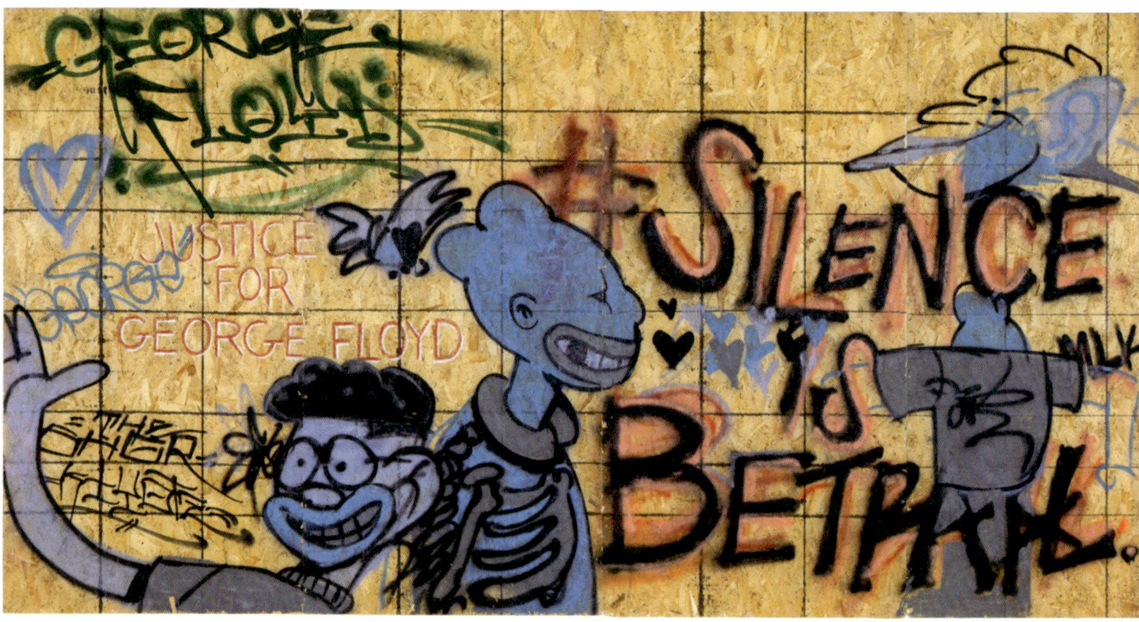

Plate 61

Papa Young Vision, *Silence is Betrayal*, 2020

Eastside Food Co-op, 2551 Central Ave. N.E., 96 x 192 in.

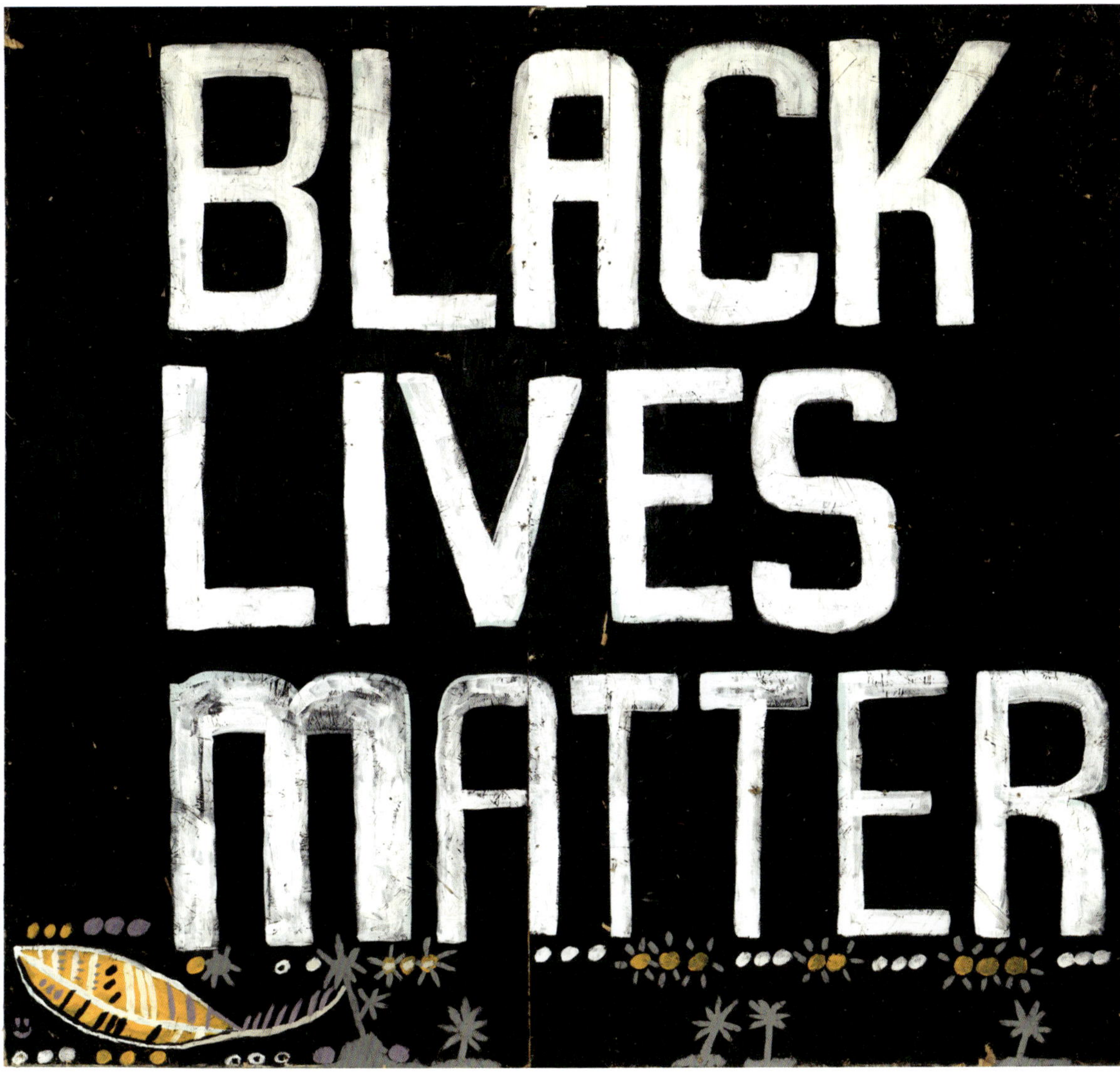

Plate 62

Artist Unidentified, *Black Lives Matter (Feather)*, 2020
Denny Kemp Salon, 605 Central Ave. N.E., 96 x 96 in. approx.

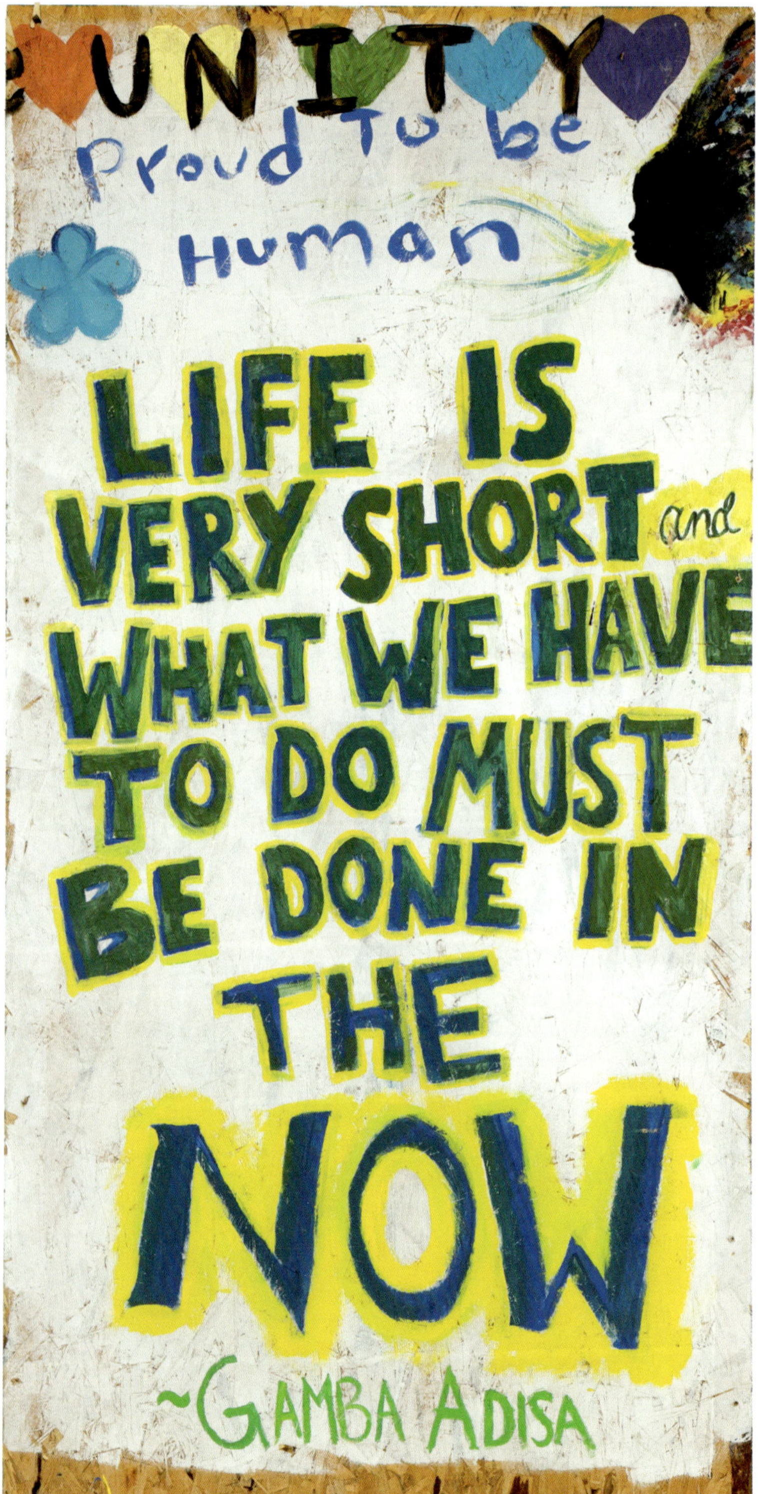

Plate 63

Artist Unidentified, *Proud to Be Human*, 2020, Eastside Food Co-op, 2551 Central Ave. N.E., 96 x 48 in.

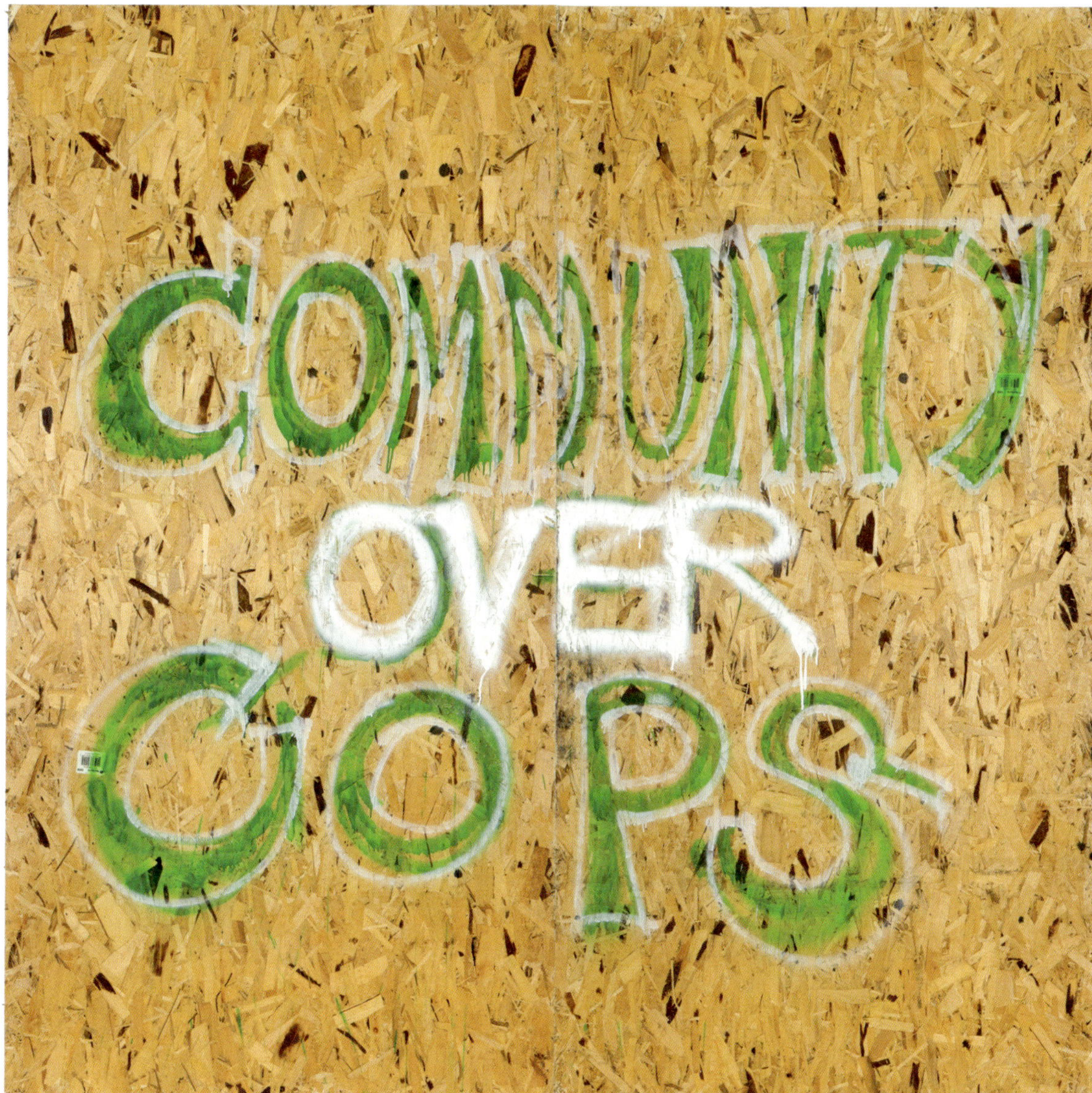

Plate 64

Artist Unidentified, *Community Over Cops*, 2020

Eastside Food Co-op, 2551 Central Ave. N.E., 96 x 96 in.

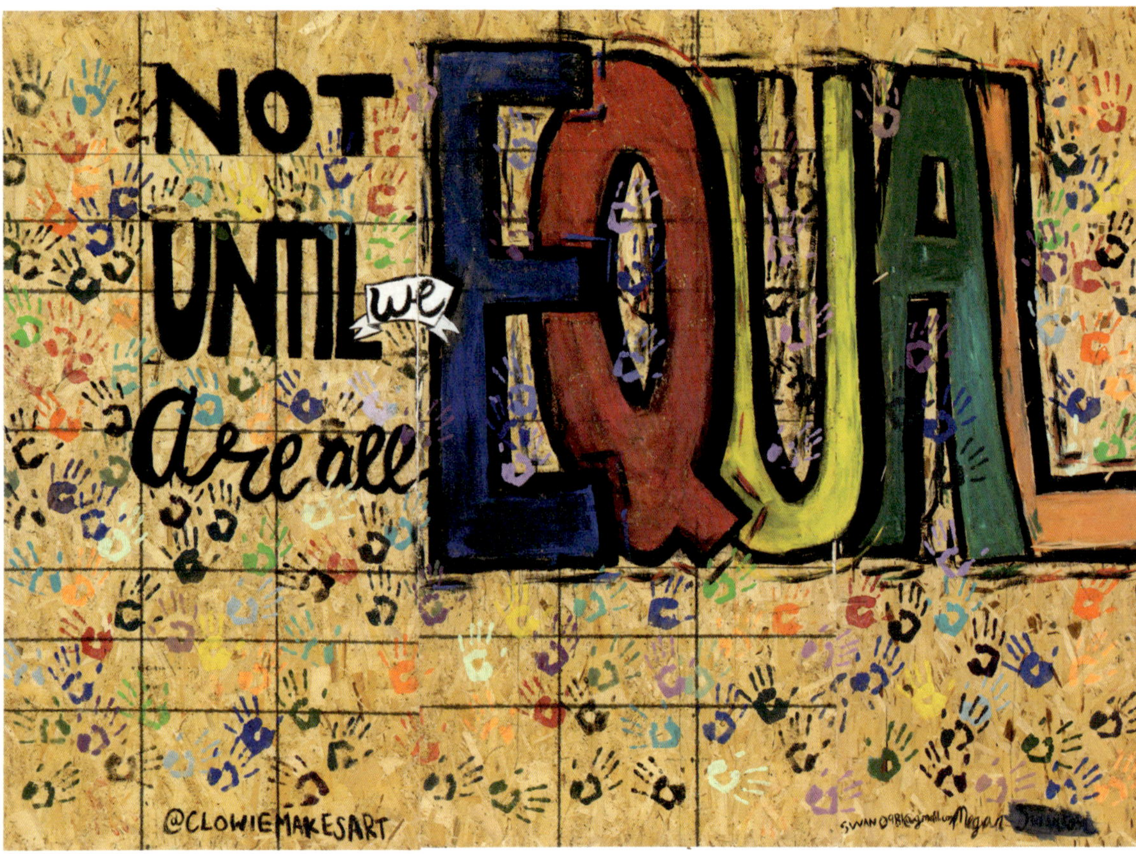

Plate 65

Clowie Makes Art, *Not Until We Are All Equal*, 2020

Eastside Food Co-op, 2551 Central Ave. N.E., 96 x 144 in. approx.

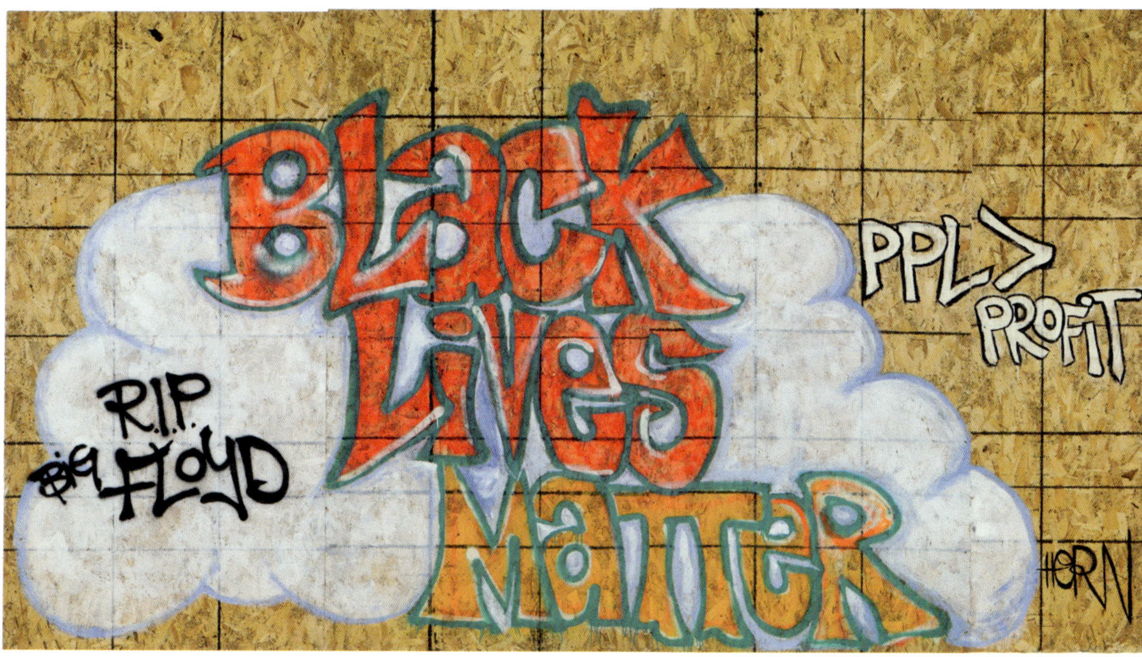

Plate 66

Horn, *Black Lives Matter, People Over Profit*, 2020

Eastside Food Co-op, 2551 Central Ave. N.E., 96 x 168 in.

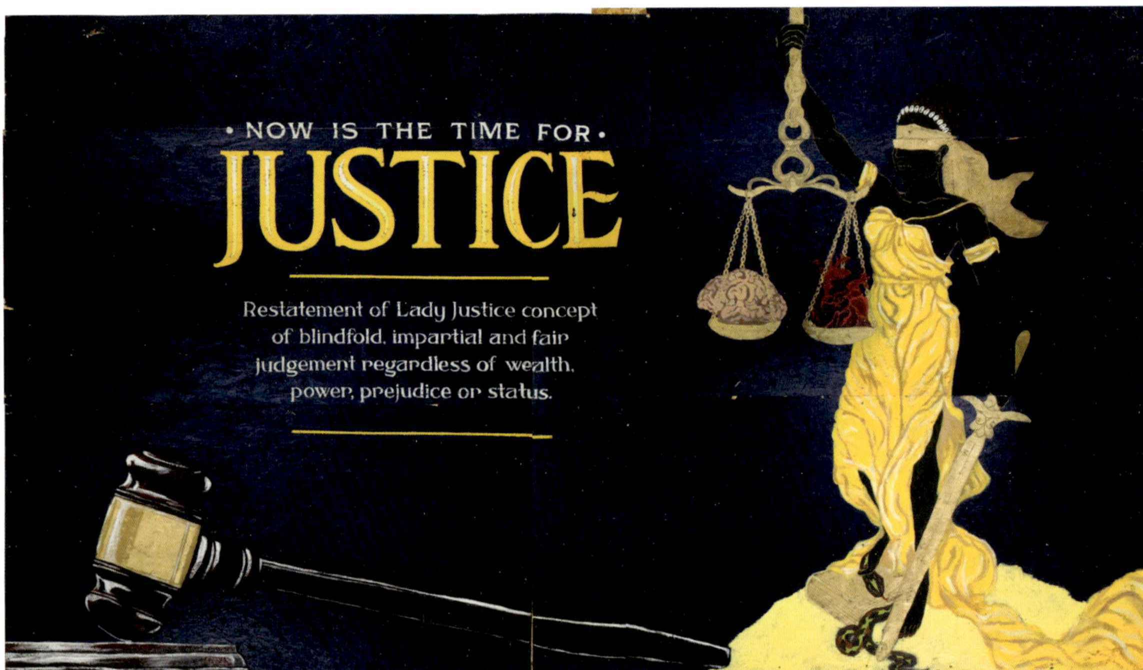

Plate 67

Artist Unidentified, *Now is the Time for Justice*, 2020

Denny Kemp Salon, 605 Central Ave. N.E., 116 x 192 in. approx.

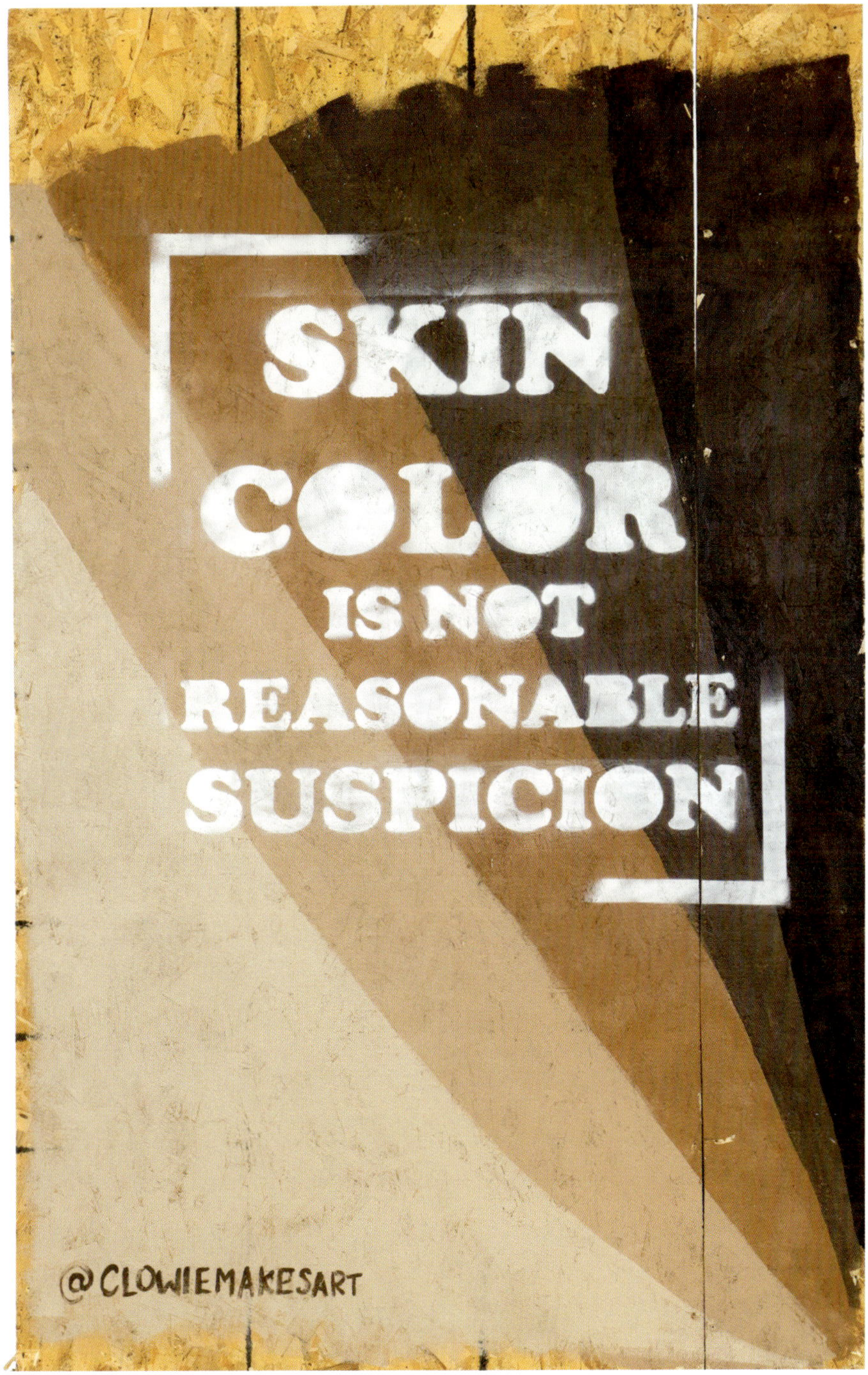

Plate 68

Clowie Makes Art, *Skin Color is Not Reasonable Suspicion*, 2020
Eastside Food Co-op, 2551 Central Ave. N.E., 96 x 56 in. approx.

ST. PAUL

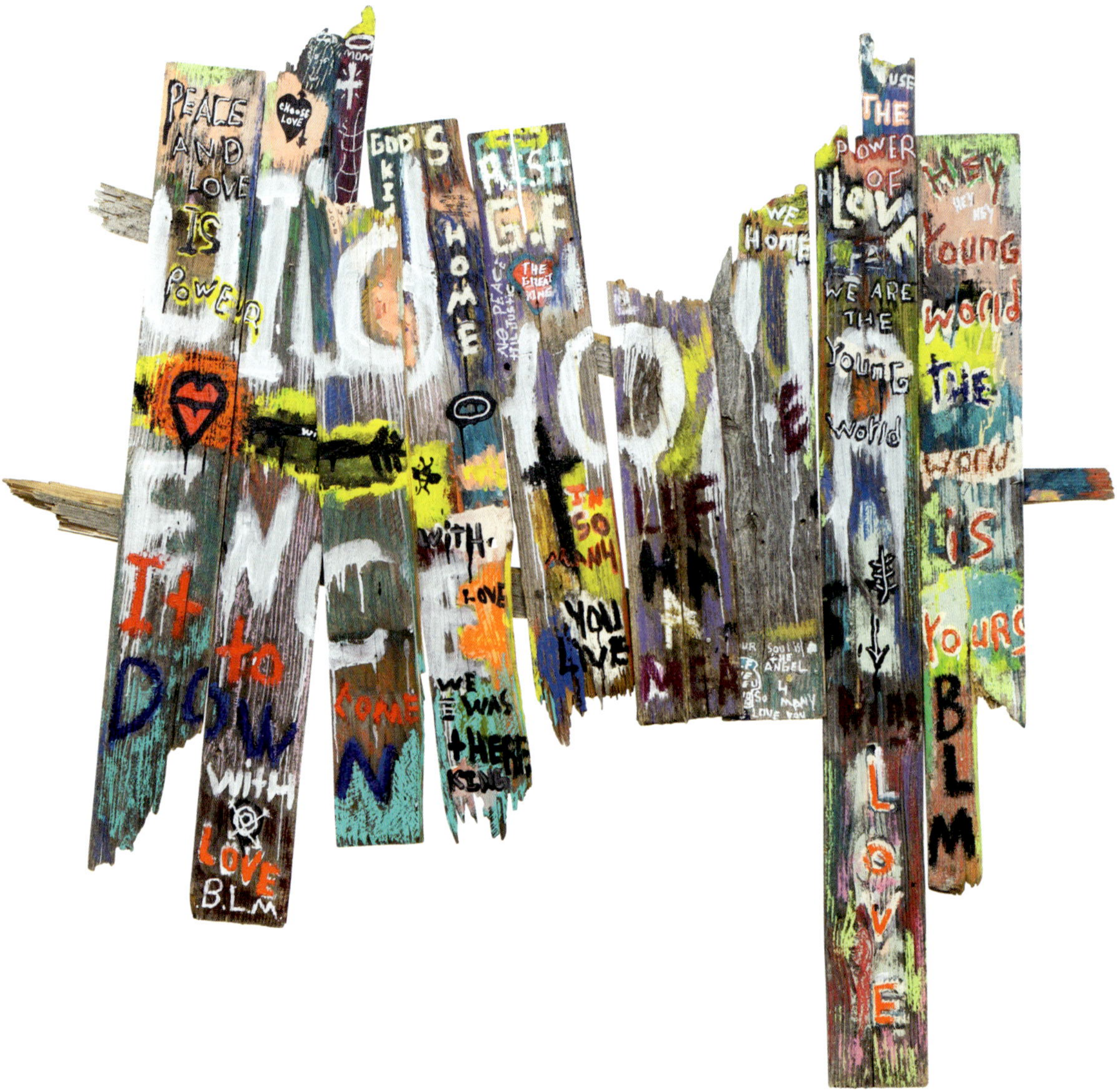

Plate 69

Artist Unidentified, *Mural on Fence*, 2020

Payne Ave., Payne-Phalen, 62 x 59 in. approx.

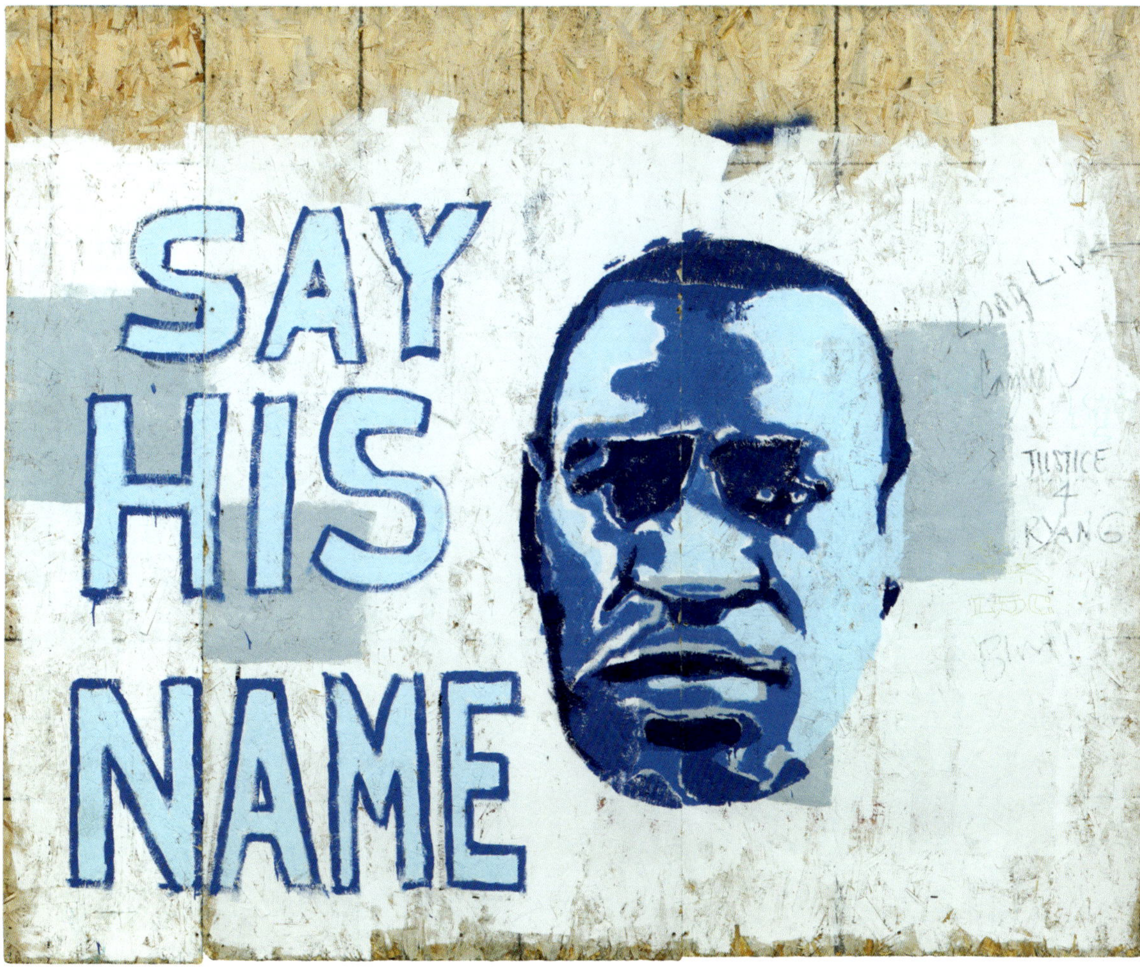

Plate 70

Seitu Jones, *Blues for George*, 2020

Springboard for the Arts, 262 University Ave. W., 96 x 116 in.

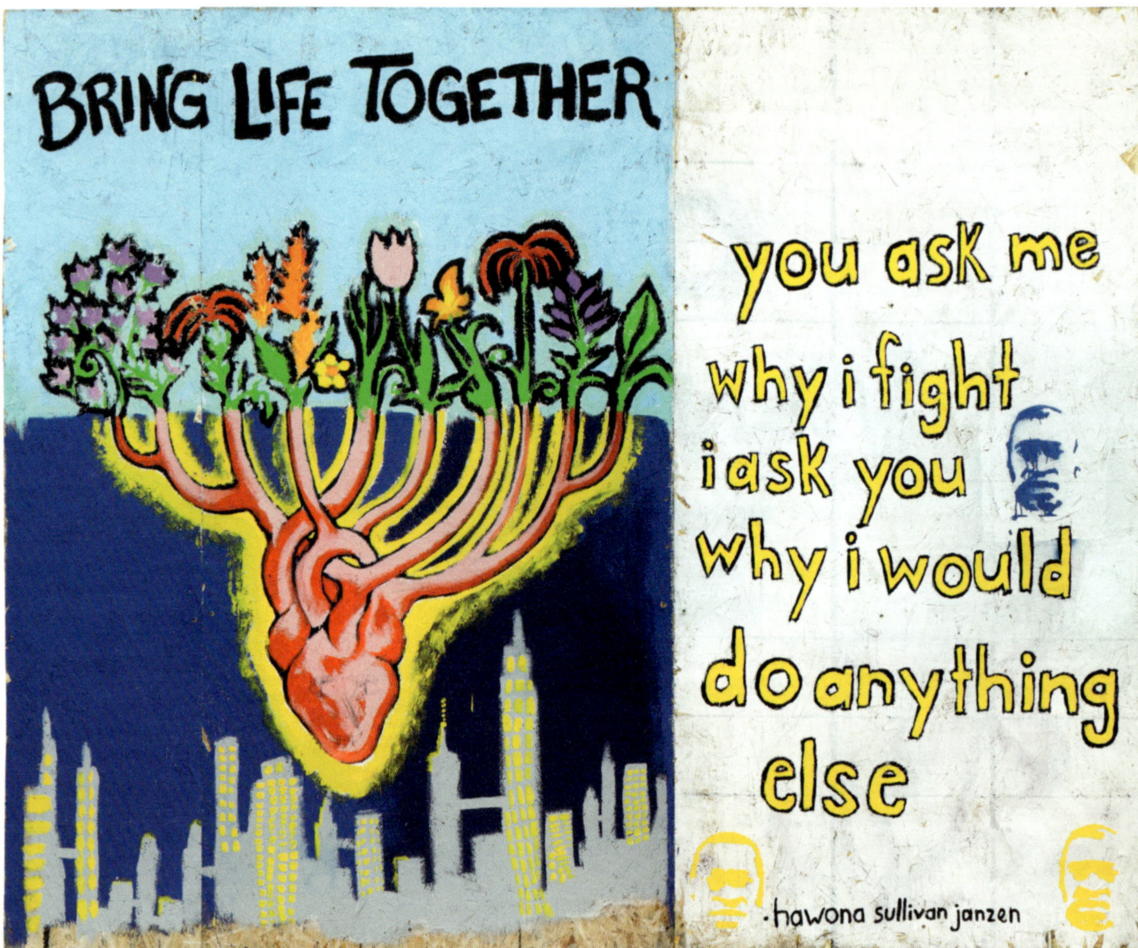

Plate 71

Community painted mural; poem by Hawona Sullivan Janzen, *Bring Life Together*, 2020
Springboard for the Arts, 262 University Ave. W., 96 x 116 in.

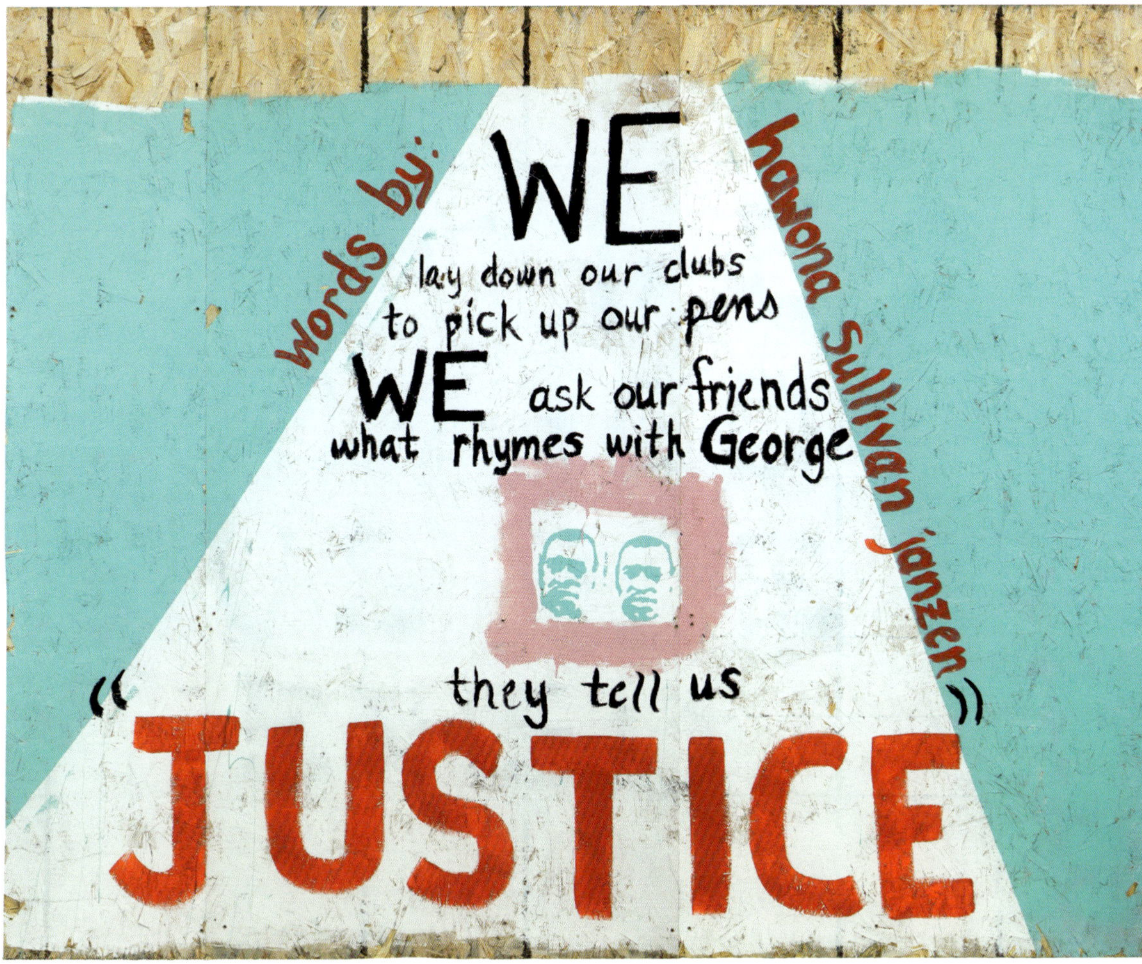

Plate 72

Community painted mural; poem by Hawona Sullivan Janzen, *We Lay Down Our Clubs to Pick Up Our Pens*, 2020
96 x 116 in. approx.

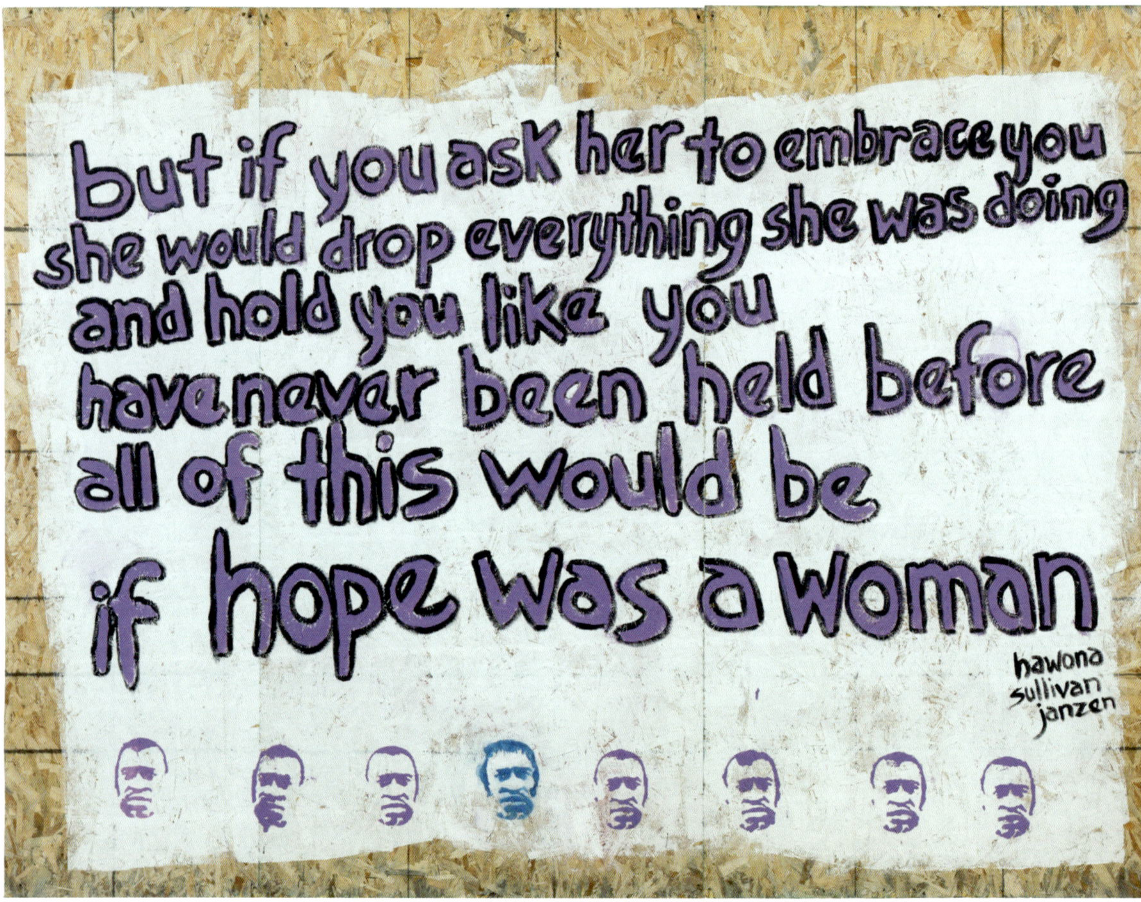

Plate 73

Community painted mural; poem by Hawona Sullivan Janzen, *But if You Ask Her to Embrace You*, 2020
Springboard for the Arts, 262 University Ave. W., 96 x 124 in.

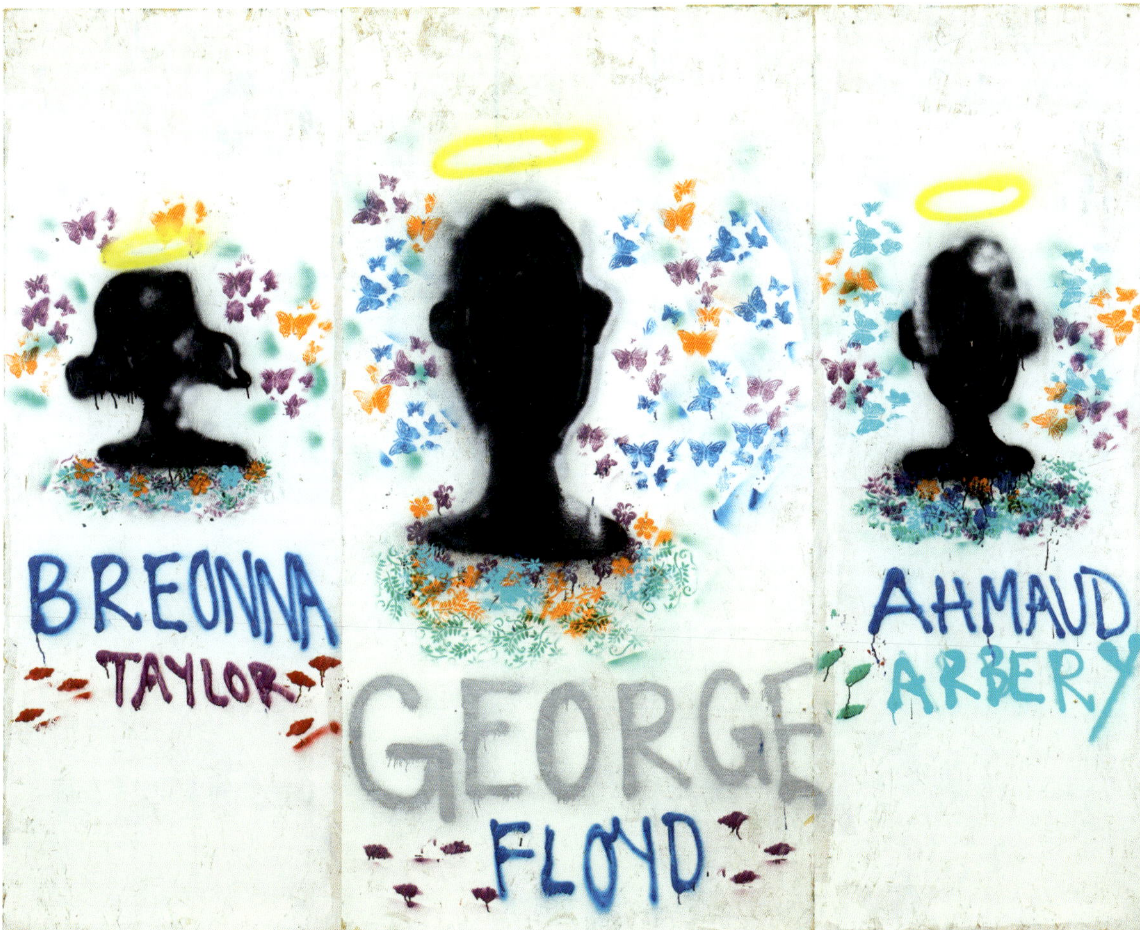

Plate 74

Artist Unidentified, *Breonna Taylor, George Floyd, Ahmaud Arbery*, 2020

Model Cities, 839 University Ave. W., 96 x 116.5 in.

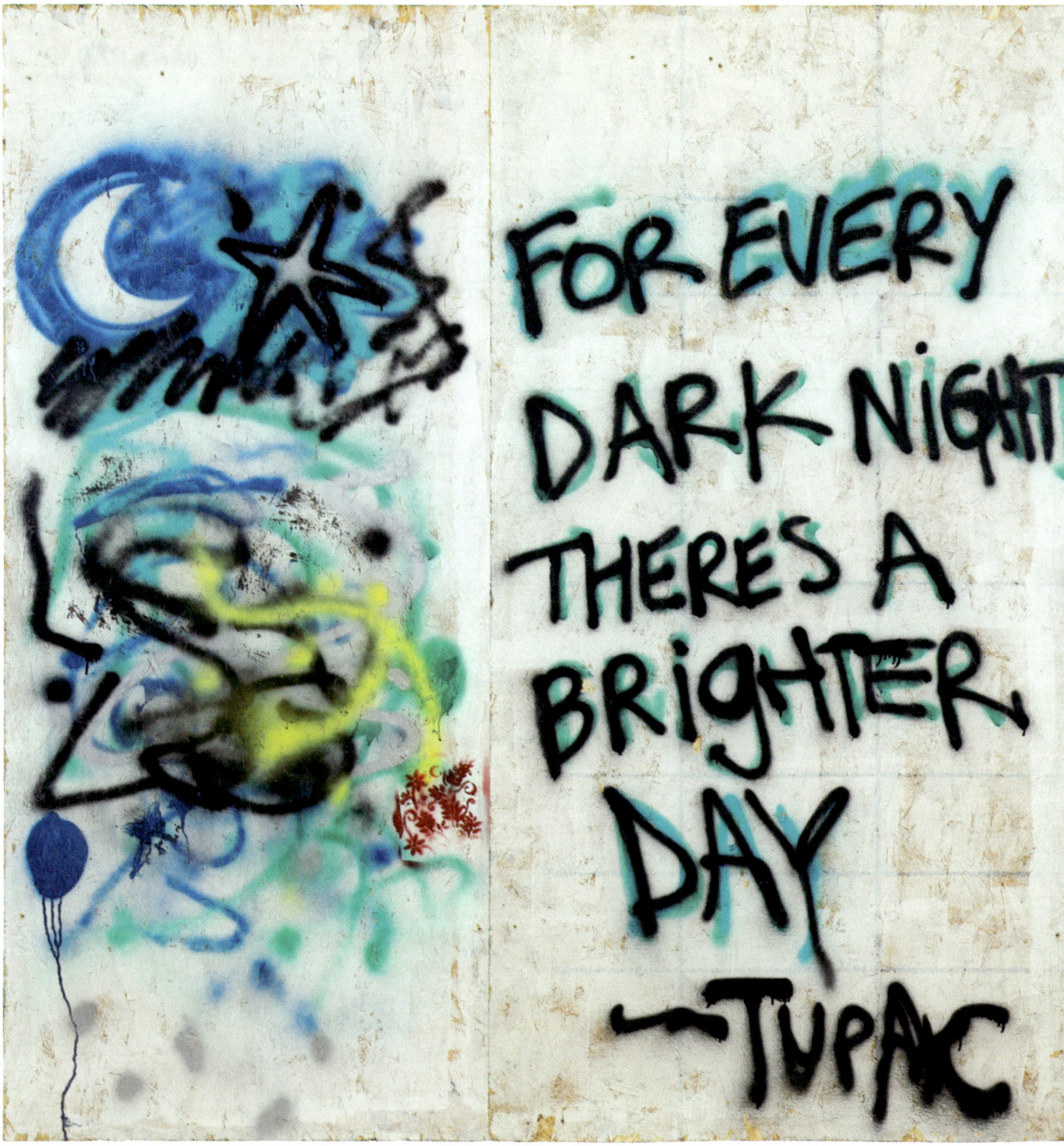

Plate 75

Artist Unidentified, *For Every Dark Night, There's a Brighter Day*, 2020
Model Cities, 839 University Ave. W., 96 x 89.5 in.

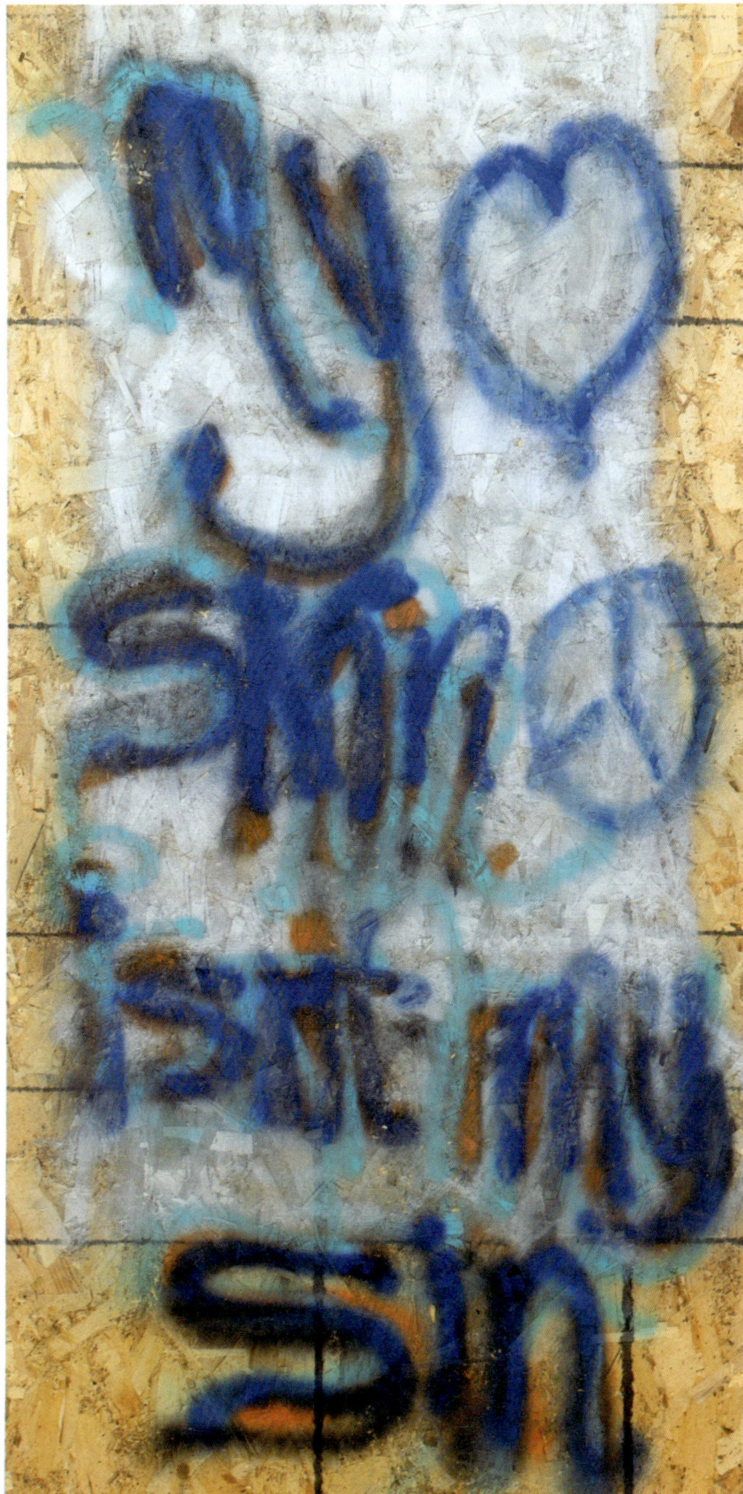

Plate 76

Artist Unidentified, *My Skin is Not My Sin*, 2020, Model Cities, 839 University Ave. W., 96 x 39 in.

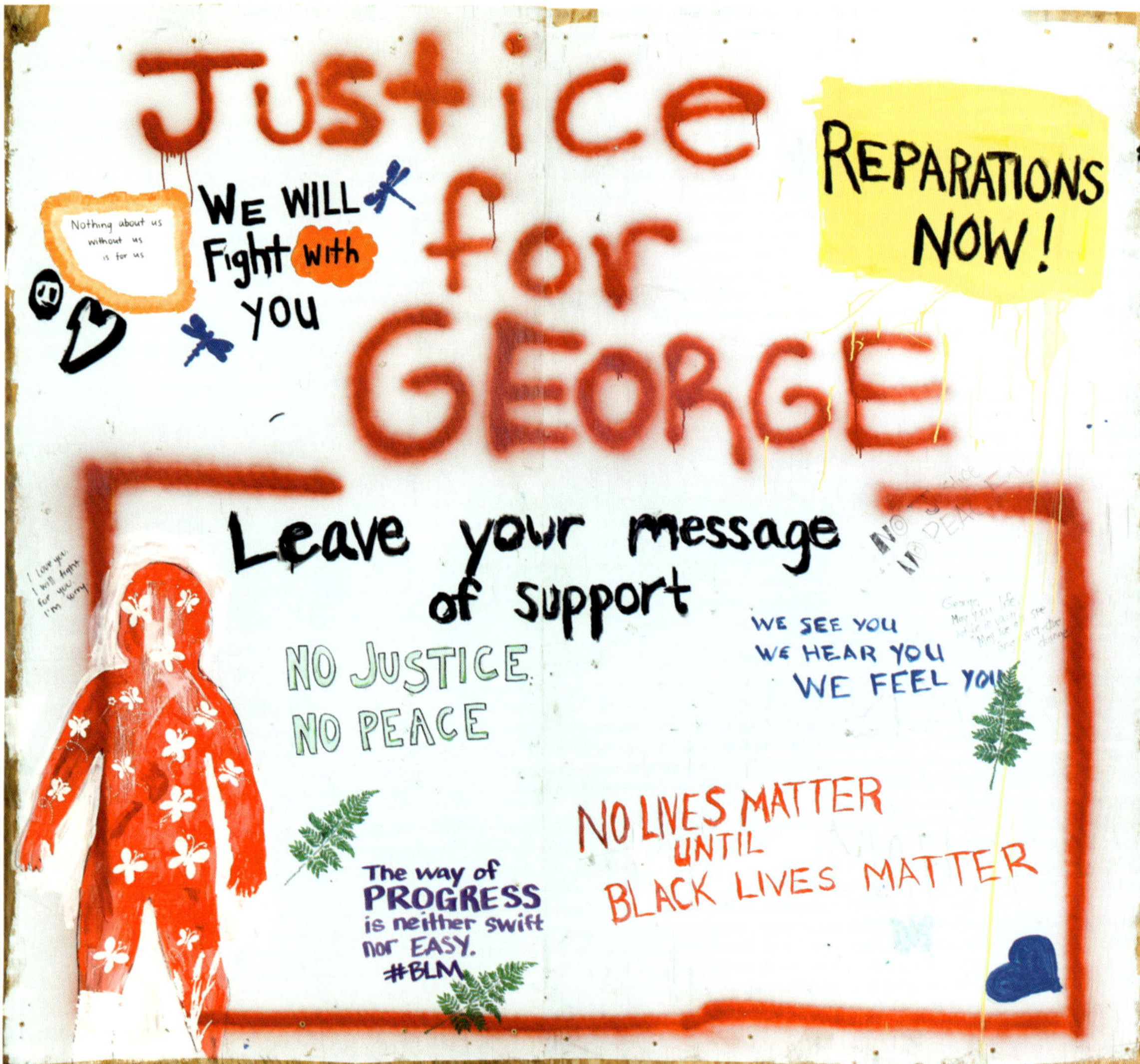

Plate 77

Community Painted Mural, *Justice for George, Leave Your Message of Support*, 2020
West St. Paul, 84 x 96 in.

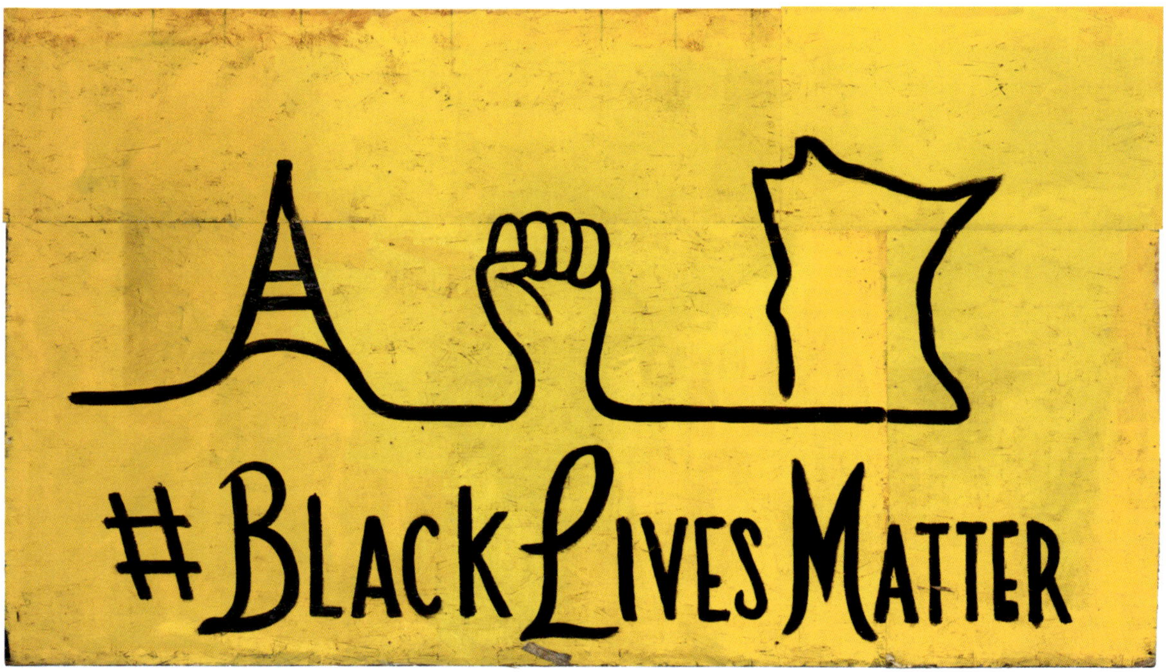

Plate 78

Ua Si Creative (formerly ArtCrop), *Minnesota Hmong Strong*, 2020
Marc Heu Patisserie, 383 University Ave., 71 x 98 in. approx.

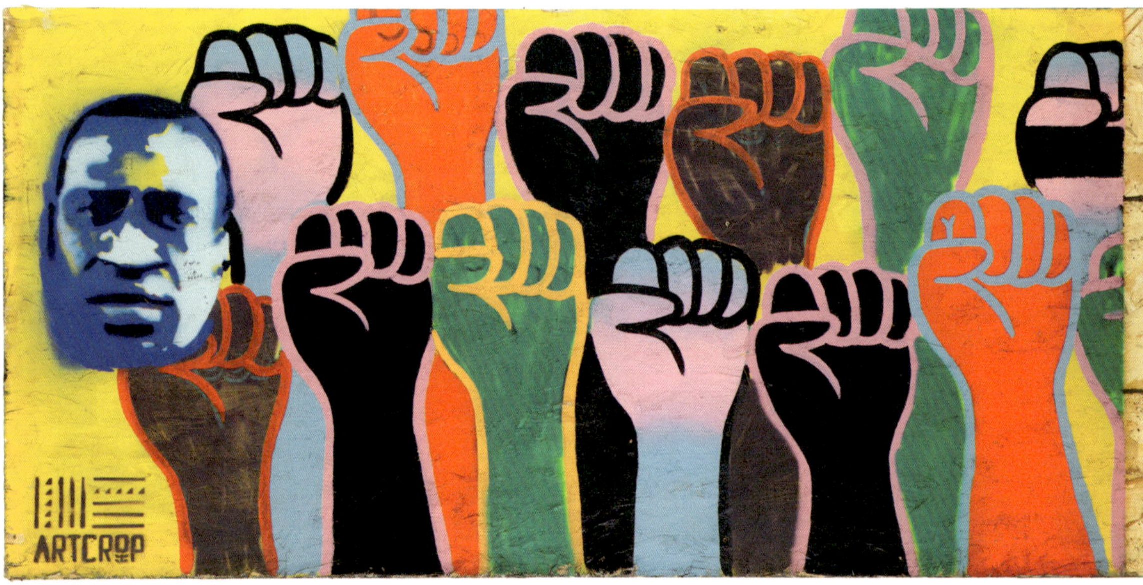

Plate 79

Ua Si Creative (formerly ArtCrop), *Many Colored Fists*, 2020

Marc Heu Patisserie, 383 University Ave., 48 x 96 in.

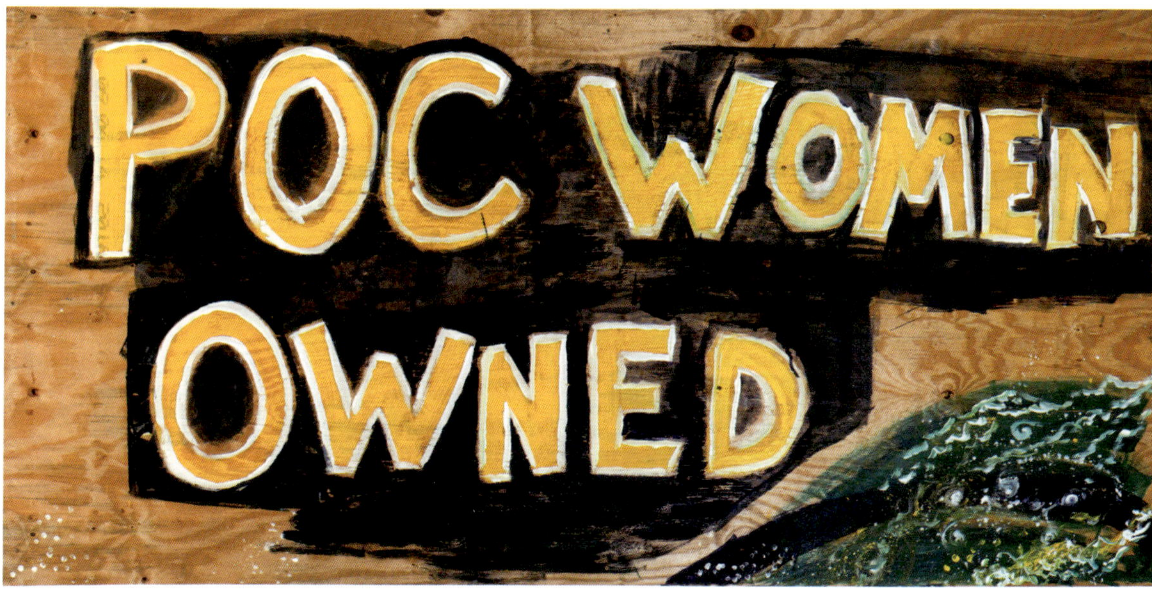

Plate 80

Ananya Dance Theatre Community, *POC Women Owned*, 2020

Ananya Dance Theatre, 1197 University Ave. W., 48 x 96 in.

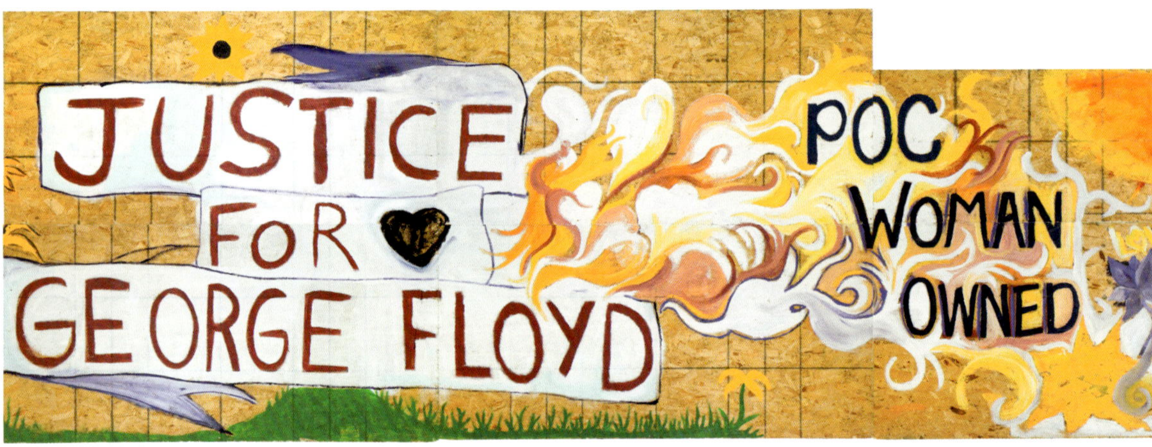

Plate 81

Ananya Dance Theatre Community, *Justice for George Floyd, POC Woman Owned*, 2020
Ananya Dance Theatre, 1197 University Ave. W., 96 x 258 in. approx.

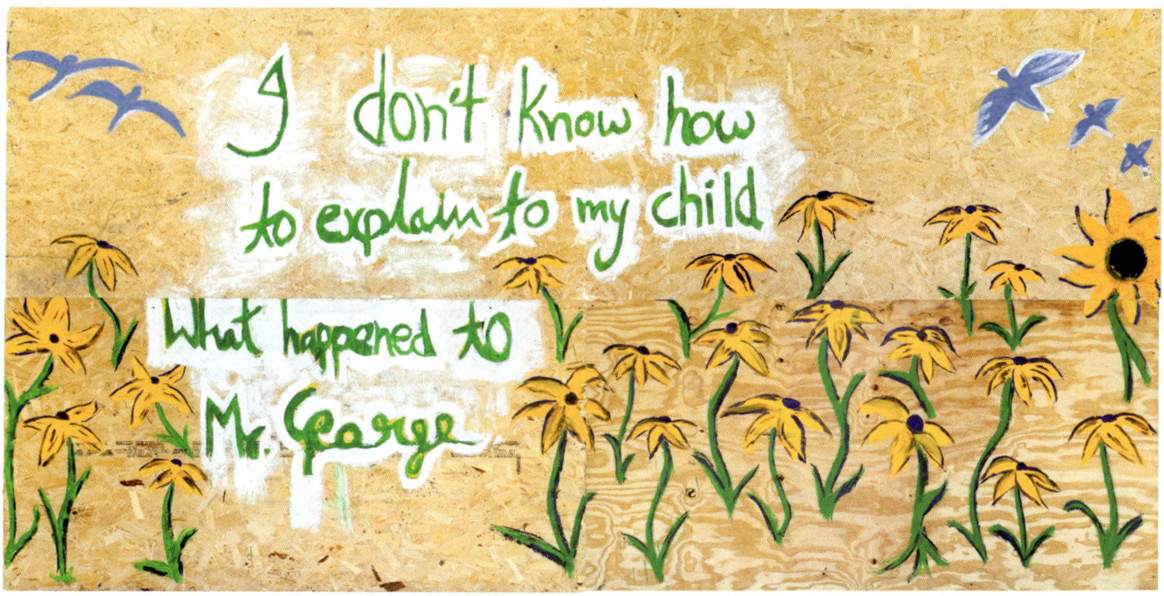

Plate 82

Ananya Dance Theatre Community, *I Don't Know How to Explain to My Child*, 2020
Ananya Dance Theatre, 1197 University Ave. W., 96 x 192 in.

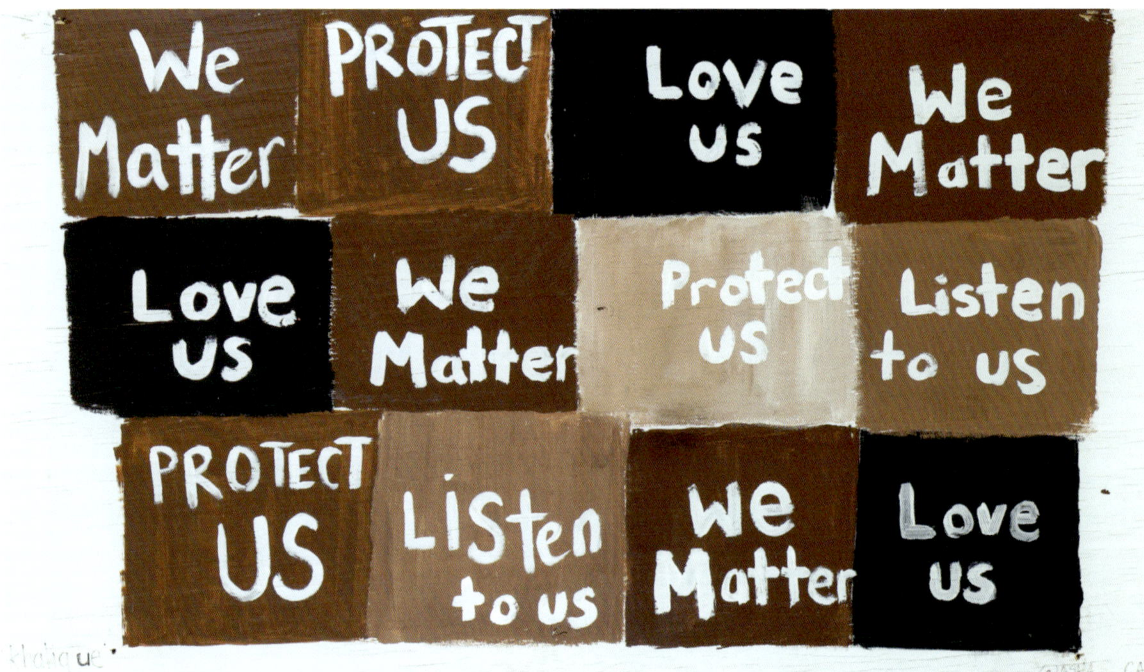

Plate 83

Khalique Rogers, Asha Cadeey, *We Matter, Protect Us, Love Us*, 2020

Gordon Parks High School, 1212 University Ave. W., 48 x 96 in.

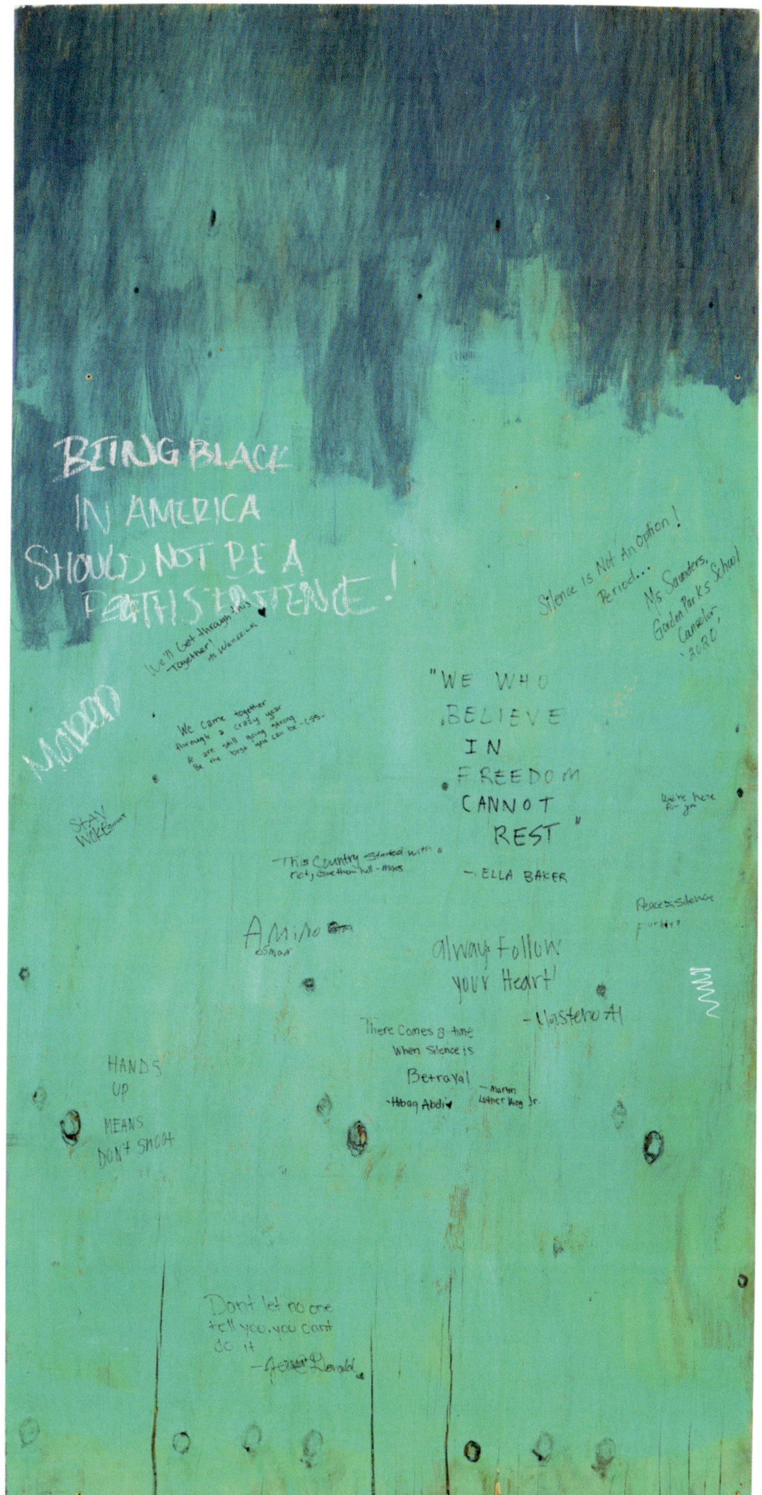

Plate 84
Gordon Parks School Students, Staff, Faculty, *Messages from Gordon Parks High School*, 2020, Gordon Parks High School, 1212 University Ave. W., 96 x 48 in.

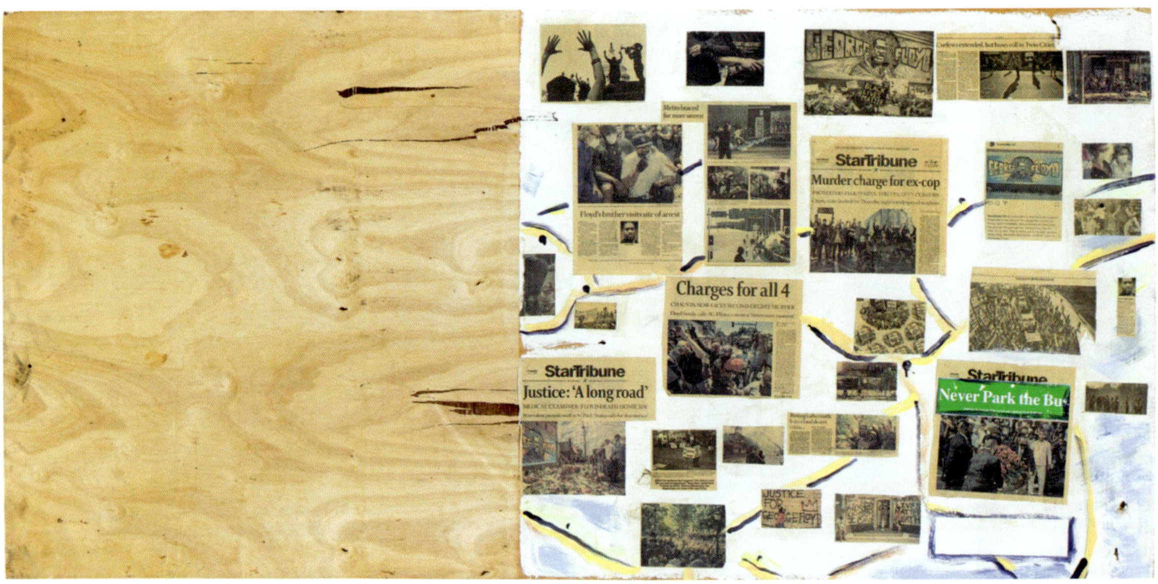

Plate 85

Gordon Parks School Students, Staff, Faculty, *Newspaper*, 2020
Gordon Parks High School, 1212 University Ave. W., 48 x 96 in.

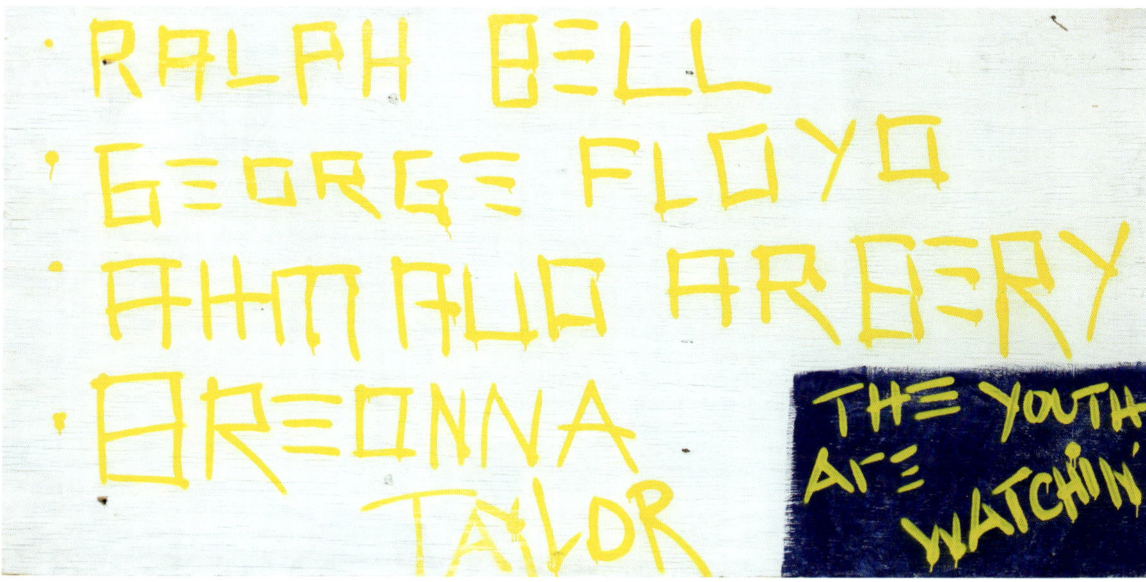

Plate 86

Gordon Parks School Students, Staff, Faculty, *The Youth are Watching*, 2020

Gordon Parks High School, 1212 University Ave. W., 48 x 96 in.

Plate 87

Gordon Parks High School Students, Staff, Faculty, *Take Your Knee Off Our Neck*, 2020
Gordon Parks High School, 1212 University Ave. W., 48 x 96 in.

BODY SHIELDS

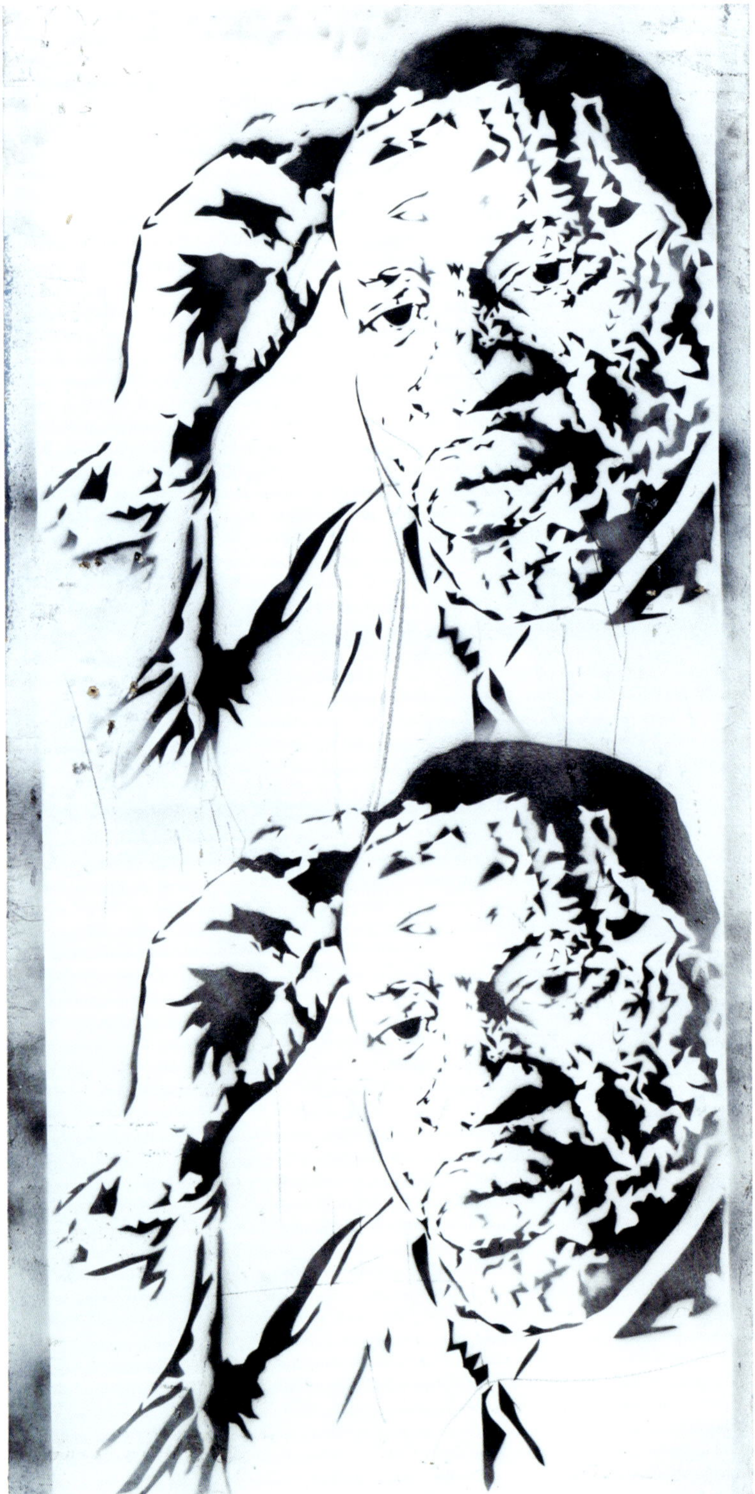

Plate 88
Artist Unidentified, *Body Shield (front)*, 2020, Made during protest to protect protestors from police brutality, 48 x 24 in.

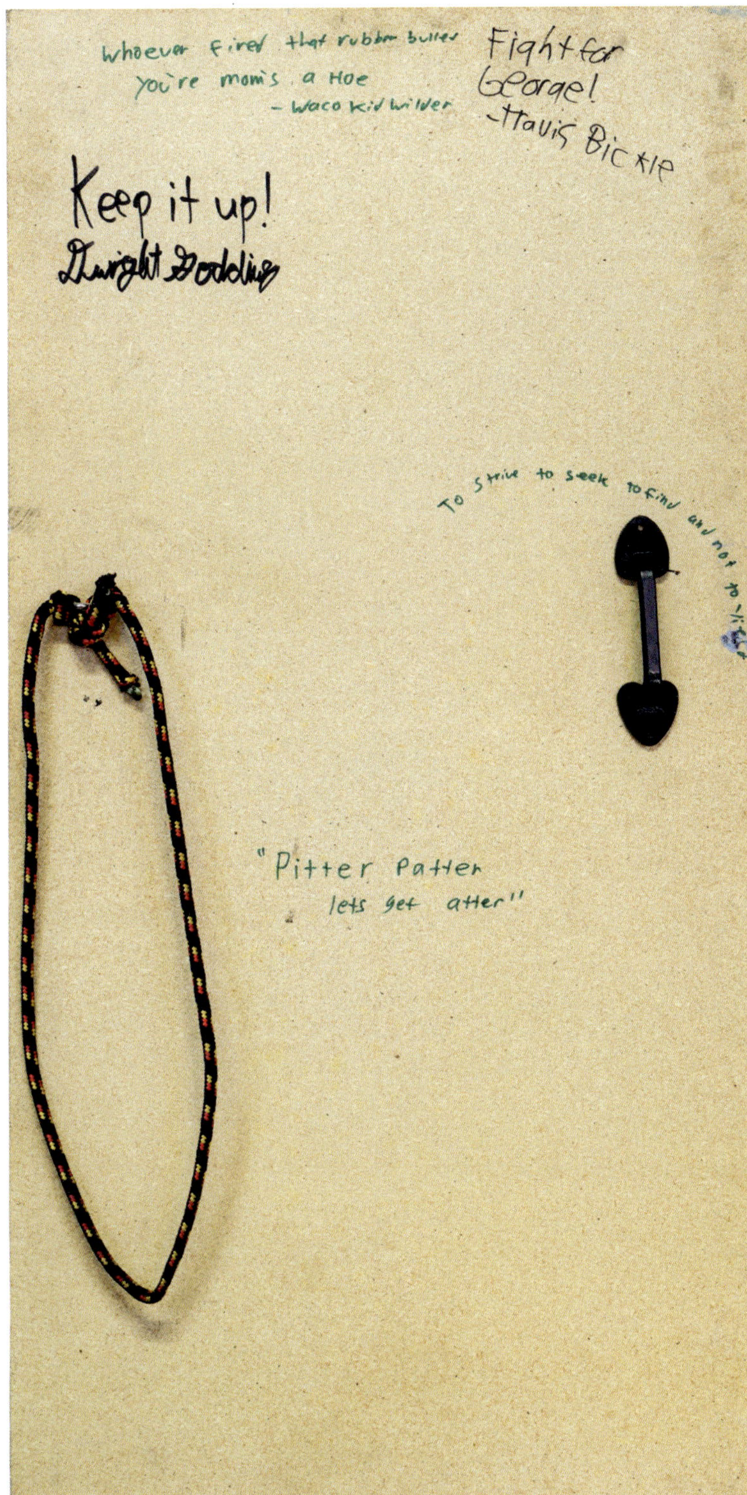

Plate 89

Artist Unidentified, *Body Shield (back)*, 2020, Made during protest to protect protestors from police brutality, 48 x 24 in.

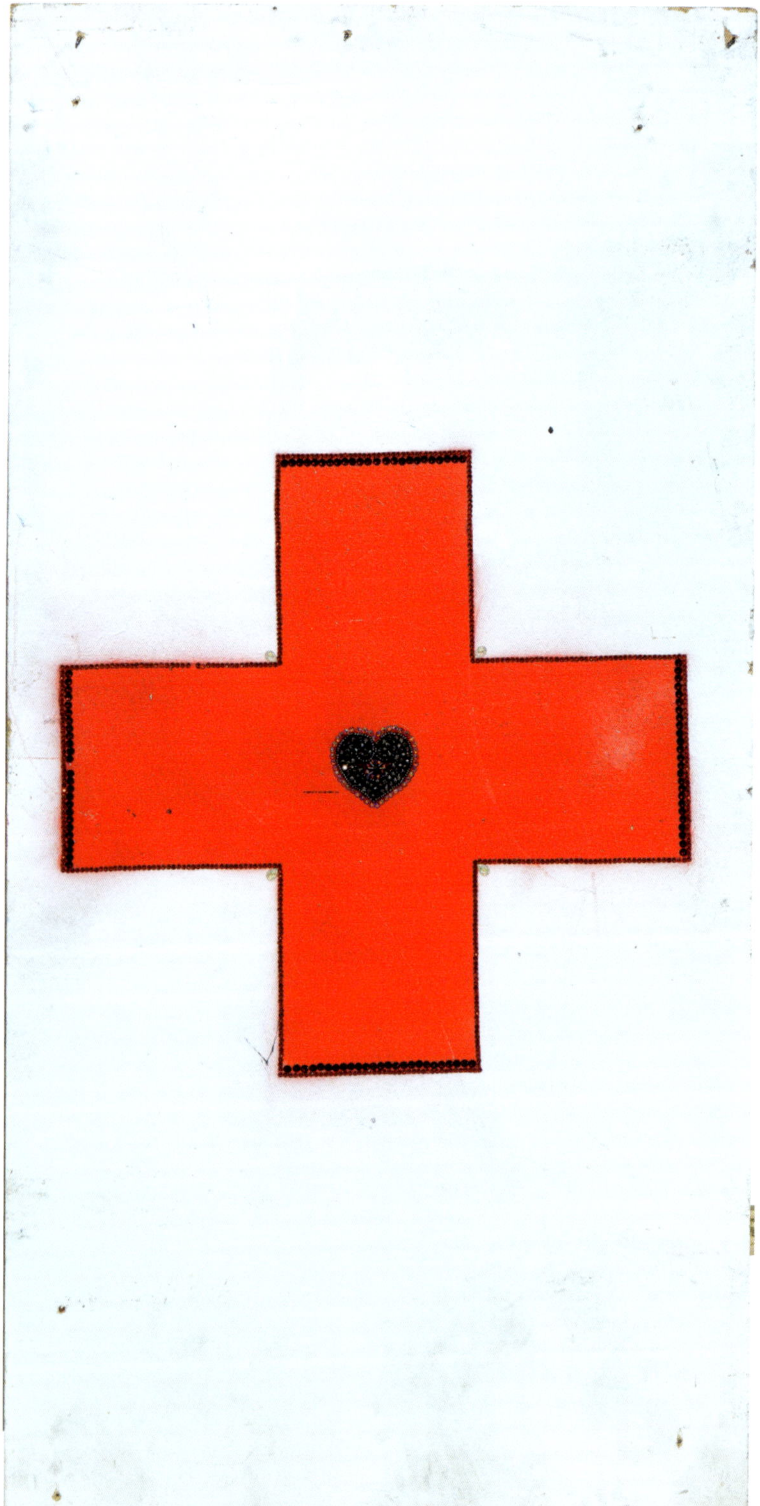

Plate 90
Artist Unidentified, *Body Shield*, 2020, Made during protest to protect protestors from police brutality, 48 x 24 in.

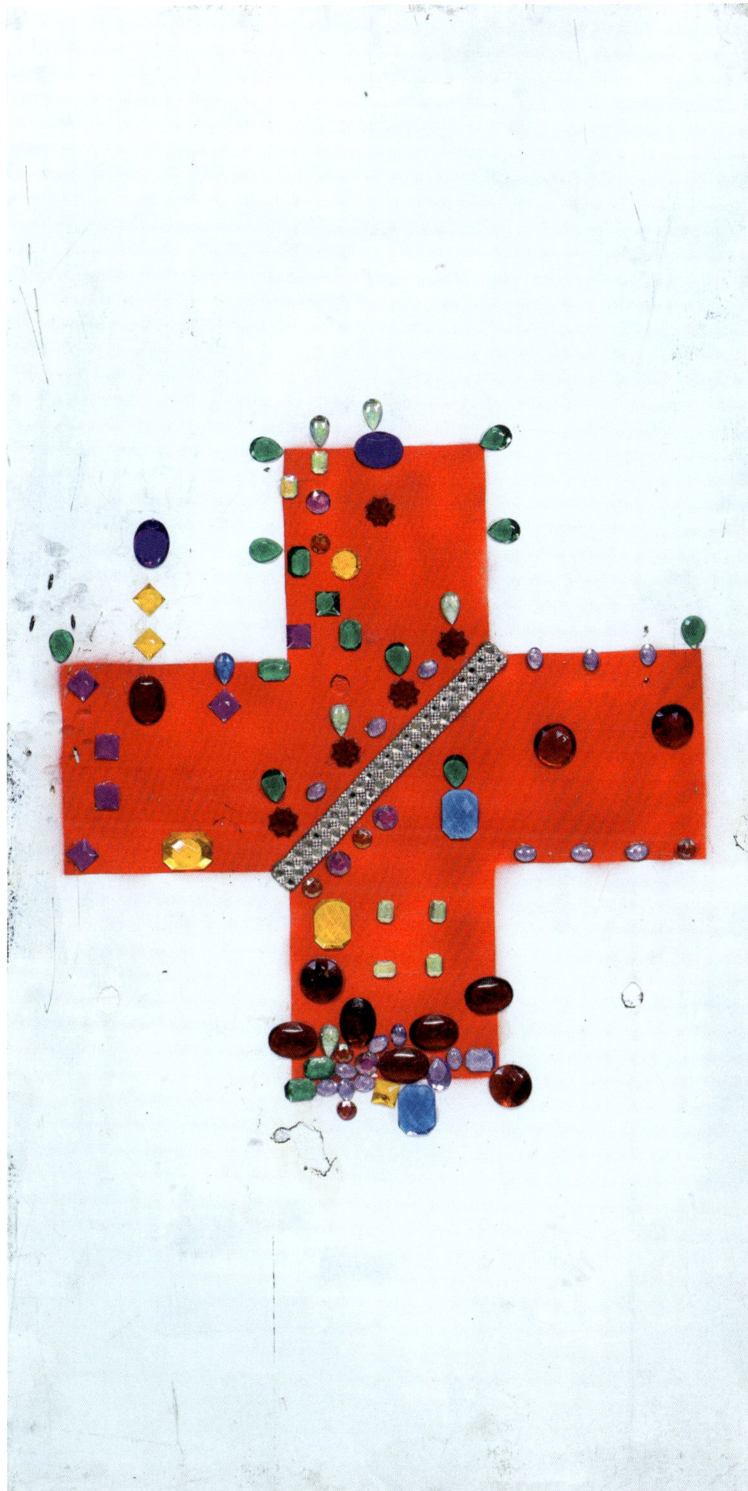

Plate 91
Artist Unidentified,
Body Shield, 2020, Made during protest to protect protestors from police brutality, 48 x 24 in.

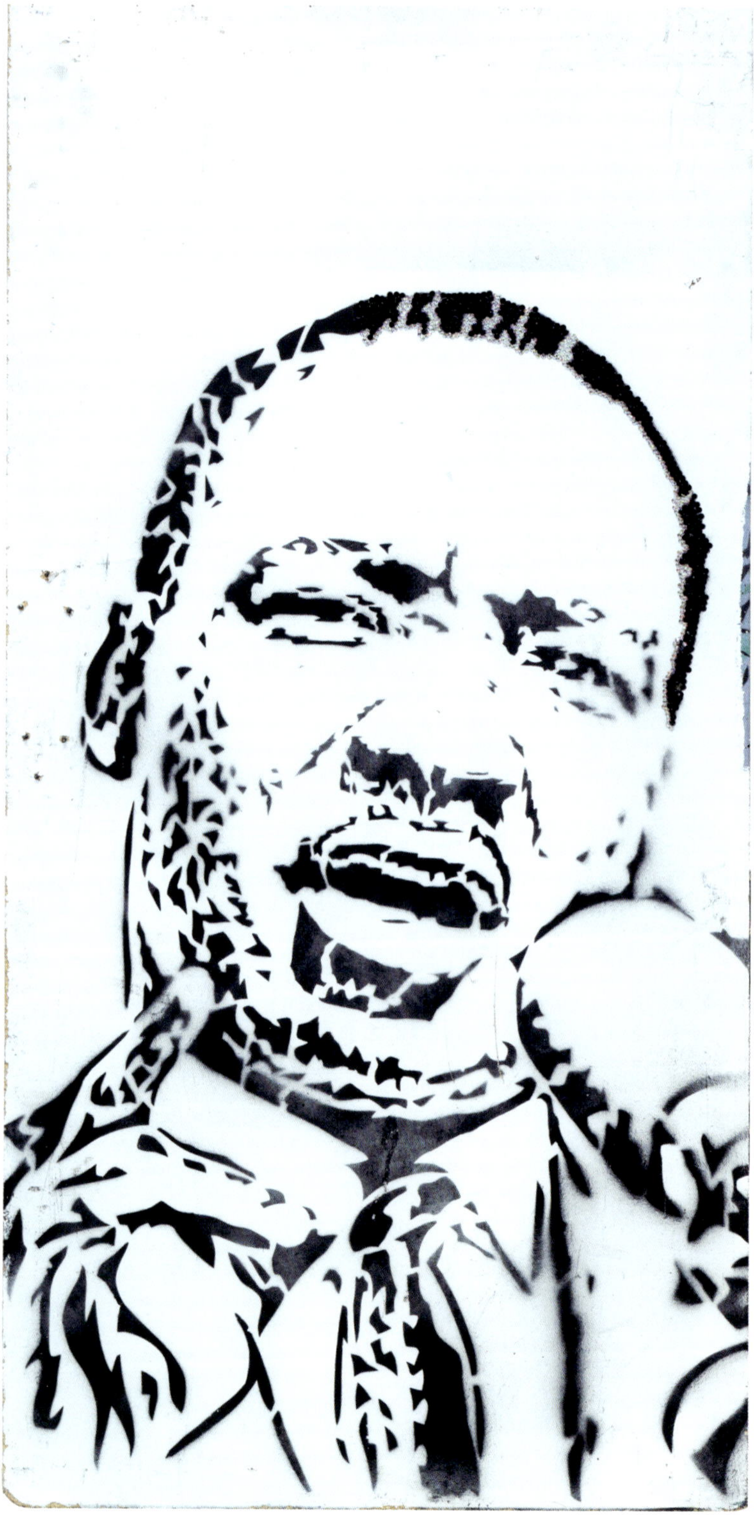

Plate 92
Artist Unidentified, *Body Shield*, 2020, Made during protest to protect protestors from police brutality, 48 x 24 in.

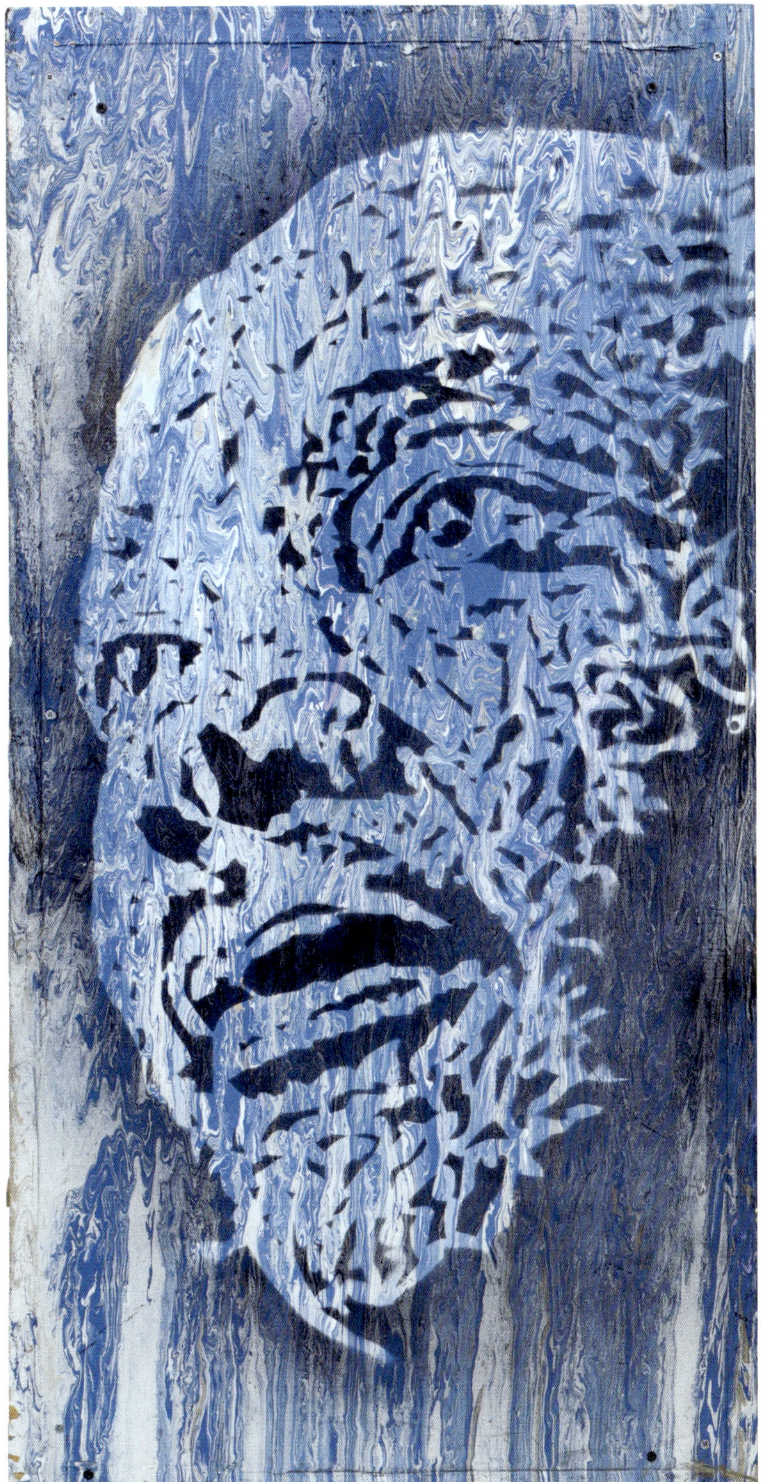

Plate 93
Artist Unidentified, *Body Shield*, 2020, Made during protest to protect protestors from police brutality, 48 x 24 in.

JUSTICE FOR GEORGE

Justice for George is an annual event hosted by Memorialize the Movement to commemorate the murder of George Floyd by Minneapolis police officers on May 25th, 2020. Justice for George themes change each year, but the key elements remain the same: a large-scale exhibition of the murals in their stewardship, live mural paintings, and a vendor fair highlighting small businesses and makers in their community. This event provides an opportunity for visitors to experience the stories being told through the murals. The murals in this section were created at Justice for George 2021, 2022, 2023, and 2024. Each mural was created by a local Black, Brown, or Indigenous artist with varying experience levels. The final mural in this section was commissioned by local artists to commemorate the first Justice for George event in Memorialize the Movement's new home.

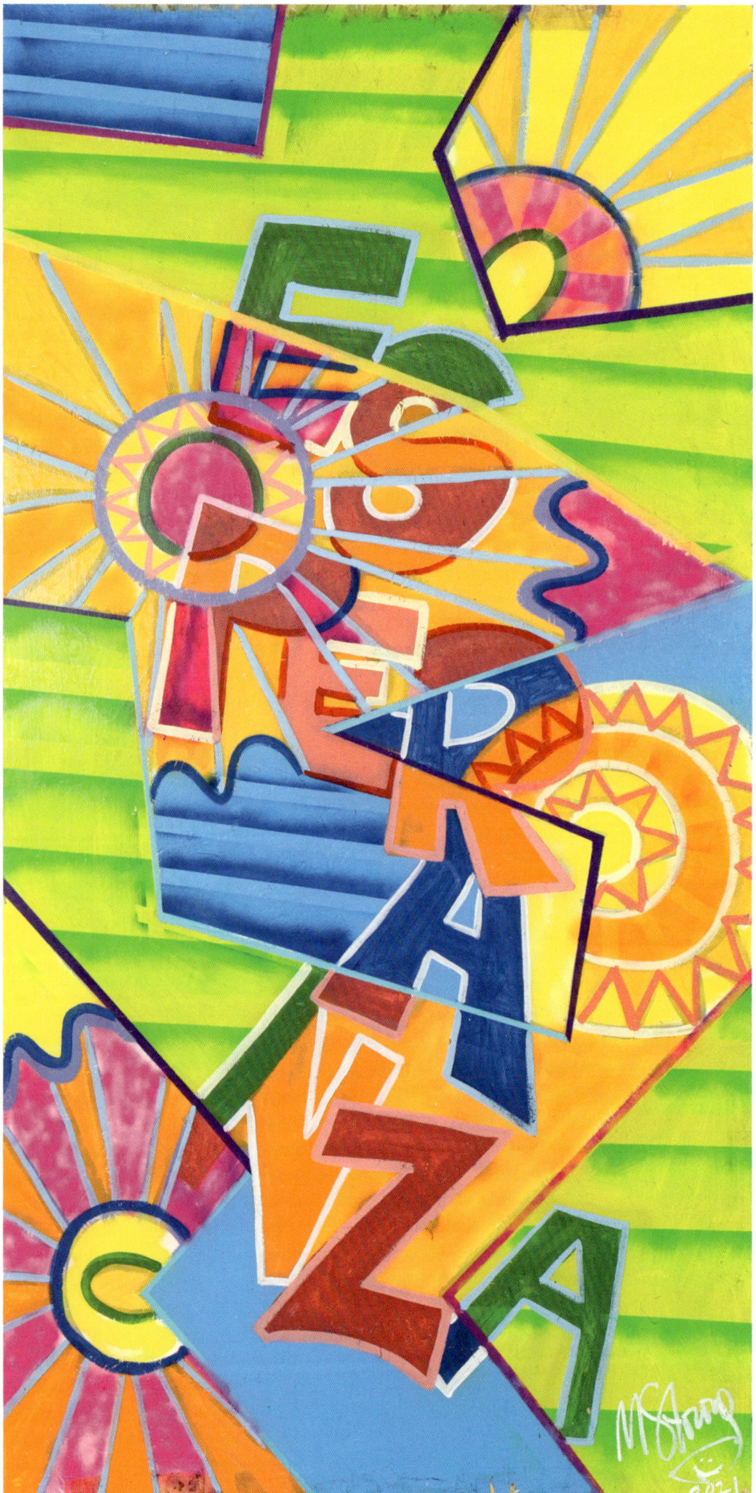

Plate 94
Melodee Strong, *Esperanza*, 2021, Justice for George: Messages from the People, 96 x 48 in.

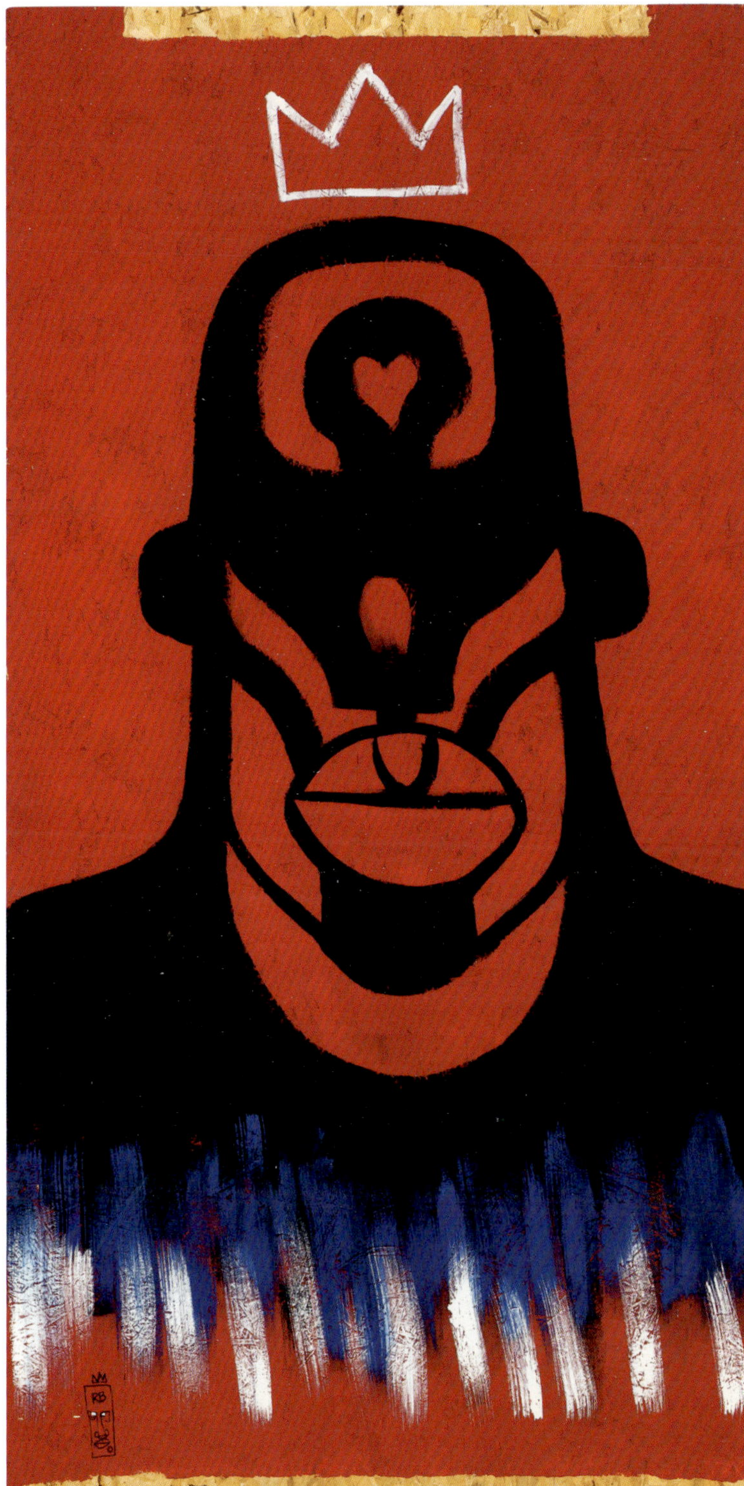

Plate 95

Ron Brown, *Red Portrait of George*, 2021, Justice for George: Messages from the People, 96 x 48 in.

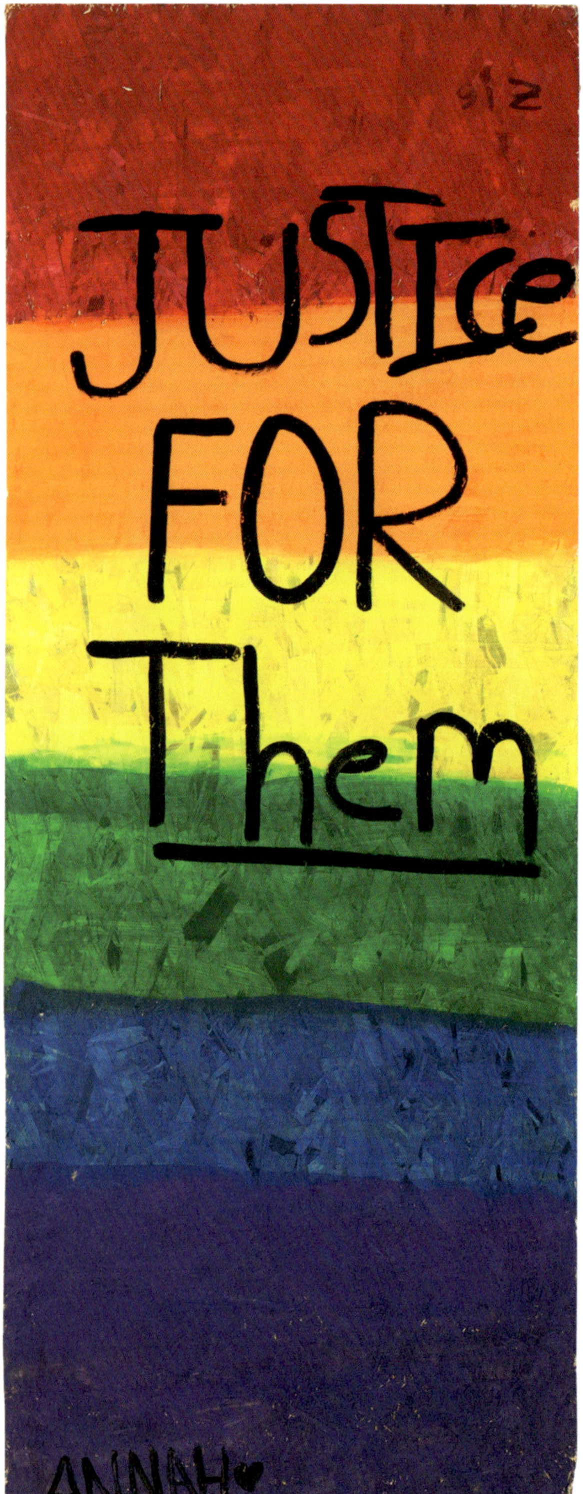

Plate 96

Girl Scouts Connectz, *Justice for Them*, 2022, Justice for George: Our Strength, Our Story, 96 x 36 in.

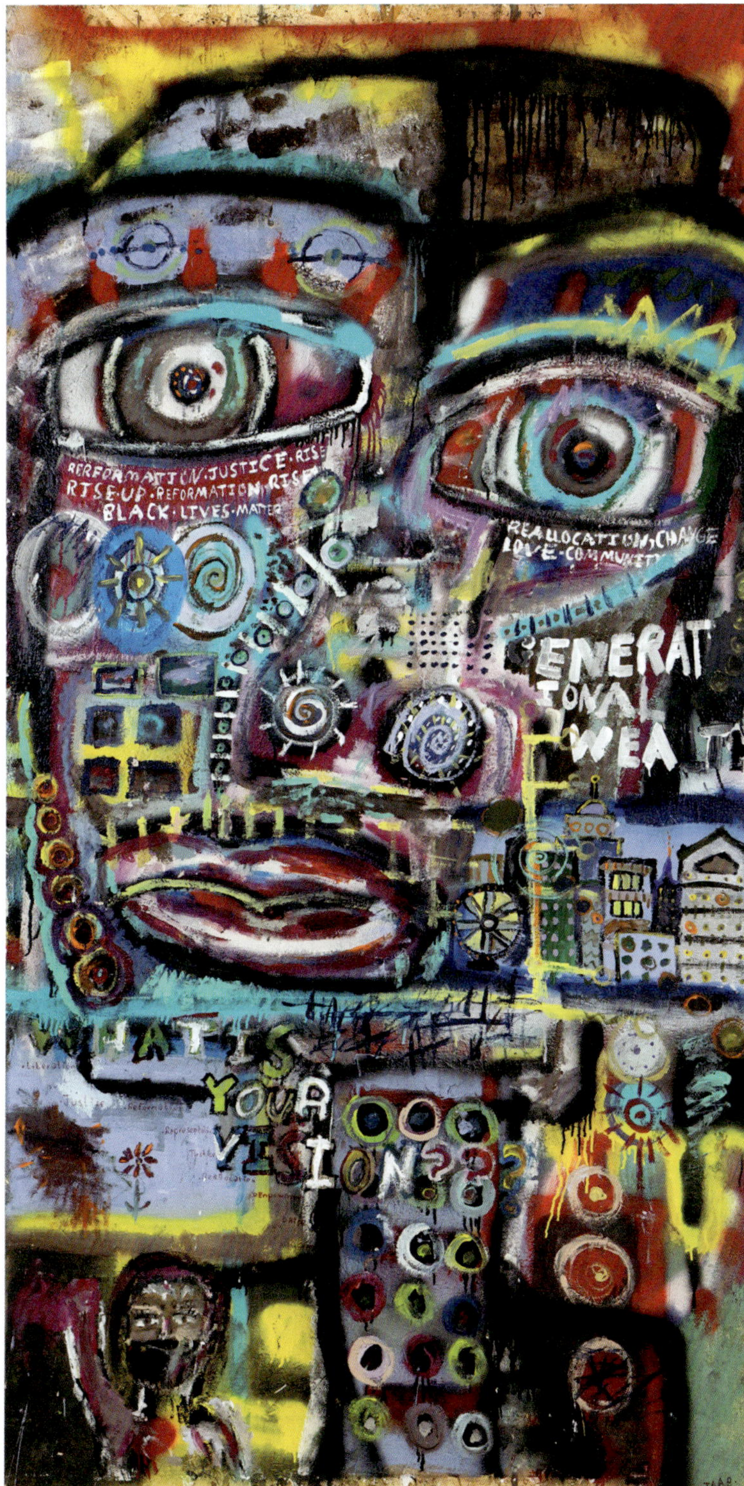

Plate 97
Theo Simmons, *Visionary*, 2022, Justice for George: Our Strength, Our Story, 96 x 48 in.

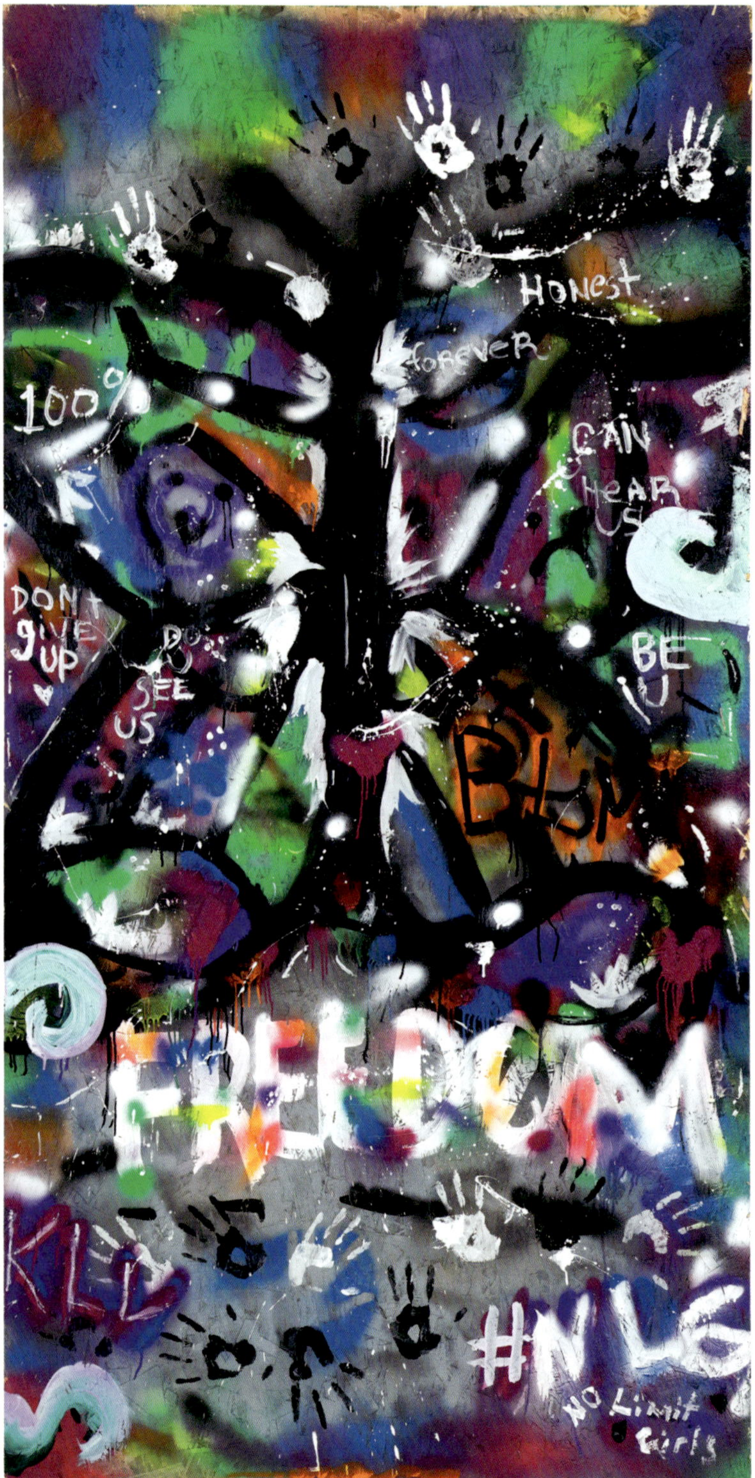

Plate 98

Kamille Vaughn, *Freedom Butterfly*, 2022, Justice for George: Our Strength, Our Story, 96 x 48 in.

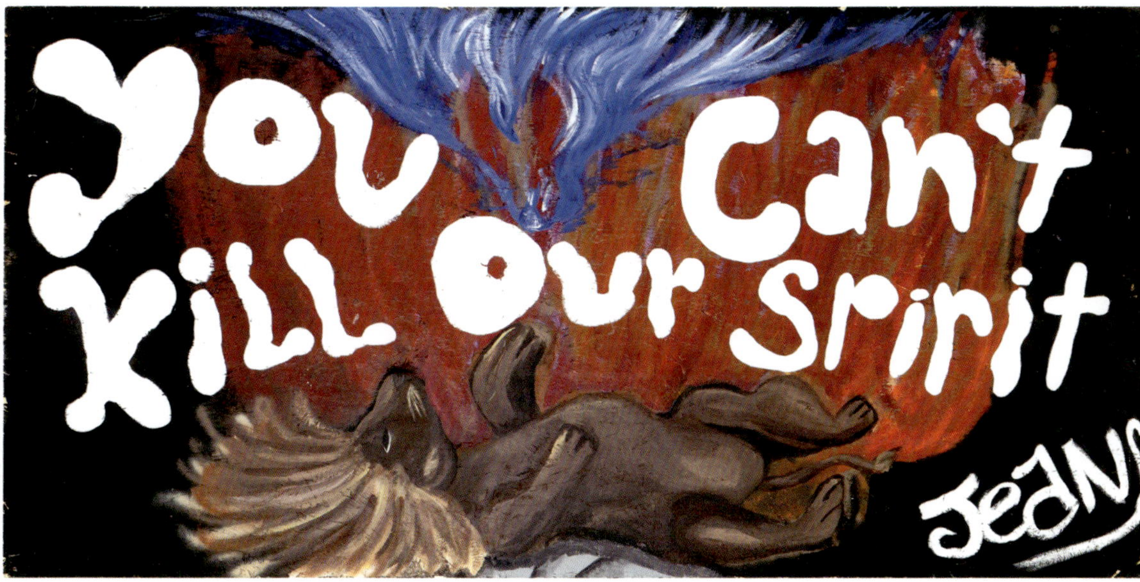

Plate 99

Rogen Abdalla, *You Can't Kill Our Spirit*, 2022

Justice for George: Our Strength, Our Story, 48 x 96 in.

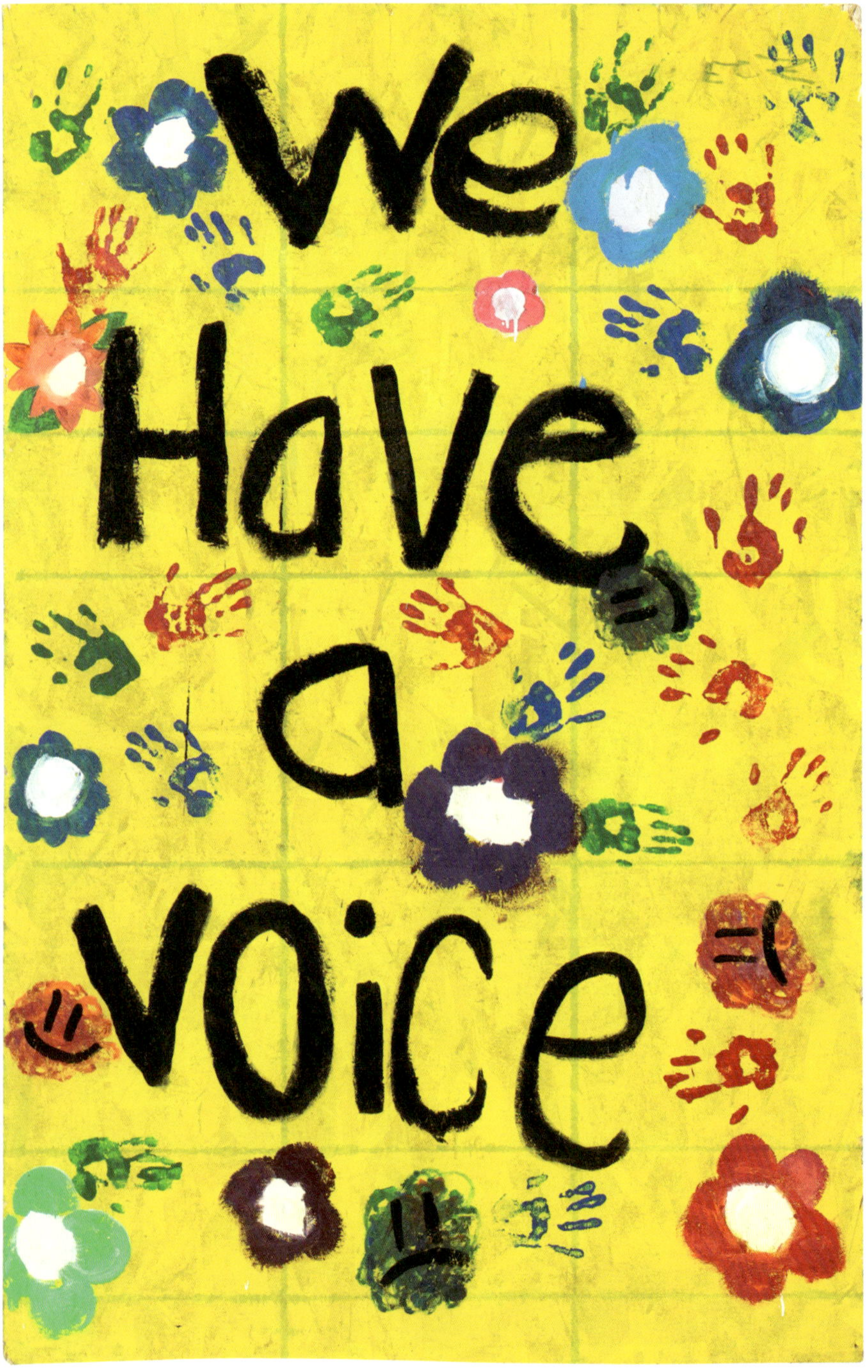

Plate 100

Girl Scouts Connectz, *We Have a Voice*, 2022

Justice for George: Our Strength, Our Story, 76 x 48 in.

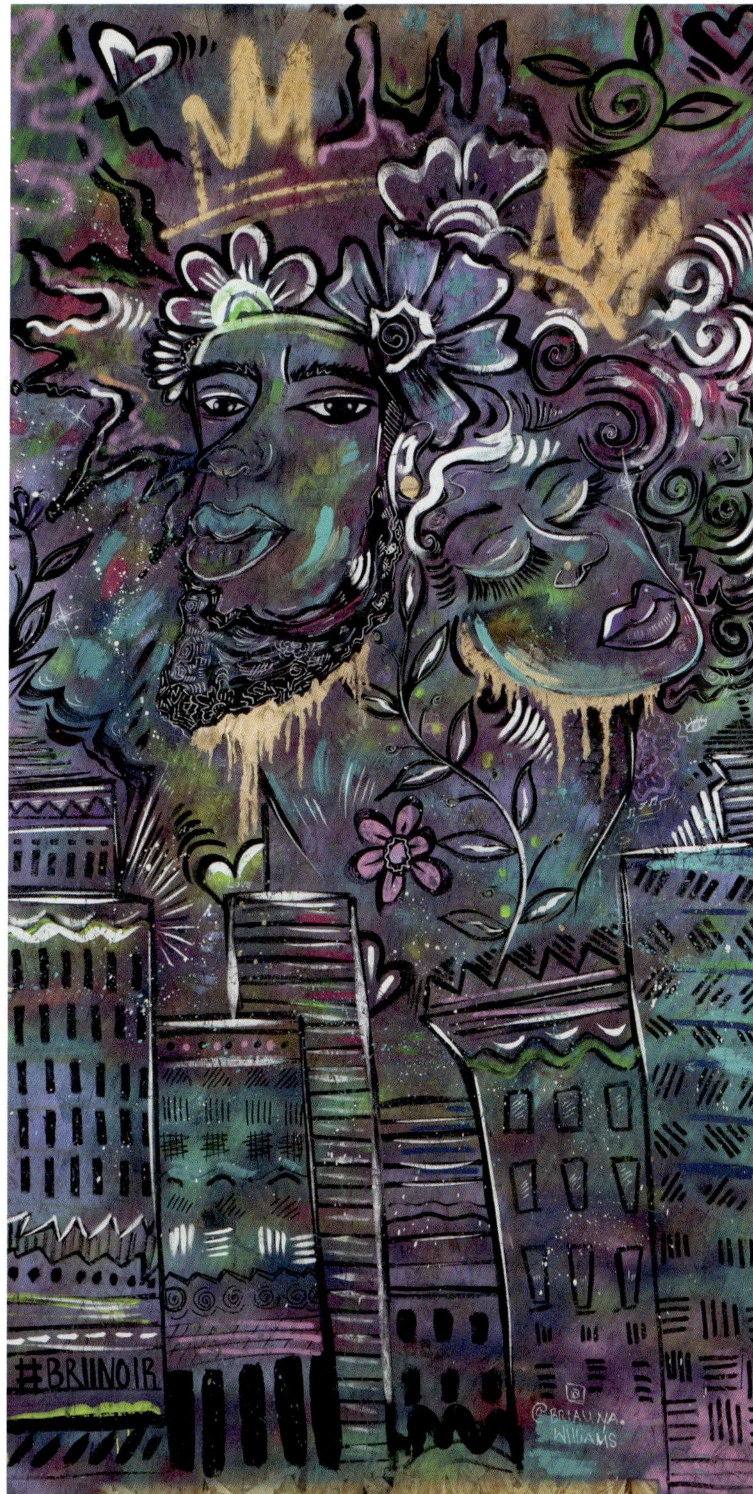

Plate 101
Briauna Williams, *The Foundation; Rooted in Love*, 2023, Justice for George: Breaking Barriers, Building Bonds, 96 x 48 in.

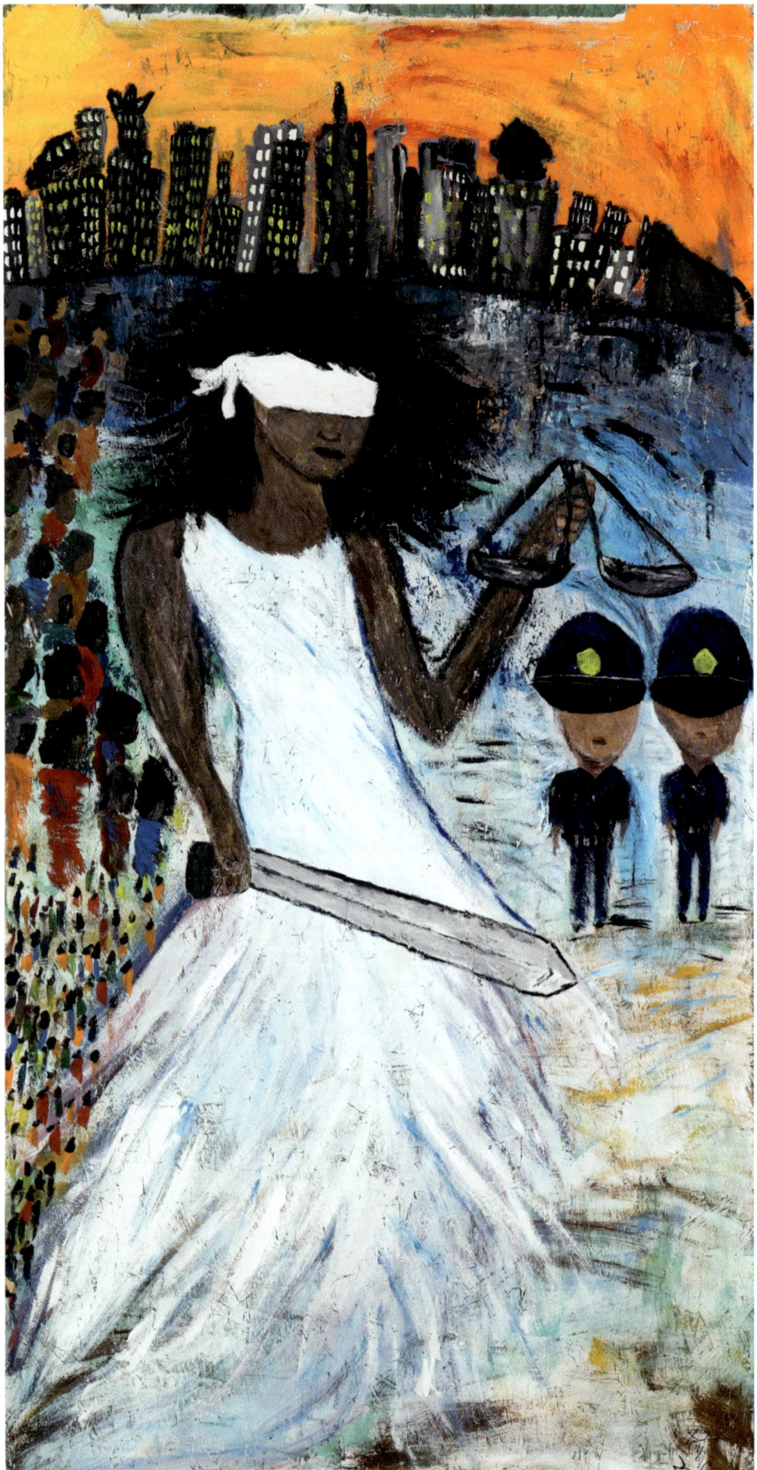

Plate 102

Sophia Ponce, *Justice for All*, 2023, Justice for George: Breaking Barriers, Building Bonds, 96 x 48 in.

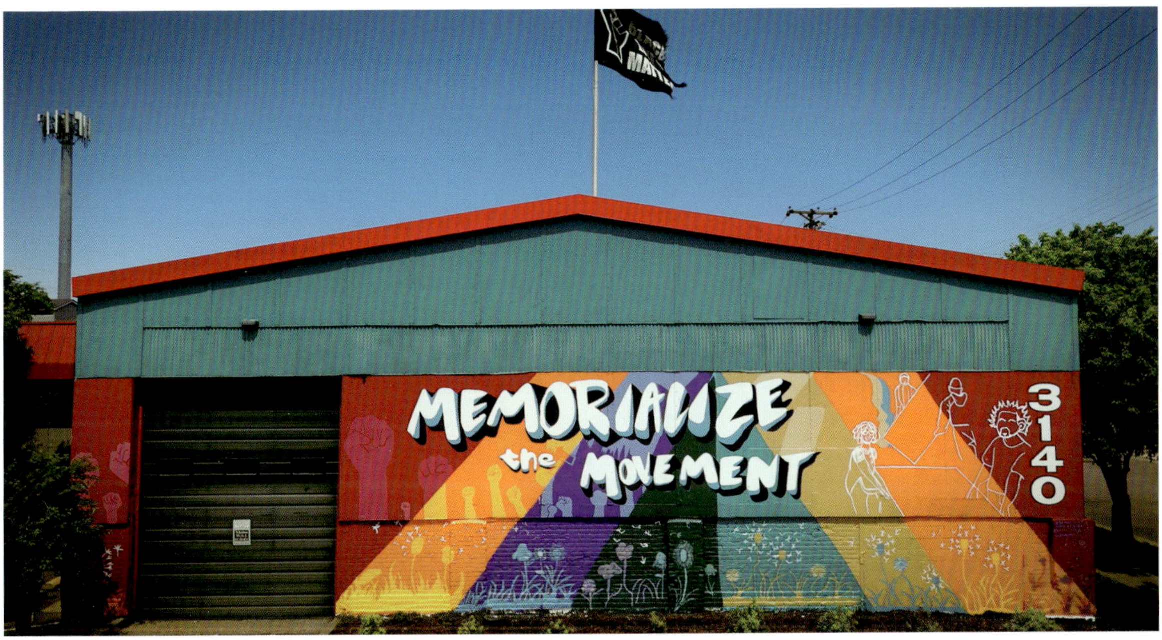

Plate 103

Kira Bass, Kim Nathe, Crystal Sokuu, Briauna Williams, *Memorialize the Movement*, 2024
Justice for George: Space as Canvas. Memorialize the Movement Headquarters, 3140 Snelling Ave.
Photo by Axel Santo Domingo

CONTRIBUTOR BIOGRAPHIES

Leslie Guy - After over twenty-five years of experience in the cultural sector, Leslie Guy founded LG Consultancy specifically to be a catalyst for change, a bridge between past and present, and a connector between communities. LG Consultancy values the collaborative creative process and conducts its work in partnership with clients and stakeholders to create meaningful and relevant programming and provide ethical and culturally sensitive collections stewardship. In 2021 Ms. Guy started Conduit: A Midwestern Black Visual Art Preservation Initiative, to support the preservation of community-based Black art. Ms. Guy has held the positions of chief curator at the DuSable Museum of African American History; curator of collection, director of curatorial services at the African American Museum in Philadelphia; and conservator at the University of Pennsylvania Museum of Archaeology and Anthropology. She received a BA in biological chemisty from Wellesley College and an MA from the Winterthur/University of Delaware Program in Art Conservation.

Seitu Jones - Artist and advocate Seitu Ken Jones has been tending the soil of community through art for more than forty years. Throughout his career, he has harnessed the tools of visual art, infrastructure, and civic engagement to create work that links history to the present and honors the community's assets—from its historic figures to natural resources to cultural traditions. His large-scale sculptural installation *Turnip Greens* was dedicated in 2019 in the Nashville Farmers Market, inspired by the city's bounty of food and Black culture. First enacted in St. Paul in 2014, *A Community Meal* convened two thousand people over dinner at a table half a mile long. Jones's site-specific art installations for the Twin Cities Light Rail Transit system blends visual beauty with local history. In 2013, Jones cofounded Frogtown Farm, a five-acre urban farm in a St. Paul city park, created with and for neighborhood residents. Jones holds a BS in landscape design and an MLS in environmental history from the University of Minnesota. He served on the board of the Capitol Region Watershed District and resides in St. Paul, Minnesota, with his partner, the poet Soyini Guyton.

Leesa Kelly - Leesa Kelly is an activist, writer, public speaker, and curator. Leesa is the Founder and Executive Director of Memorialize the Movement, a grassroots organization that preserves, displays, and educates the public on the protest plywood murals that emerged after George Floyd's death in Minneapolis in 2020. Through her work with Memorialize the Movement, Leesa has spoken at over 20 conferences and universities, organized large-scale exhibitions in the Twin Cities and New York, and has led workshops on cultivating BIPOC representation and visibility in the museum and conservation industry. She believes in dismantling oppressive systems and rebuilding new systems that work for ALL people.

Howard Oransky - Howard Oransky was appointed director of the Katherine E. Nash Gallery in 2011. Since then, he has organized numerous exhibitions of work by students, staff, faculty, and artists from Minnesota, across the United States, and around the world. He cocurated, with Lynn Lukkas, *Covered in Time and History: The Films of Ana Mendieta*, the first full-scale exhibition and publication devoted to the artist's work in the filmic medium. The exhibition premiered at the Nash Gallery in 2015 and traveled to the NSU Art Museum, the UC Berkeley Art Museum and Pacific Film Archive, the Bildmuseet, the Martin-Gropius-Bau, and the Jeu de Paume. In 2022 he cocurated, with Herman Milligan, *A Picture Gallery of the Soul*, a group exhibition of work by one hundred Black American artists whose practice incorporates the photographic medium. With Brenda J. Child he cocurated *Dreaming Our Futures: Ojibwe and Očhéthi Šakówiŋ Artists and Knowledge Keepers*. The exhibition premiered at the Nash Gallery in 2024 and traveled to the Rochester Art Center and the Tweed Museum of Art.

Amira McLendon - Amira McLendon is a visual artist and emerging curator from Apple Valley, Minnesota, currently based in Minneapolis. She received her BA in art from the University of Minnesota. In her artistic practice, she focues on digital illustration and explores diverse storytelling from a curatorial lens. McLendon views art and curation as one medium for calling upon social change and justice, and her interests reflect that. She is interested in the untold stories of people that historically haven't always been given the space to tell their stories themselves, such as LGBTQ+ individuals, Black and Indigenous people, and People of Color. She developed her interest in curation and other areas like collections management and archiving through her work with Memorialize the Movement.

Seph Rodney - Seph Rodney, PhD, was born in Jamaica, and came of age in the Bronx, New York. He is a former senior critic and opinions editor for Hyperallergic, and now regularly contributes to the *New York Times*. He has written for CNN, NBC, *Art in America*, and *American Craft*, and penned catalogue essays on Gary Simmons, Lisa Corinne Davis, Pope.L, Teresita Fernandez, Sarah Oppenheimer, and Meleko Mokgosi, among others. His book, *The Personalization of the Museum Visit*, was published by Routledge in 2019. In 2020 he won the Rabkin Prize for arts journalism and, in 2022, the Andy Warhol Foundation Arts Writers Grant. He is a cocurator of *Get in the Game*, the largest exhibition that SFMOMA has undertaken, which opens in October 2024.

NOTES

FROM RED OCHRE TO EGYPTIAN BLUE - Howard Oransky

Epigraph: Ida B. Wells, *A Red Record: Tabulated Statistics and Alleged Causes of Lynchings in the United States, 1892–1893–1894* (Chicago: Donohue & Henneberry, 1895), 97.

1. James Allen, *Without Sanctuary: Lynching Photography in America* (Santa Fe: Twin Palms, 2000), Plate 30.
2. Chris Julin and Stephanie Hemphill, "A Mob Lynches Three Black Men," Minnesota Public Radio, June 2001, accessed April 12, 2024, https://news.minnesota.publicradio.org/projects/2001/06/lynching/page1.shtml.
3. "Duluth Lynchings: Resources relating to the tragic events of June 15, 1920: People," Minnesota Historical Society, accessed on April 14, 2024, https://www.mnhs.org/duluthlynchings/people.
4. Clayton Jackson McGhie Memorial, accessed April 12, 2024, https://claytonjacksonmcghie.org/the-memorial/. The American musician Bob Dylan was born in Duluth twenty-one years after Elias Clayton, Elmer Jackson, and Isaac McGhie were killed there. He memorialized the lynching in the opening lines of his 1965 song "Desolation Row": "They're selling postcards of the hanging / They're painting the passports brown / The beauty parlor is filled with sailors / The circus is in town."
5. Rachel Treisman, "Darnella Frazier, Teen Who Filmed Floyd's Murder, Praised for Making Verdict Possible," NPR, April 21, 2021, https://www.npr.org/sections/trial-over-killing-of-george-floyd/2021/04/21/989480867/darnella-frazier-teen-who-filmed-floyds-murder-praised-for-making-verdict-possib.
6. Christopher S. Henshilwood et al., "An abstract drawing from the 73,000-year-old levels at Blombos Cave, South Africa," *Nature* 562, no. 7725 (October 2018): 115–18, available at https://www.geo.umass.edu/climate/papers2/Henshilwood_2018.pdf.
7. Seitu Jones, email message to author, March 15, 2024. "He [George Washington Carver] created many beautiful colors, including one blue which was believed to be a rediscovery of an old Egyptian blue for which modern pigment makers had been searching for years." *Dr. George Washington Carver Biographical Information*, 10; PDF available at the George Washington Carver Museum & Cultural Center, Austin, Texas, accessed April 13, 2024, https://www.austintexas.gov/sites/default/files/files/Parks/Carver_Museum/Carver_Bio_and_Information.pdf. Carver's process of producing paints and stains was patented on June 14, 1927, under patent US1632365A, exactly seven years to the day after Elias Clayton, Elmer Jackson, and Isaac McGhie arrived in Duluth with the John Robinson Circus.
8. Graham Bowley, "Museums Collect Protest Signs to Preserve History in Real Time," *New York Times*, June 10, 2020, https://www.nytimes.com/2020/06/10/arts/design/museums-protest-signs.html.
9. "The Killing of Daunte Wright and Trial of Kimberly Potter," Minnesota Public Radio News, accessed April 12, 2024, https://www.mprnews.org/crime-law-and-justice/killing-of-daunte-wright.

MEMORIALIZING A MOVEMENT - Leesa Kelly

1. "Fatal Minneapolis police shooting case goes to prosecutors," CBS News, February 10, 2016,

https://www.cbsnews.com/news/minneapolis-police-fatal-shooting-case-goes-to-prosecutors-jamar-clark/.
2. Mitch Smith, "Minnesota Officer Acquitted in Killing of Philando Castile," *New York Times*, June 16, 2017, https://www.nytimes.com/2017/06/16/us/police-shooting-trial-philando-castile.html.
3. Maritza Vasquez Reyes, "The Disproportional Impact of COVID-19 on African Americans," *Health and Human Rights Journal* 22, no. 2 (December 2020): 299–307.
4. "Conservator Demographics and Statistics in the US," Zippia: The Career Expert, updated April 5, 2024, https://www.zippia.com/conservator-jobs/demographics/; "Historian Demographics and Statistics in the US," Zippia: The Career Expert, updated April 5, 2024, https://www.zippia.com/historian-jobs/demographics/; Loureen Ayyoub, "Curator at Museum of African Diaspora in San Francisco amplifies Black voices," CBS News, April 10, 2024, https://www.cbsnews.com/sanfrancisco/news/curator-at-museum-of-african-diaspora-in-san-francisco-amplifies-black-voices/.

WHAT ARE WE DOING TO SAFEGUARD OUR HISTORY?

- Leslie Guy

1. Memorialize the Movement website, accessed April 8, 2024, https://www.memorializethemovement.com/.
2. "Governor DeSantis Announces Legislative Proposal to Stop W.O.K.E. Activism and Critical Race Theory in School and Corporations," Office of Governor Ron DeSantis, December 15, 2021, https://www.flgov.com/2021/12/15/governor-desantis-announces-legislative-proposal-to-stop-w-o-k-e-activism-and-critical-race-theory-in-schools-and-corporations/#:~:text=Activism%20and%20Critical%20Race%20Theory%20in%20Schools%20and%20Corporations.
3. Rep. Avila and Sen. Diaz, "OPPOSE HB 7/SB 148 So-called 'Stop WOKE Act,'" Equality Florida, accessed April 10, 2024, https://www.aclufl.org/sites/default/files/stop_woke_act_one-pager_2022_v2.pdf.
4. Allyson Henning, "Sarasota school district pulls 'BLM' passage from 5th grade textbooks," WFLA News Channel 8, October 19, 2021, https://www.wfla.com/news/sarasota-county/sarasota-school-district-pulls-blm-passage-from-5th-grade-textbooks/.
5. "Florida bill banning 'identity politics' from teacher prep programs headed to DeSantis," CBS News Miami, March 6, 2024, https://www.cbsnews.com/miami/news/florida-bill-banning-identity-politics-from-teacher-prep-programs-headed-to-desantis/.
6. Unite Against Book Bans, accessed April 8, 2024, https://uniteagainstbookbans.org/2023-book-bans/.
7. Mike Kaszuba, "Tears for a lost landmark; Amid protests, workers preparing for a housing project tear down a much-loved mural in north Minneapolis," *Minneapolis Star Tribune* (Metro Edition), January 1, 2002, 1B.
8. Ibid.
9. Judgment in the U.S. Supreme Court Case Dred Scott v. John F. A. Sandford; 3/6/1857; *Dred Scott, Plaintiff in Error, v. John F. A. Sandford*; Appellate Jurisdiction Case Files, 1792–2010; Records of the Supreme Court of the United States, Record Group 267; National Archives Building, Washington, DC.
10. Olive Jensen Theisen, *Walls That Speak: The Murals of John Thomas Biggers* (Denton: University of North Texas Press, 2010), 106.
11. "Celebration of Life by John Biggers et al., 1996, relic," Hennepin County Library, accessed April 9, 2024, https://www.hclib.org/about/art/art-list-container/art-list/su/celebration-life.
12. Terry Fiedler, "Freeway mural is coming down; Panels in north Minneapolis won't be moved," *Minneapolis Star Tribune* (Metro Edition), December 30, 2001, 3B.
13. The John Biggers Seed Project (Seed), Public Arts Administration, City of Minneapolis, accessed April 9, 2024, https://www2.minneapolismn.gov/business-services/planning-zoning/city-plans/public-art-long-range-planning/the-john-biggers-seed-project.
14. Milton Gustafson, "Travels of the Charters of Freedom," Prologue 34, no. 4 (Winter 2002): https://www.archives.gov/publications/prologue/2002/winter/travels-charters.html.
15. "Declaration of Independence: A Transcription," America's Founding Documents, U.S. National Archives and Records Administration, accessed April 9, 2024, https://www.archives.gov/founding-docs/declaration-transcript.
16. "Learn More About the Charters of Freedom," press release, July 4, 1999, U.S. National Archives and Records Administration, https://www.archives.gov/press/press-releases/1999/nr99-73.html.
17. Rich Rennicks, "The History of Vellum and Parchment," *The New Antiquarian* (blog), December 29, 2022, https://www.abaa.org/blog/post/the-history-of-vellum-and-parchment.
18. "One later theory as to why the Declaration was aging so soon after its creation stems from the

common 18th-century practice of taking 'press copies.' Press copies were made by placing a damp sheet of thin paper on a manuscript and pressing it until a portion of the ink was transferred. The thin paper copy was retained in the same manner as a modern carbon copy. The ink was reimposed on a copper plate, which was then etched so that copies could be run off the plate on a press. This 'wet transfer' method may have been used by William J. Stone when in 1820 he was commissioned by Secretary of State John Quincy Adams to make a facsimile of the entire Declaration, signatures as well as text. By June 5, 1823, almost exactly 47 years after Jefferson's first draft of the Declaration, the (Washington) National Intelligencer was able to report 'that Mr. William J. Stone, a respectable and enterprising Engraver of this City, has, after a labor of three years, completed a fac simile of the original of the Declaration of Independence, now in the archives of the government; that it is executed with the greatest exactness and fidelity; and that the Department of State has become the purchaser of the plate.'" "The Declaration of Independence: A History," America's Founding Documents, U.S. National Archives and Records Administration, accessed April 9, 2024, https://www.archives.gov/founding-docs/declaration-history.

19. "The Centennial Exhibition: A History of the Project," *Daily Evening Telegraph* (Philadelphia), June 17, 1870, 8.
20. Ulysses S. Grant, Special Message, February 25, 1874, The American Presidency Project, University of California, Santa Barbara, https://www.presidency.ucsb.edu/documents/special-message-1878.
21. "Documenting Reconstruction Violence: Known and Unknown Horrors," chapter 3 of *Reconstruction in America: Racial Violence after the Civil War*, 1865–1876, Equal Justice Initiative, accessed April 9, 2024, https://eji.org/report/reconstruction-in-america/.
22. On August 3, 1876, Congress adopted a joint resolution providing "that a commission, consisting of the Secretary of the Interior, the Secretary of the Smithsonian Institution, and the Librarian of Congress be empowered to have resort to such means as will most effectually restore the writing of the original manuscript of the Declaration of Independence, with the signatures appended thereto." "The Declaration of Independence: A History."
23. Rexford Stead, introduction to *Two Centuries of Black American Art*, by David C. Driskell (Los Angeles: Los Angeles County Museum of Art; New York: Alfred A. Knopf, 1976), 9.

LISTENING TO WHAT THE MURALS ARE TELLING US

- Seph Rodney

1. Derrick Bryson Taylor, "George Floyd Protests: A Timeline," *New York Times*, November 5, 2021, https://www.nytimes.com/article/george-floyd-protests-timeline.html.

COLLEGE OF LIBERAL ARTS

UNIVERSITY OF MINNESOTA

This catalogue is published to accompany the exhibition *Art and Artifact: Murals from the Minneapolis Uprising*, September 10–December 7, 2024, curated by Amira McLendon. The exhibition is produced by the Katherine E. Nash Gallery, operated by the Department of Art, in association with Memorialize the Movement. The University of Minnesota is on Mní Sóta Makhóčhe, the land of the Dakhóta Oyáte.

Art and Artifact: Murals from the Minneapolis Uprising was made possible with the generous support provided by the Associate Dean for Art and Humanities, College of Liberal Arts; College of Liberal Arts Public Engagement; the Office of Diversity, Equity, and Inclusion, College of Liberal Arts; the Department of American Studies; the Department of History; The Imagine Fund Special Events Award; the Institute for Advanced Study; Minnesota Transform: A Mellon Foundation Just Futures Project at the University of Minnesota; The Givens Foundation for African American Literature; Harlan Boss Foundation for the Arts; Stuart and Kate Nielsen; Rosalie O'Brien; and an anonymous donor.

Published by the Katherine E. Nash Gallery in association with Memorialize the Movement
405 21st Avenue S., Minneapolis, MN 55455
https://cla.umn.edu/art

Distributed by the University of Minnesota Press
111 Third Avenue South, Suite 290, Minneapolis, MN 55401-2520
http://www.upress.umn.edu

Editors: Leesa Kelly, Howard Oransky
Copy Editor: Miles Champion
Designer: Emily Swanberg
Photographer: Easton M. Green

ISBN 978-1-5179-1898-9
A Cataloging-in-Publication record for this book is available from the Library of Congress
Printed in Canada by Friesens